Blueprint Reading for Construction

SECOND EDITION

James A. S. Fatzinger, CPE, ME

American Society of Professional Estimators

PEARSON

Prentice
Hall

Upper Saddle River, New Jersey
Columbus, Ohio

Library of Congress Cataloging-in-Publication Data
Fatzinger, James A. S.
  Blueprint reading for construction / James A. S. Fatzinger.—2nd ed.
    p. cm.
Includes index.
ISBN 0-13-110811-5
1. Building—Details—Drawings. 2. Blueprints. I. Title.

TH431.F38 2004
6921.1—dc21   2003040507

Editor in Chief: Stephen Helba
Executive Editor: Ed Francis
Development Editor: Linda Cupp
Production Editor: Holly Shufeldt
Production Coordination: Carlisle Publishers Services
Design Coordinator: Diane Ernsberger
Cover Designer: Thomas Mack
Cover Image: Corbis
Production Manager: Matt Ottenweller
Marketing Manager: Mark Marsden

This book was set in Schneider, Humanist 777, and Courier by Carlisle Communications, Ltd. It was printed and bound by Banta Book Company. The cover was printed by Phoenix Color Corp.

Pearson Education Ltd.
Pearson Education Australia Pty. Limited
Pearson Education Singapore Pte. Ltd.
Pearson Education North Asia Ltd.

Pearson Education Canada Ltd.
Pearson Educación de Mexico, S. A. de C. V.
Pearson Education—Japan
Pearson Education Malaysia Pte. Ltd.

10 9 8 7 6 5 4 3 2 1
ISBN 0-13-110811-5

Preface

To an inexperienced person, a *blueprint* is nothing more than lines, numbers, letters, arrows, short statements, abbreviations, and pictures on large sheets of blue paper with dark blue lines or white paper with black or multi-colored lines. This text is written to explain the types of information on these sheets of paper so that one can begin to visualize and understand what they mean. There are two purposes of *blueprint reading*—to establish a picture of the structure in one's mind and the construction team can make the picture a reality. The blueprint further shows the necessity for coordination between trades so that the structure can be finished with the fewest problems and the most cooperation.

A picture is indeed worth a thousand words, especially in the construction industry. This text endeavors to communicate, in words, an idea, show it to other participants with varying skills and individual areas of expertise, and enable them to transform that idea into a physical reality. Therefore, *Blueprint Reading for Construction* relies heavily on schematics in general and blueprints in particular. As a further aid to the reader, each chapter concludes with exercises that promote better understanding of the material covered.

FEATURES OF THE BOOK

Part I, "Introduction to Blueprint Reading," focuses on the basics. Chapter 1, "Blueprint Reading Fundamentals," explains the physical appearance of the blueprints, their components, and meanings. Chapter 2 includes surveying of areas and individual properties.

Part II, "Residential Blueprint Reading," transports the reader from the drawing table to the job site. There the reader can relate the plan to the process and thence to the product. All phases of construction of a home—from before the first spadeful of earth to the last nail in the last roof tile and afterward—are examined, and their origins are traced from the blueprint. Included are off-site and site improvement, and on-site work. Chapter 8, "The Lee Residence Plans and Specifications," is especially helpful to readers because it relates all previous information and construction phases to the blueprints for one particular home.

In Part III, "Commercial Blueprint Reading," readers can gain insight into the complex legal issues and multiparty interrelationships of nonresidential construction. The leadoff chapters examine the legal documents and contracts, the project manual, and off-site and site improvements. The ensuing chapters review the similarities and differences in planning and constructing two major families of commercial projects: office complexes and manufacturing/warehouse facilities.

Four appendixes conclude this book. The first is an optional review chapter, "Fundamental Everyday Mathematics." The other useful appendixes include construction abbreviations and symbols, reference tables, and contract documents.

Finally, the glossary defines common terms used in architecture and the construction trades.

The author has practical experience in construction as a crewmember in the field as well as a contractor and professional estimator. This text is written based on the knowledge gained from these experiences and professional guidance from friends in the industry.

ACKNOWLEDGMENTS

The author sincerely thanks all persons who have assisted in making this text possible. The author further thanks the following reviewers for their insightful critiques and helpful suggestions: Eugene H. Wright, University of Nebraska-Lincoln, and Dianne H. Kay, Southern Illinois University.

James A. S. Fatzinger

Contents

PART I

Introduction to Blueprint Reading

CHAPTER 1

Blueprint Reading Fundamentals

The urge to produce a design drawing (plan) for a construction project is as old as time. The ancient structures of the Middle East indicate that a great deal of planning went into logical layout and construction of temples, palaces, and whole communities. The same is true of structures built by the Polynesians, Incas, Mayans, and Aztecs. Some plans were engraved in stone and others were painted on walls, examples of which still exist today.

As humankind continued to dream of larger structures, details (specifications) were written describing exactly how the structure was to be built. One of the best examples of such instructions is found in the Bible for Solomon's temple. The necessity to actually design a structure became stronger as better writing utensils and materials (ink, graphite, and papyrus) were used to better describe their thoughts. Projects of today are also designed on paper and built to the specifications and drawings of the architect and engineer. The development and improvement in paper quality, and the variety of available blueprinting processes have increased the ability to make plans for all types of structures. These plans are called **blueprints.**

THE BLUEPRINT

The term *blueprint* has two definitions. The first definition refers to the initial *blueprint sheet,* a drawing developed from the blueprint process. The individual blueprint sheet, best described as a *plan* or *drawing,* is but one part of the whole design. One drawing, such as a floor plan, expresses but one view of a project.

The second definition of the term *blueprint* refers to a *composite* of several plans (such as the foundation plan, floor plan, elevations, sections, and details) that must be assembled into an organized *set of drawings* to show as much about a project as can be placed on paper in one- or two-dimensional views. The completed set of drawings is a pictorial description of a construction project prepared by a construction designer, an architect, and/or an engineer.

3

COMPUTER-AIDED DRAFTING (CAD) AND DESIGN DRAFTING (CADD)

See figure 1–1, Computer-aided Design Drafting (CADD). The growth of the personal computer industry has resulted in the development of two computer-aided drafting systems. One is the **computer-aided drafting (CAD)** program, used for standard one- and two-dimensional drawings. The second drafting system is a **computer-aided design drafting (CADD)** program, used for both two-dimensional and three-dimensional design development. Most present-day blueprints are produced from these programs.

A draftsperson with computer experience can produce a set of drawings in a much shorter time than it takes to produce them manually. A completed drawing can be revised simply by making a computer command change. The completed plans can be saved within the computer itself or placed on a computer *disc* in lieu of *vellum* or *mylar* sheets that require filing in large storage cabinets.

The Plotter.   *See figure 1–2, Plotter.* The *plotter* is designed for the purpose of producing the finished computer drawing on paper. The computerized drawings can be in black and white, or color, or in combination, as desired. The plotter is connected to the computerized drawing system. The plans are copied from the computer as directed by the draftsperson. The drawings can then be reproduced by standard copy methods rather than through the use of blueprint machines.

The major problem with plotters is the scanning device. There are areas in which measurements may be confused because of the inability of the scanner to differentiate between numbers, such as 3, 6, and 8. Also, the finished product may not be exactly to scale because of inaccurate draftsmanship or plotter inaccuracies.

FIGURE 1–1
Computer-Aided Design Drafting (CADD). [Permission of Autodesk, Inc.]

FIGURE 1–2
Inkjet technology is used in the HP DeskJet 600 plotter, a high-resolution monochrome inkjet plotter with fast output. It uses commonly available media and offers better print quality than its predecessor.

LINES OF CONSTRUCTION

See figure 1–3, Lines of Construction. In order to properly communicate in blueprint reading the draftsperson and the individual(s) reading the completed drawing must "speak" a common language. Standard symbols and lines make up the "alphabet" for this graphic language. Lines play a very important part in defining meanings on a drawing. Identification of some of the more common types is as follows:

1. *Dimension lines.*   Used to establish the dimensions of a portion of a structure and terminated with arrows (open or closed), dots, or slashes at a termination line drawn perpendicular to the dimension line and concluding at a desired point.

2. *Leaders and arrowheads.*   A line with an arrowhead at the end pointing to a specific object for identification purposes. Used with words, abbreviations, or keynotes (see the following sections).

3. *Property lines.*   Define the boundaries of a property. These lines are normally heavier than any other lines on site or plot plans.

4. *Cutting planes.*   Used to indicate the plane at which a cross section is taken on a plan and the view direction of the object to be identified. Like property lines, these lines are normally heavier than any other lines on a drawing.

5. *Section cut.*   Shows areas not included in identification on the cutting plane view.

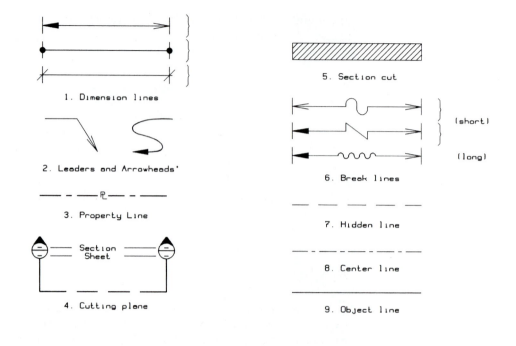

FIGURE 1–3
Lines of Construction

6. *Broken line.*   Notes that the identified object continues beyond the drawn view.

7. *Hidden line.*   Identifies a portion of a structure hidden by another portion of the structure such as a footing hidden under the basement slab.

8. *Centerline.*   Identifies symmetry about an object, such as the centerline of a wall.

9. *Object line.*   Identifies the object of primary interest or closeness. This line is slightly heavier than the hidden lines, centerline, or broken lines on a drawing.

Note that each line has a specific design and thickness that identifies it from other lines. Some of the lines may be used for identification on the cover sheet and/or on the civil plans where they are used. This identification is referred to as the **legend**.

The geographic location, the office style used, and the portion of the plans where a line is used can produce a different meaning to the line. For example, an architectural centerline and a plumbing cold waterline may be drawn identically the same, but, because of the location within the plans, the meaning differs.

ABBREVIATIONS, SYMBOLS, AND KEYNOTES

Architects and engineers have devised systems of abbreviations, symbols, and keynotes to remove the clutter of wordy descriptions, thus making plans easier to read and understand. Again, as stated in the previous paragraph, because of geographic location and office preferences, the abbreviations, symbols, and keynote identifications may vary.

Abbreviations

See appendix II. Abbreviations used in blueprint reading are a shortening of common construction terms. For example, the term *flush* on *slab* or *face of slab* is abbreviated *F.O.S.* Abbreviations should always be written in upper-case (capital) letters. Abbreviations for a specific project should be noted on the title sheet or other introductory drawing. There are books available offering construction abbreviations and their definitions. It is recommended that the standard abbreviations be memorized. Usage will also make them easier to remember.

Symbols

Symbols are used as part of the drawings to designate a particular material required for that portion of the project. A combination of symbols, expanded and drawn to a specific size to match other material sizes on a drawing, make up the pictorial view seen on a plan. Standard graphic symbols have been established for the architectural (*figure 1–4*), civil and structural (*figure 1–5*), mechanical (*figure 1–6*), plumbing (*figure 1–7*), and electrical (*figure 1–8*) plan groups. As with the variations in lines of construction, some symbols may vary slightly in meaning from one locale to another. The symbols used for each set

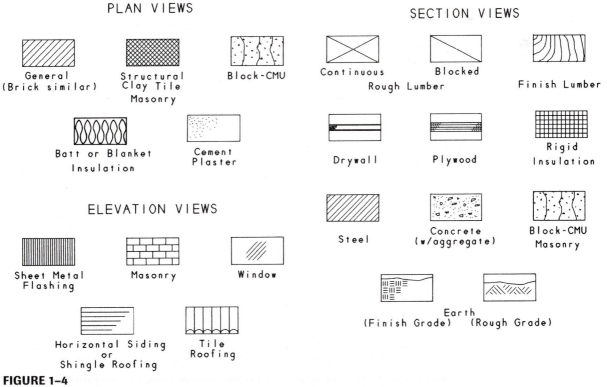

FIGURE 1–4
Architectural Symbols

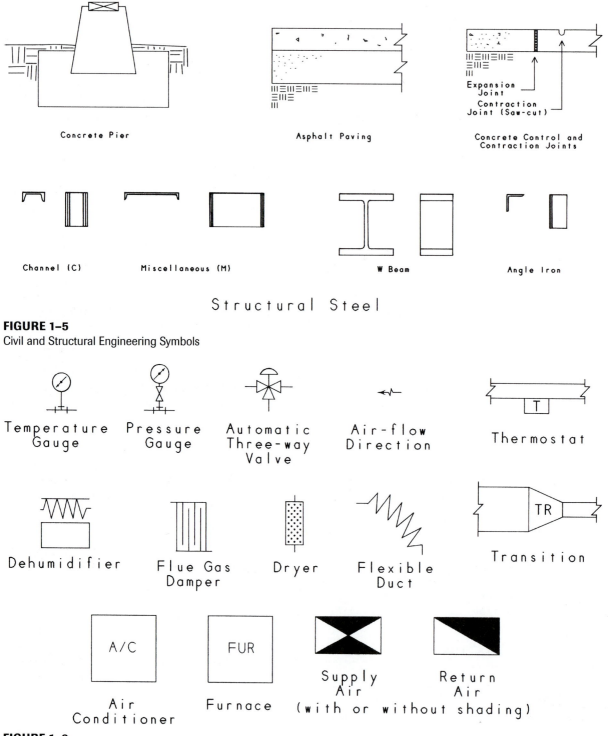

FIGURE 1–5
Civil and Structural Engineering Symbols

FIGURE 1–6
Mechanical Symbols

of plans should be indicated on the title sheet or other introductory drawing. By so doing, the person reading the set of plans can better identify the object or material indicated. Many code books, manufacturers' brochures, and specifications also include symbols and their meanings.

FIGURE 1–7
Plumbing Symbols

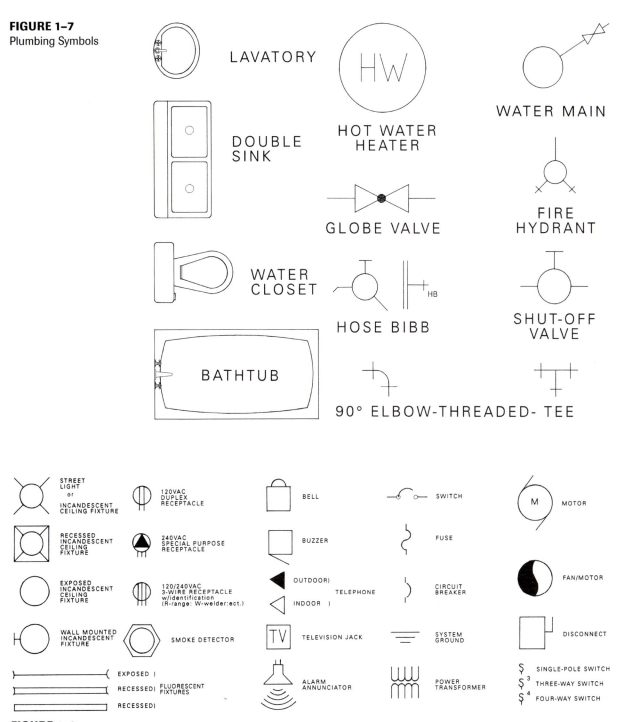

FIGURE 1–8
Electrical Symbols

Keynotes

See figure 1–9, Keynotes. A more recent trend to reduce cluttering on a plan is the *keynote*. A number or letter (usually located in a square or circle) with a leader and arrowhead is used to identify a specific object. A portion of the drawing sheet is set aside for the keynotes (usually located on the right-hand

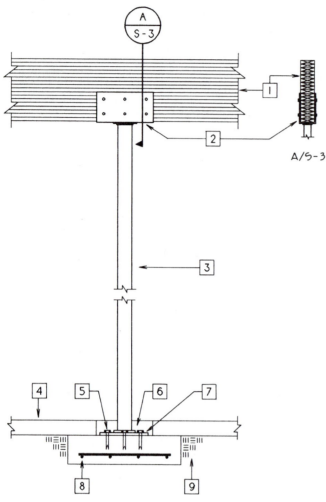

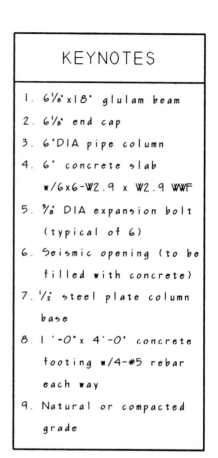

FIGURE 1–9
Keynotes

side of a drawing) with corresponding numbers or letters. These corresponding keynote numbers or letters describe the item identified on the plan. The descriptions will normally include the use of abbreviations.

THE PLANS (SET OF DRAWINGS)

Plans are made up of several types of drawings. They are identified as the plan, elevation, section, detail, and isometric views, along with schedules. The drawings are defined as follows:

1. *Plan views.* Dimensioned birds-eye or worms-eye views of the layout of a structure:
   a. The floor plan, a birds-eye view, showing the layout of rooms, room sizes, and room identification such as plan room, kitchen, or warehouse.

  b. The utility floor plans, also a birds-eye view, used for identifying the location of such items as plumbing fixtures, general power and lighting outlets and switches, or floor-mounted equipment.

  c. The reflected ceiling plan, a worms-eye view, an architectural drawing identifying the materials required for the finished ceiling along with vertical height dimensions for each area as required. Other reflected ceiling plans include drawings for required mechanical equipment, sprinkler systems, and power and lighting ceiling fixtures.

  d. The roof plan is a birds-eye view of the roof structure.

2. *Elevations.*   Vertical plan views of the structure:

  a. Exterior elevation–Pictorial views with dimensions, showing the exterior appearance of the structure and identifying finish materials such as siding, windows, and doors.

  b. Interior elevation–Detailed vertical views of materials and equipment required in each room. For example, the location of equipment for a restroom. These elevations may also be referred to as *interior detail drawings.*

3. *Sections.*   Cutting-plane views of a plan or elevation:

  a. Major section cutting-planes include:

   (1) Longitudinal section: the vertical cutting plane parallel to the longest side of a structure. In residential, it is usually parallel to the roof ridge.

   (2) Transverse section: the vertical cutting plane at 90° from the longitudinal section, or the shorter length of a structure.

   (3) Wall section: the vertical cutting-plane view of a portion of any vertical section view (longitudinal or transverse).

4. *Details.*   Blown-up portions of a plan or section views identifying specific construction details and material requirements for the area shown. Each detail may be drawn in differing scales to aid in clarification of the area chosen.

5. *Isometric plans.*   These plans are used primarily with the utility plans for identifying items for plumbing and piping drawings.

6. *Schedules.*   Information regarding the materials of construction, location and placement. These may be located on the plans themselves or in a separate cover referred to as a *specification* or *project manual.*

The Title Block

See all plans and figure 1–10, Title Block.   General information regarding the project is found in the title block of each drawing. Included in the title block should be the following information:

1. Name of project.
  a. Owner's name and project address is also included.

2. Name of architect and/or engineer, address and telephone number.
  a. A certification or confirmation such as a state seal indicating the architect's or engineer's registration.

3. Project number of architect and/or engineer.

4. Date plans are completed.

FIGURE 1–10
Typical Title Block

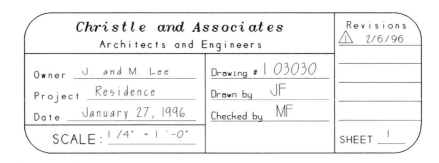

5. Initials of draftsperson and date.

6. Initials of plan checker and date.

7. Revision(s) and revision date(s) noted, if any.

8. Scale of plan.
   a. If more than one scale is used on the plan (such as found on detail sheets), or the scale is noted with the drawing, the space for indication of scale should read "as shown" or "as noted."

9. Plan sheet number located along the bottom or the right side of the sheet.

DRAWING SCALES

The three drawing scales commonly in use for the development of plans are the architectural, civil engineering, and metric scales. The scales may be designed in triangular (open divided), flat, or beveled shapes. Each type includes varying sizes indicated on each face of the rule. The open-divided triangular scales are 12" in length, whereas the flat or bevel scales may be 4" to 18" in length. Some scales are made into tape measures and others are included in wheels. These other scales may not include all of the scales identified in the following paragraphs.

Many architects also include a statement warning that *"dimensions shown on the plans take precedence over scaling."* The term **scaling** means to physically measure with some form of scale (architectural, engineering, metric, measuring wheel, or tape measure) rather than reading the dimensions. This means that the person reading the plans should *not* scale a drawing. The reasons for not scaling a plan are as follows:

1. The change in the size of the drawing due to reproduction methods.

2. Forced dimension changes on a drawing at the last minute.

3. The skill and accuracy of the draftsperson.

Architectural Scale

See figure 1–11, Architectural Scale. Most building plans are designed by the architect. The architects have developed a set of scales (rulers), referred to as the *architectural scales*. The scales are designed to measure feet, inches, and fractions of an inch. The scales are designated by a fraction of an inch equal to one foot, such as ¼" = 1'-0", which is actually ¹⁄₄₈ of one foot

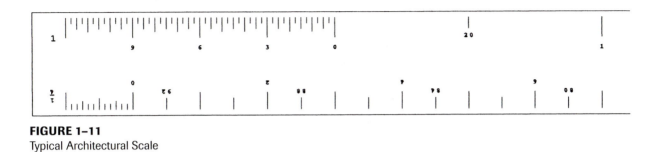

FIGURE 1–11
Typical Architectural Scale

(4-¼ inch × 12 inches = 48, therefore ¹⁄₄₈, or 1:48 scale). The architectural scale includes four[1] measurements on each face for a total of twelve scales. The twelve scales are as follows:

Face 1:

Full Scale = 12″
$\frac{1}{16}$″ = 1′-0″ (the 16 marked on the Full Scale)[1]
$\frac{3}{32}$″ = 1′-0″
$\frac{3}{16}$″ = 1′-0″

Face 2:

$\frac{1}{8}$″ = 1′-0″
$\frac{1}{4}$″ = 1′-0″
$\frac{1}{2}$″ = 1′-0″
1″ = 1′-0″

Face 3:

$\frac{3}{8}$″ = 1′-0″
$\frac{3}{4}$″ = 1′-0″
1 $\frac{1}{2}$″ = 1′-0″
3″ = 1′-0″

Reading Architectural Scales.   Architectural scales are challenging to read. On an open-divided scale, each line of scales on every face except the full scale (12″ ruler) contains the same information. The left and right ends show a small ruler broken down into either inches or inches-and-fractions-of-an-inch. The size of the scale is also designated on each end. The smaller scales on each level of each face are always half the size of the larger scale, that is, $\frac{3}{32}$″ and $\frac{3}{16}$″ are on one level; $\frac{1}{8}$″ and $\frac{1}{4}$″ on another; $\frac{3}{8}$″ and $\frac{3}{4}$″ on another; $\frac{1}{2}$″ and 1″ on another; and, finally, 1 $\frac{1}{2}$″ and 3″ on another. The remaining two scales are the

---

[1.] This scale is not recognized by many architects as a scale on the ruler, but many plans have been drawn to this $\frac{1}{16}$″ = 1′-0″ scale and is, therefore, to be considered.

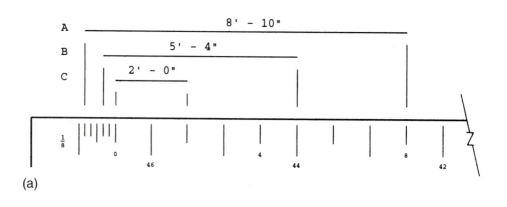

(a)

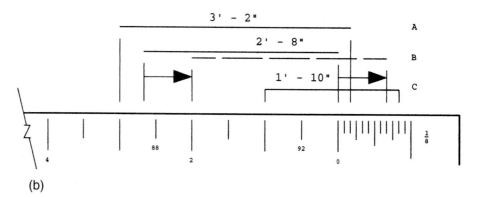

(b)

FIGURE 1–12
Reading Architectural Open-Divided Scale

"full scale" (12″ ruler) and the "16" scale. The "16" scale is the 12″ ruler broken down into ¹⁄₁₆″ increments (¹⁄₁₆″=1'-0″).

See figure 1–12a. The sizes indicated on the drawing are for the ¹⁄₈″=1'-0″ and ¼″=1'-0″ scales. As mentioned above, both scales are on the same face and on the same level.

Figure 1–12a shows a portion of the ¹⁄₈″ scale. The very small lines left of the zero represent increments of 2″, adding up to 1'-0″. Reading from the zero on the left toward the right, there are two different size lines and two groups of numbers with differing values. The space between *all* of the lines (shortest and longest) is the ¹⁄₈″ scale. Starting at the zero and reading from left-to-right, each fourth line is numbered starting with 4 (lineal feet) and ending with 92 (lineal feet).

See figure 1–12b. The drawing shows a portion of the ¼″ scale. The breakdown for the very small lines from the zero to the right shows 1″ increments, totaling 1'-0″. Starting at the zero and reading from right to left, the numbers start with 2 and end with 46. Only the larger lines represent the ¼″ scale.

To read a measurement with the scales, use the following procedure:

1. Place the zero (0) on the scale to be read at the end of the line to be measured or drawn.

2. If the line ends on one of the vertical scale lines, read the length on the scale being measured.

3. Where the line extends beyond one of the scale indicators but does not extend to the next measurement, use the following procedure:
   a. Move the scale so that the end of the line is located at the nearest lower measurement. This moves the end of the line at the zero into the inch increments.
   b. Read the number of inches and/or fractions of an inch and add the inches to the foot measurement of the scale.

For example, the length of line "C" in figure 1–12a (the ⅛" scale) is exactly 2 lineal feet (lf) (0.61 m). All other lines are longer and include both feet and inches, that is, line "A" is 8'-10" (2.69 m) long and line "B" is 5'-4" (1.62 m).

Figure 1–12b (the ¼" scale) shows how these measurements are obtained. Line "B" on the right extends beyond the *nearest lower whole foot*. In this case the nearest lower whole foot is 2 lf (0.61 m). The scale is moved (see arrows) so that the left end of the line aligns with the 2 lf (0.61 m). The reader then looks to the right of zero to see how many inches the line extends into the inch ruler on the right. In this case it extends 8" (203.2 mm). The line, therefore, is 2'-8" (0.81 m). It is in this same manner that all lines are measured. No matter which scale is used, move the scale to the *nearest lower whole foot* to the left or right (depending upon the scale), and read the inches to the left or right of the zero.

Civil Engineering Scale

See figure 1–13, Engineering Scale. Site plans, street improvements, and utility installations are designed by civil engineers. Engineering and surveying typically use feet and tenths of a foot as the units of measure. Therefore, engineers have developed scales designed to measure feet per inch only (for example, 1" = 10 lf). The engineering scale, similar to the triangular open-divided architectural scale, has six scales on the three faces. They are as follows:

Face 1:

1" = 10'-0"
1" = 50'-0"

Face 2:

1" = 20'-0"
1" = 40'-0"

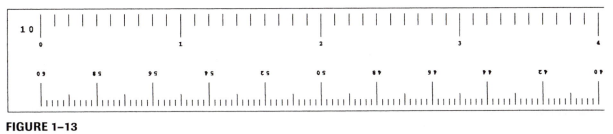

FIGURE 1–13
Typical Engineering Scale

Face 3:

1″ = 30′-0″

1″ = 60′-0″

Each line on any scale is equal to 1 lineal foot. The lines that are numbered must have the zero added. Thus, number 1 = 10 lf, 2 = 20 lf, and so on, no matter which scale is read. This scale may be used for very large plans and maps using multiples of the base scales. For example, the 1″ = 20 lf scale can be read as 1″ = 200 lf or 1″ = 2000 lf.

Metric Scale

See figure 1–14, Metric Scale, and appendix III. Many countries have been using the International System (SI) metric system. Appendix III identifies some metric measurements and their English equivalents. Metric scales, once required for all federal government plans, are now an option. There are also variations in the shapes of the metric scales, but the most common type used is the triangular open-divided scale.

The metric scale has a total of six measurements on three faces. The faces of a metric scale are as follows:

Face 1:

.01 - 1:100   (where 100 mm = 1 m)

.025 - 1:40   (where 40 mm = 1 m)

Face 2:

.0125 - 1:80   (where 80 mm = 1 m)

.02 - 1:50   (where 50 mm = 1 m)

Face 3:

.05 - 1:20   (where 20 mm = 1 m)

1:33 ⅓   (where 30 mm = 1 m)

The decimals located on the faces of the scales—.01, .0125, .02, .025, and .05—indicate the decimal length of a meter on the particular scale. The meaning of the ratios on the face is indicated (such as 100 mm = 1 m).

The metric drawing scales use the *millimeter (mm)* as the base linear measurement. Metric measurements are set up in *multiples of 10.*

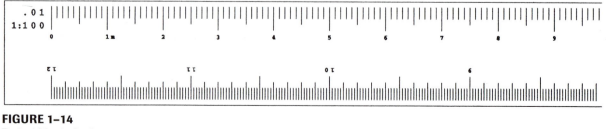

FIGURE 1–14

Typical Metric Scale

1 millimeter (mm) = $\frac{1}{10}$ centimeter (cm) = $\frac{1}{100}$ decimeter (dm) = $\frac{1}{1000}$ meter (m)

1 centimeter (cm) = $\frac{1}{10}$ of a decimeter (dm) = $\frac{1}{100}$ of a meter (m)

1 decimeter (dm) = $\frac{1}{10}$ of a meter (m)

10 meters (m) = 1 dekameter (dkm)

100 meters (m) = 10 dekameters (dkm) = 1 hectometer (hm)

1000 meters (m) = 100 dekameters (dkm) = 10 hectometers (hm) = 1 kilometer (km)

The numbers are expressed in whole and decimal parts of whole numbers. For example:

$$500 \text{ millimeters (mm)} \begin{cases} 0.5 \text{ meter (m)} \\ 5.0 \text{ decimeters (dm)} \\ 50.0 \text{ centimeters (cm)} \end{cases}$$

Square and cubic measures are calculated in the same manner as the English measure. The same measurements indicated for linear measure (*meter*) also hold true for volume (*liter*) and for mass (*gram*).

Throughout the text, English and metric dimensions are noted. These metric figures are called "hard" metrics using the English to metric and metric to English conversions, (*conversion tables 1–2 and 1–3 in appendix III*). Also, *table 1–5 in appendix III* is an example of the "soft" dimensions because the metrics are rounded off to the nearest 100 millimeters.

CHAPTER EXERCISES

Abbreviations

1. What do the following abbreviations mean?

a. CJ	e. HDW	i. L	m. DIA
b. FTG	f. TOP	j. MO	n. DO
c. GI	g. BM	k. CC	o. ENCL
d. d	h. REINF	l. A.F.F.	p. SHTHG

Scales

The student should already have the three scales, or the instructor may supply scales for the following examples.

Architectural Scale

1. Draw a line that is 6 $\frac{3}{16}$" long. Using an open-divided architectural scale, determine the length of the line for each of the following scales in inches, feet, or feet and inches.

a. $\frac{1}{8}$" = 1'-0" scale _____		g. $\frac{3}{8}$" = 1'-0" scale _____	
b. $\frac{3}{32}$" = 1'-0" scale _____		h. 1" = 1'-0" scale _____	
c. 1 $\frac{1}{2}$" = 1'-0" scale _____		i. $\frac{1}{2}$" = 1'-0" scale _____	
d. $\frac{3}{16}$" = 1'-0" scale _____		j. $\frac{1}{16}$" = 1'-0" scale _____	
e. $\frac{1}{4}$" = 1'-0" scale _____		k. $\frac{3}{4}$" = 1'-0" scale _____	
f. Full scale _____		l. 3" = 1'-0" scale _____	

Engineering Scale

2. Draw a line that is 5⅞″ long. Using an open-divided civil engineering scale, determine the length of the line for each of the following scales:
   a. 1″ = 10′ _____   d. 1″ = 50′ _____
   b. 1″ = 60′ _____   e. 1″ = 20′ _____
   c. 1″ = 30′ _____   f. 1″ = 40′ _____

Metric Scale

3. Draw a line that is 7″ long. On the metric scale, this line measures:
   a. .025 (1:40) scale =   _____ m
   b. .30 (1:33 ⅓) scale =   _____ m
   c. .05 (1:20) scale =   _____ m
   d. .02 (1:50) scale =   _____ m
   e. .0125 (1:80) scale =   _____ m
   f. .01 (1:100) scale =   _____ m

4. *Figure 1–15* is a *footprint* of a structure with various measurements indicated by letters only. Using the following scales, give the length of the line corresponding with the letter next to the scale:

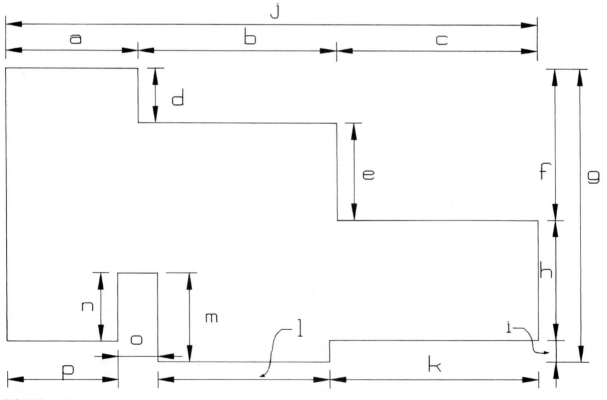

FIGURE 1–15
Footprint

a. $\frac{1}{8}'' = 1'\text{-}0''$ _____   i. $\frac{3}{32}'' = 1'\text{-}0''$ _____
b. $1'' = 1'\text{-}0''$ _____   j. $3'' = 1'\text{-}0''$ _____
c. $1\frac{1}{2}'' = 1'\text{-}0''$ _____   k. $1'' = 60'$ _____
d. $\frac{1}{2}'' = 1'\text{-}0''$ _____   l. $\frac{3}{16}'' = 1'\text{-}0''$ _____
e. $\frac{3}{4}'' = 1'\text{-}0''$ _____   m. $\frac{1}{16}'' = 1'\text{-}0''$ _____
f. $1'' = 10'$ _____   n. $\frac{3}{8}'' = 1'\text{-}0''$ _____
g. $\frac{1}{4}'' = 1'\text{-}0''$ _____   o. $1'' = 40'$ _____
h. $1'' = 20'$ _____   p. $1'' = 30'$ _____

5. Why are both architectural and structural sections drawn in a set of plans?

2

The Survey

Identifying the limits and direction of one's property and property lines has been, and is, important to the owner in many ways. The identification helps prevent encroachment by others onto the property; it aids in the determination of one's wealth; but the **survey,** primarily, establishes the location and boundaries of a property.

The materials used in earlier times to measure and locate the length and direction of a property line included the *rod* (a specific length of *chain*) and a mariner's *compass*. The rod, measuring 16'-6" (5.03 m), is used for horizontal measurement and is still in use today. Another type of rod is the *Philadelphia rod,* a type of vertical ruler used with a scope or laser beam to determine elevations. It is divided into either ⅛" or ¹⁄₁₀₀" increments.

See figure 2–1, Mariner's (a) and Surveyor's (b) Compass. The third instrument used for surveying is the compass. There are two types of compasses, the *mariner's compass,* used to determine an **azimuth,** and the *surveyor's compass,* used to determine a **bearing.** Using a mariner's compass, an *azimuth* is a horizontal angle measured in degrees (from 1° to 359°) using true or magnetic north as the reference (zero) line. The survey compass aids in the location of a *bearing,* a horizontal angle indicated in respect to one of four quadrants of the compass (northeast, southeast, northwest, or southwest). A bearing is measured clockwise or counterclockwise from the *north-south meridian,* and the angle east or west of it. Both of the survey systems in the following sections use the surveyor's compass to assist in determining property lines.

TYPES OF SURVEYS

Metes and Bounds

See figure 2–2, Metes and Bounds. The *Metes and Bounds* system, in use since colonial times, is primarily used for individual property surveys in the eastern states. The Metes and Bounds system is best described as *the measurement and location of a specific piece of property.* A survey team locates,

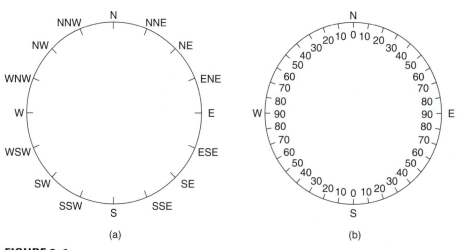

FIGURE 2–1
(a) Mariner's and (b) Surveyor's Compass

identifies, and uses as a reference point the nearest **datum point** (described in the following sections) to the property. The team then proceeds to locate the distance and direction from that point to the nearest corner of the property.

The bearing and length of all property lines are determined from this point (called the *point of beginning*—See the following section on the point of beginning). The bearings are in reference to the north-south meridian along the property lines. For example, in figure 2–2, the northerly direction is noted with the large "N" symbol. The shaded section in the quadrant symbol at each property line is the angle from the nearest meridian quadrant. The north property line reads S 79° 47′ 24″ E. This states that the property line is in the *southeast* quadrant and is read as south 79 degrees, 47 minutes (^{47}⁄₆₀ of a degree), 24 seconds (^{24}⁄₆₀ of a minute), *east*. These references continue until all directions and terminal points are located and plotted. The length of this property line is determined in feet and decimal fraction of a foot, such as 235.42′ (71.76 m).

The Area Survey

See figure 2–3, Range, Township, Section, and Quarter-Section. The second system is the survey used for the location of *ranges, townships, sections, quarter-sections* and *plats* for location and identification of areas. Each portion of the area survey has a principal *meridian* line and a *base* line to establish position and location on a topographical map. As previously mentioned, the meridian line is the north-south (longitudinal) boundary of the area. The east-west line, called the *base line,* is the (latitudinal) boundary of the area from which the meridian is determined. The size of each system is noted in figure 2–3.

The longitude and latitude are recorded for each range, township, section, quarter-section, **plat,** and subdivision *lot* (individual properties). These directions are recorded as the legal description of a property. For example, the legal description of a property may read as follows:

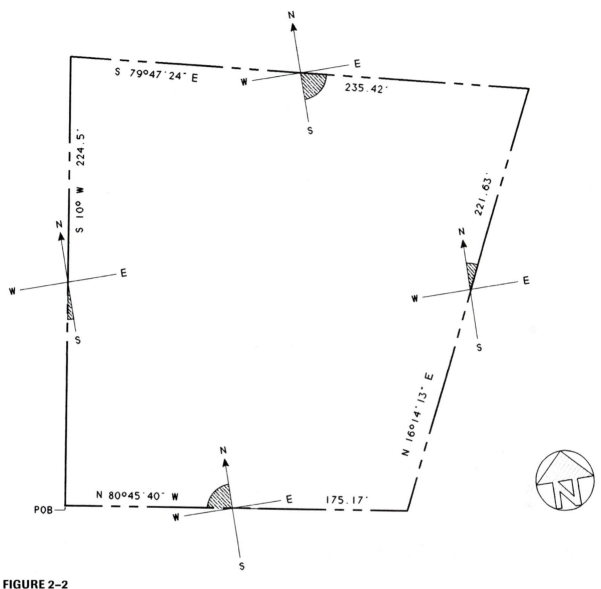

FIGURE 2–2
Metes and Bounds, the "C" Residence

"Plat_____, lot_____."

"This property is located in the northeast quarter-section of the south-west section of township number _____, located in the northwest portion of range number _____, as recorded in the Book of Records in the County of _____, State of _____."

Plats are maps of an area that may vary in size and may include town-ships, or even quarter-sections, with subdivisions showing many smaller lots. The plat map normally includes streets and other improvements.

The Datum Point. Datum points are established during the survey. The datum points are usually identified by a brass cap located in the center of a street intersection, on a curb near the intersection, or any other location

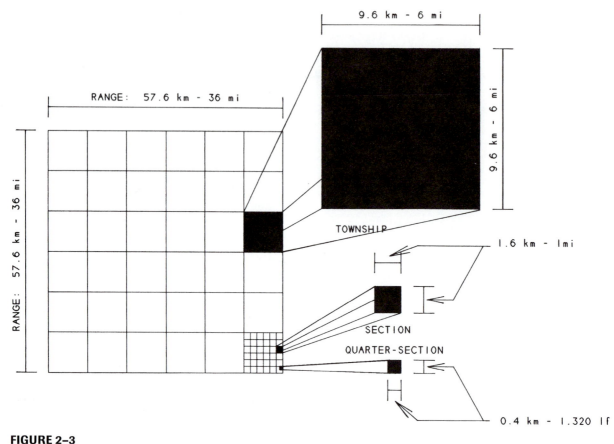

FIGURE 2–3
Range/Township/Section and Quarter-Section

that can be prominently displayed for the surveyors. The datum point nearest a project is usually written on the site plan and/or plot plan indicating its location in relationship to the project.

Point of Beginning and Stations.   The point of beginning (POB) is usually the corner of a property nearest the datum point where the survey starts. It is identified primarily as a reference point for horizontal dimensioning and determining vertical elevations of a property. The remaining points, at the junction of two of the property lines, are referred to as **stations.** Each junction of the boundaries may have a marker and an elevation established for it. On a set of plans the stations may be identified by letters and/or numbers.

Contours.   *See figures 2–4, Development of Contour Profile, and refer to 2–5, Site (Survey) Plan, Garland Residence.* The natural **contour lines** are the elevations, drawn as curved lines on a topographical map, including site and plot plans. The contour elevations may be scaled in increments of 1.0′, 5.0′, 10.0′ (0.30 m, 1.52 m, 3.05 m), or larger elevations (for very large area topographical maps). The elevation is usually noted above mean sea level. In some locales the elevation for a site and plot plan may be noted at the nearest datum point.

The example in figure 2–4 identifies the natural contour elevations in a plan view spaced at 5.0′ intervals. A centerline is drawn through the plan

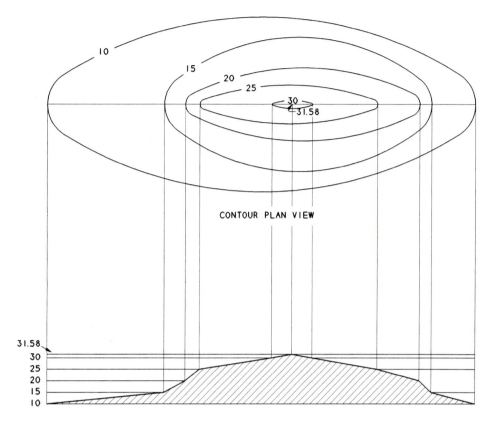

CONTOUR PLAN VIEW

CONTOUR PROFILE

FIGURE 2–4
Development of Contour Profile

view for its full length. The contour profile portion of the drawing also has the
5.0′ (1.52 m) intervals drawn vertically in horizontal lines extending the length
of the plan view. Perpendicular lines are drawn from the contours at the junction of the centerline to the matching elevation line on the profile. When all
the intersections on the profile are determined, a line drawn through
those intersections produces the profile. This profile is actually an elevation, or
a section, of the plan. A second profile, or section, can be done at any angle over
the plan view in the same manner. The plan view can be dissected even further
to get a more accurate picture of the elevations. Reverse the procedure to
develop a plan view from actual elevations.

This is the manner in which civil engineers produce contours shown
on a site plan. The elevations are plotted and the contour plan produced.
All natural contours are normally shown with dashed lines (refer to figure 2–5).

The Benchmark.   A **benchmark** usually indicates the lowest elevation
above mean sea level for an area. For example, a map may show the point as
the junction of two streams, or the junction of highways, or at street intersections. The benchmark may be a marker such as a steel or wood post, or
a concrete or stone monument established for the purpose. The United States
Army Corps of Engineers established many of the original benchmarks.
Other government organizations, such as the Bureau of Land Management
(BLM), now do their own surveys. The elevations are noted on the maps as the

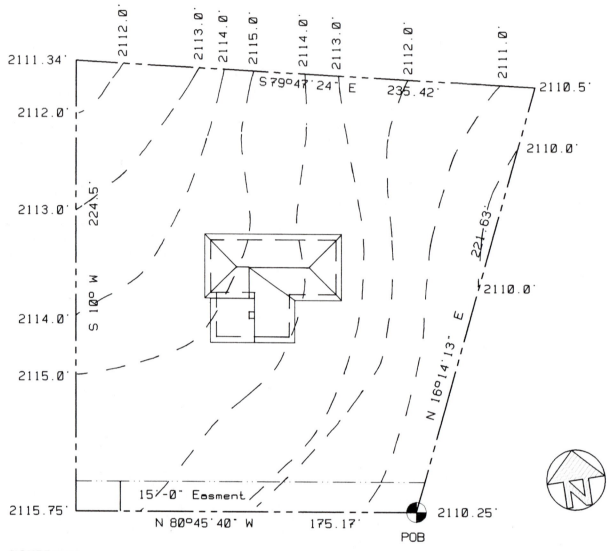

FIGURE 2–5
Site (Survey) Plan, Garland Residence

elevation above mean sea level in feet and decimal parts of a foot, where necessary, such as elev. 2575.38′ (784.98 m). The measurements are identified as the *elevation,* not as the height.

THE SITE AND PLOT PLANS

Site Plan

See figure 2–5, Site (Survey) Plan, Garland Residence. The site plan (also referred to as the survey plan) includes the location of the property in regards to the nearest *datum point,* the boundary *bearings* and dimensions, and the *natural contours* developed from a survey. The contours are normally drawn as dashed lines through the property. The survey is used as the base map for the civil site plans.

Plot Plan

See figure 2–6, Plot Plan, Garland Residence. A plot plan is a layout of a project, including the placement of the residence and/or other structure(s). The finish grades are drawn through the property in the same way as the natural contours, except that solid lines are used. The *finish contours* are identified in the same manner as the natural contours, that is, as an elevation above mean sea level, or above the nearest datum point, after excavating and grading work is completed.

All construction within the property such as excavating and grading, trenching, landscaping, driveways, sidewalks and free-standing structures, other than the main structure, up to, or a fixed distance from, the main structure are considered *site improvements*. Any or all of these items may be included as part of the plot plan.

An alternative to the finish grade contours is the use of grade *points.* A point, identified thus (+), is drawn with an elevation next to it—for example, +2193.7′ (+668.7 m). The points are located at all grade changes for finish surfacing such as asphalt or concrete finish elevations, curbs, and steps.

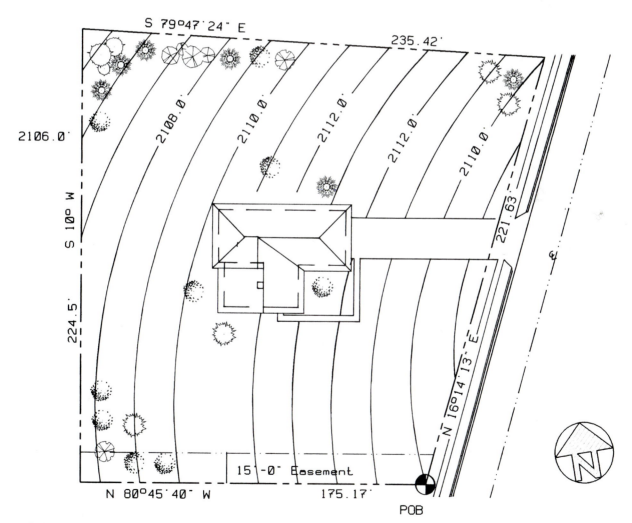

FIGURE 2–6
Plot Plan, Garland Residence

Easements.   An easement is a portion of the property reserved as the *right-of-way* for utilities whether they are installed above grade, on grade, or below grade. The property owner may not build any structures or obstructions on the easement, but the area may be landscaped. The exception to the "no structure" regulation may be the installation of property perimeter walls. This may be done only with permission from the utilities or local authorities. An easement may vary in width.

Setbacks.   A setback is the distance that the front and one side of a structure is measured at right angles from the nearest intersecting property lines. The setback locations are dependent upon the location and size of the property (tract or custom construction). The setbacks may be noted on the site plan if a structure *footprint* is shown; otherwise they are identified on the plot plan. A footprint is a perimeter outline of the foundation of the structure indicating the finish floor elevation—again, above mean sea level or from a datum point.

Minimum setbacks are established by local codes and ordinances. Where the population is sparse, such as in some suburban areas, the setback minimums may extend 25'-0" (7.62 m) or more. In locales where high-density construction is allowed, the setbacks may be as little as 2'-0" (0.61 m) or as far as 10'-0" (3.05 m) from the nearest property lines. Density is determined by the number of units per acre allotted by the local authorities.

CONTINUING SURVEYS FOR A PROJECT

Surveying does not stop with the site survey. A survey may be necessary for such construction as street improvements or utility installations. The excavation and grading contractor must continue surveying a project until the earth has been properly graded in accordance with the finish grade elevations. Where a mass excavation (discussed in chapter 3) is required, another survey is necessary for the layout of the area to be excavated. Upon the completion of the excavating and grading, the concrete, plumbing, and electrical contractors must be certain that the trenches are in the proper locations for the structure as well as determining the proper widths and depths for the footings and service installations. And, finally, the proper location of the structure itself requires the services of a land surveyor.

The specialty contractors, or subcontractors, use a variety of survey equipment to determine if the floor or ceilings are being installed to the proper levels. The survey equipment varies according to necessity and to how technical the work is, but surveys are necessary from beginning to end of a project.

CHAPTER EXERCISES

Multiple Choice

_____   1. The individual property survey common since colonial times is:
   a. A range survey
   b. A quarter-section survey
   c. A Metes and Bounds survey
   d. None of the above

_____   2. The base point from which a survey is started for a specific
               property is called:
               a. The point of beginning
               b. The found
               c. The nearest datum point
               d. The benchmark

_____   3. An area survey includes the following:
               a. Ranges, quarter-sections, and plats only
               b. Townships, sections, and plats only
               c. Ranges and townships only
               d. Ranges, townships, sections, quarter-sections, and plats

_____   4. The benchmark is also known as:
               a. A found
               b. A datum point
               c. A secondary elevation point
               d. None of the above

_____   5. The property survey includes the following:
               a. The point of beginning
               b. Stations
               c. A datum point
               d. All of the above

_____   6. The survey drawing is also referred to as:
               a. The plot plan
               b. The site plan
               c. The range layout
               d. None of the above

_____   7. There are two types of contours identified in civil drawings.
               They are:
               a. The natural contours and finish grades
               b. The azimuths
               c. The property perimeter lines
               d. The bearings

_____   8. A range map is also referred to as one of the following:
               a. A topographical map
               b. A plat
               c. A subdivision
               d. None of the above

_____   9. A subdivision is made up of individual:
               a. Townships
               b. Sections
               c. Quarter-sections
               d. Plots

_____ 10. A site survey is:
               a. Required on all preliminary property investigations
               b. The determination of the property limits
               c. Both a and b
               d. Neither a nor b

True or False

T F 1. The natural contours are the finish grades on a plot plan.

T F 2. The utility companies have a "right-of-way" called the boundary.

T F 3. The individual property survey most commonly uses the system of Metes and Bounds.

T F 4. The azimuths of a Metes and Bounds survey are the lengths of the property lines.

T F 5. All latitudes and longitudes are given in reference to true or magnetic north.

T F 6. A natural contour is the contour of the land prior to excavating or grading.

T F 7. A setback is the distance from the rear and one side of the property.

T F 8. The point of beginning is usually the point nearest the local datum point.

T F 9. The location of the corners of a property is identified as a found.

T F 10. The number shown at a datum point is identified as the height above mean sea level.

T F 11. The identification of the direction of a property line is given in hours, minutes, and seconds.

T F 12. A township is 36 mi by 36 mi square.

T F 13. A plat is a map of subdivisions of multiple lots.

T F 14. An easement is a reference to an elevation of a property.

T F 15. The surveyor of a property identifies the angle formed by a bearing and a meridian line as north-by-east, south-by-east, north-by-west, and south-by-west.

Completion

1. The _____ is the area of a property used by the utility companies as a right-of-way.

2. A property line has a bearing reading that states the line is north 35 degrees, 21 minutes, and 30 seconds by west. It is written as _____.

3. The larger survey maps are made up of _____.

4. A quarter-section is _____ in length each way.

5. The original individual property survey, since colonial times, is called a _____ survey.

6. Surveys were made using chains and _____.

7. The Philadelphia rod is divided into increments of $1/100''$ or _____".

8. The length of a rod in today's survey is _____.

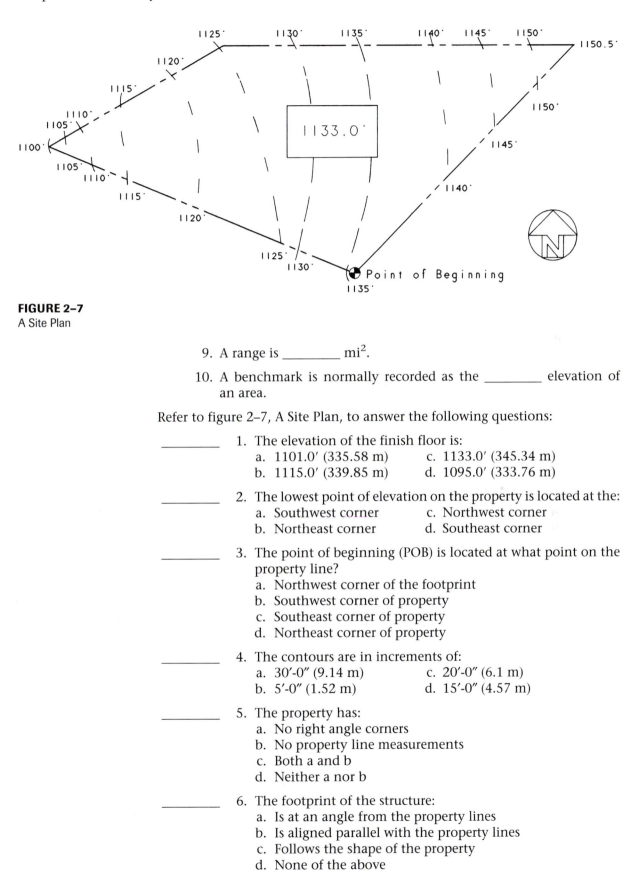

FIGURE 2–7
A Site Plan

9. A range is _____ mi².

10. A benchmark is normally recorded as the _____ elevation of an area.

Refer to figure 2–7, A Site Plan, to answer the following questions:

_____ 1. The elevation of the finish floor is:
a. 1101.0′ (335.58 m)   c. 1133.0′ (345.34 m)
b. 1115.0′ (339.85 m)   d. 1095.0′ (333.76 m)

_____ 2. The lowest point of elevation on the property is located at the:
a. Southwest corner   c. Northwest corner
b. Northeast corner   d. Southeast corner

_____ 3. The point of beginning (POB) is located at what point on the property line?
a. Northwest corner of the footprint
b. Southwest corner of property
c. Southeast corner of property
d. Northeast corner of property

_____ 4. The contours are in increments of:
a. 30′-0″ (9.14 m)   c. 20′-0″ (6.1 m)
b. 5′-0″ (1.52 m)   d. 15′-0″ (4.57 m)

_____ 5. The property has:
a. No right angle corners
b. No property line measurements
c. Both a and b
d. Neither a nor b

_____ 6. The footprint of the structure:
a. Is at an angle from the property lines
b. Is aligned parallel with the property lines
c. Follows the shape of the property
d. None of the above

Residential Blueprint Reading

CHAPTER 3

Off-Site and Site Improvements

New construction projects require a considerable amount of work on and in the ground before a structure can be built. The work includes both off-site construction and site improvements. Off-site work includes any construction outside the property limits. Whereas off-sites are not always required, site improvements are. The work may encompass excavating, grading, paving, landscaping, concrete work and masonry. Other trades, such as plumbing and electrical, may also be involved. The terms and the work involved are defined and expanded upon in the following sections.

SOILS REPORTS

See table 3–1, Types and Classifications of Soil. Any contractor involved with work directly on or excavating in the earth must know the soil conditions in which the project is located. This area of instructions must be understood and adhered to prior to any work being started on a construction project. A special report, called the *soils report,* is included in the legal documents for the project. This report identifies the type, content, and stability of the soil.

The sieve sizes designed for soil classifications range in size from a no. 4 to a no. 200. The sieve is a pie-shaped pan with a wire mesh in the bottom. The sieves are graded as no. 4, no. 8, no. 16, no. 30, no. 50, no. 100, and no. 200 for fine aggregates. The larger the sieve number, the finer the openings in the sieve. There are larger sieves for larger aggregates ranging in size from 6″ (152.4 mm) square to ⅛″ (3.17 mm) square. The smaller sizes are calculated in the number of meshes (openings) in 1 in². The larger sized sieves have square holes of the size indicated. For example, a no. 4 sieve has 16-¼″ (6.35 mm) square openings.

OFF-SITE CONSTRUCTION

Off-site construction includes all work outside of a property that may be required as well as any approaches into the property up to the property line. This may include grading and paving of a public street upon completion

TABLE 3–1
Soil Classifications

Types and Classifications of Soil

Class 1: Gravel—a mixture of natural or crushed rock from ¼″ (0.64 cm) to 3″ (7.62 cm) DIA.

Class 2: Sand—actually, a crushed gravel (rock) that is ⅜″ (0.95 cm) DIA maximum, will pass through a no. 4 sieve, but will be retained in a no. 200 sieve.

Class 3: Clay—a compact soil primarily of a silica and alumina mixture. When dry, it is brittle, when wet, very plastic (malleable).

Class 4: Loam—a rich, smooth soil consisting of clay, sand, and organic matter.

Class 5: Loam with sand (sandy loam)—a mixture of class 2 and class 4.

Class 6: Silt and loam—a very fine sand (passes through a no. 200 sieve) and class 4.

Class 7: Clay and loam—a mixture of class 3 and class 4.

of utility work or for street improvements only; curb and gutter installation; driveway entrance aprons; sidewalk improvements and **berms.** *Berms* are mounded areas of earth that may be located between the curb and sidewalk or between the sidewalk and the property line to form a privacy barrier. Additional plans may be prepared by the utilities or the local authorities to be included with the set of plans. The requirements may also be inferred by local ordinance.

SITE IMPROVEMENTS

Site improvements include all construction within the property limits up to, or a fixed distance from, the main structure. All or part of this construction area may be identified on the *site plan, plot plan,* or both. The allowable fixed distance surrounding the major structure on the property may vary outward from 4′-0″ (1.22 m) to 10′-0″ (3.05 m) in all directions from the foundation of the structure. This distance is determined by local codes and ordinances.

Excavating and Grading

Refer to figures 2–5 and 2–6, Site (Survey) Plan and *Plot Plan, Garland Residence.* Any change deliberately created in the earth from the natural grade elevations (site plan) to the finish grade elevations (plot plan) is referred to as *excavating* and *grading.* An excavating and grading contractor must have a survey (layout) prepared so that the natural contour elevations are changed to match the specified finish contour elevations on the property.

Earth that is to be excavated or removed from the project is called the *cut.* Earth that is added at any portion of a project is referred to as *fill.* Grading is the *leveling and compacting* of the fill soils and *leveling* the excavating to achieve the required finish elevation.

See figure 3–1, Mass Excavation Layout. Any excavation required, such as a sub-grade foundation for a subterranean garage or basement, is referred to as a *mass excavation.* This is one of the areas where the general contractor or excavating contractor must do a special survey to locate the exact ends of the excavation. Stakes, batter boards (horizontal pieces of lumber attached to

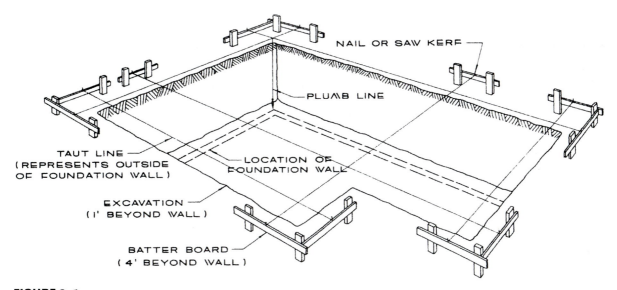

FIGURE 3–1

Mass Excavation Layout

the stakes), and taut strings are placed approximately 2'-0" (0.61 m) at each side of each corner of the excavation in the manner shown in the drawing. The strings define the outer perimeter of the excavation to identify the layout in the event of weather problems.

Where such work is done, care must be taken to ensure that the earth is sufficiently stable to support itself. Otherwise, *forms* and *shoring* may be necessary. Where such materials are necessary, the forms, shoring, or any bracing must remain until the footings and walls are properly cured.

Landscaping

Refer to figure 2–6, Plot Plan, Garland Residence. A plot plan for a single residential project usually shows the architect's and/or owner's ideas on the tree placement and some shrubbery. Additional landscape drawings include requirements for planting soil, ground cover, shrubbery, trees, watering systems (sprinklers), and sidewalks and/or driveways.

OTHER OFF-SITE/SITE IMPROVEMENTS

There are several other trades involved with the off-sites and site improvements. They include the paving contractor, concrete contractor, masonry contractor, plumbing contractor, and electrical contractor.

Paving

See figure 3–2, Paving. There are two types of paving: asphalt (*bituminous*) paving and concrete paving. Both are used for street and highway construction as well as for walkways and sidewalks.

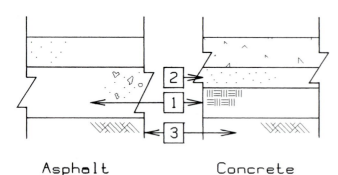

Asphalt   Concrete

KEYNOTES

1. 6" to 10" compacted base (Type II soil)

2. 4" compacted sand base

3. Natural earth

FIGURE 3–2
Paving

Asphalt is the general term for the types of materials used in asphaltic paving. One type of asphalt is **bitumen,** a natural product found in the earth. There are also two types of synthetic asphalt. One is produced from the residue of oil refining and the other is produced from the reduction of soft coal (referred to as *coal tar*).

Asphalt Paving. The normal asphalt paving application is indicated in figure 3–2. Included in the detail are the asphalt, the compacted base, and the sub-base or natural earth. A sealer may be applied over the asphalt. The quantity of base materials required is dependent upon the use of the paving. For example, asphalt used for vehicular traffic requires a deeper and better-compacted base than that used for pedestrian traffic. Asphalt paving used for vehicular traffic frequently uses a mixture of cement (or cement-like materials) with the asphalt, called *cementitious asphalt (asphalt cement).*

Concrete Paving. *Refer to figure 3–2.* The figure shows a typical concrete paving application. Included in the detail are the concrete surface, the compacted base, and the sub-base or natural earth. Concrete driveways and sidewalks should have a compressive strength of at least 2000 psi (909.1kg/cm^2).

Plumbing

The plumbing trade is divided into two major categories, *plumbing,* including waste disposal, fuel supply (gas and oil pipe and storage), and water or steam heating; and *piping* which includes all supply water (potable water). The size of pipe, the type of pipe, plumbing fixtures, accessories, and connections to both water and waste disposal systems are all part of plumbing. The materials used for plumbing include five basic groups:

1. Cast iron soil pipe and fittings. Used solely for waste disposal.
2. Galvanized iron (steel) pipe and fittings may be used for waste disposal or for potable water supply.

3. Copper tubing or pipe with solder joint or flare fittings is available in three categories referred to as:
   a. Soft copper, bendable by hand (referred to as tubing)
   b. Drawn copper, formed into rigid lengths from 12 lf (3.66 m) to 20 lf (6.1 m)
   c. Some drawn copper tubing, classified as DWV (drainage, waste, vent), used for waste disposal and treatment
4. Plastic tubing and piping, which is divided into five categories:
   a. Acrylonitrite-Butabiene-Styrene (ABS) for drainage and waste disposal
   b. Polyvinyl Chloride (PVC) for both cold water supply and drainage or waste disposal
   c. Chlorinated Polyvinyl Chloride (CPVC) use with both cold and hot water supply up to temperatures of 180° F
   d. Polyethylene (PE), for underground water supply (service)
   e. Polybutylene (PB), used for water supply
5. Black iron pipe for natural gas supply.

Supply (Potable) Water.   The water supply may be from springs, wells, or piped from water treatment, filtration, and purification plants to the consumer. Piped water supply sources are considered utility services owned privately or by local government. Wells and springs large enough to supply a neighborhood or small community may also be owned by private or government utilities. Small springs and wells are normally for use by the property owner only.

Fuel Supply.   Both natural gas and liquefied petroleum (LP) gas such as propane and butane, and oil supply line installations for residences and light commercial construction, and their storage facilities, are part of plumbing. Liquefied petroleum used by a single owner is supplied from a storage tank set apart from a structure above ground. Oil storage may be installed above ground but is usually installed below ground. Although considered part of heating, ventilation, and air-conditioning *(HVAC)* installations, the pipe work required for the installation and transmission of liquids for heat-transfer units, air-conditioning, cooling towers, and solar heating panels are also part of plumbing.

Septic Tanks and Leaching Fields (Leach Beds)

See figure 3–3, Leach Field, Garland Residence. In rural areas where sewer lines are not available, the homeowner must install an individual disposal sewage system in accordance with state and county requirements. One option is a **septic tank** and *leaching field (septic field)*. The septic tank is a holding tank used to chemically treat waste with a bacterial action. The leaching field is an area with perforated pipes buried in the ground into which the waterborne waste from the septic tank is allowed to slowly release. Any part of the septic system, tank, and leach field, must be a minimum of 25'-0" (7.62 m) from the nearest point of the structure and away from any water supply.

Electrical

See figure 3–4, Electrical Service Entrance Systems. Electrical blueprints include information for outdoor installations as well as indoor power and lighting.

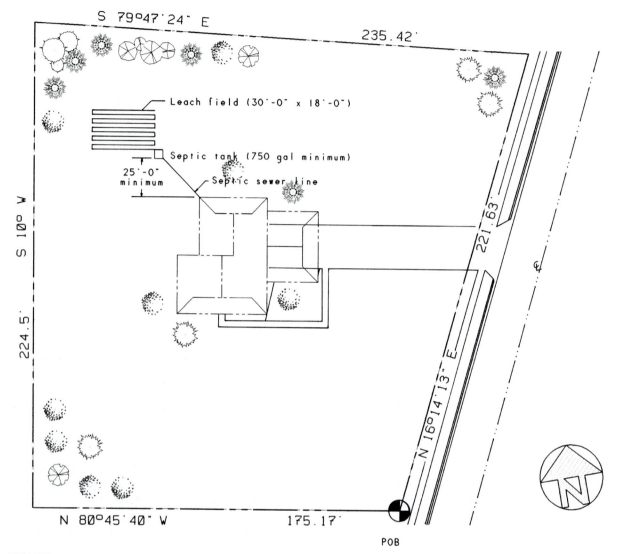

FIGURE 3–3
Leach Field, Garland Residence

Outdoor installations deal with the site lighting, power, and equipment from the utility company power supply (transformer) up to, and including, the service entrance equipment or switchgear (the protection devices for the structure). These are all included as part of the site improvements. The off-site construction (street lighting and power supply installation) is the responsibility of the electric utility or the local authorities. The electrical service entrance or switchgear equipment may be connected from an *overhead* or a *lateral* service.

Both service installations must meet the standards of the National Electric Code (NEC) and any local codes, which may supersede it. The NEC is the minimum standard established by the American Fire Protection Association (AFPA). Any local codes written that supercede these standards may not reduce the standards, they may only increase them.

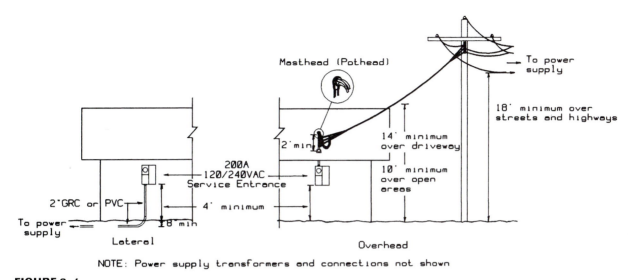

FIGURE 3–4
Electrical Service Entrance Systems

ALTERNATIVE ENERGY SOURCES

If the property is in a rural area where a power supply is not available, an electrical generating system is normally included in the property construction. The most common system is the unit powered by LP gas or an oil-fired engine, both of which are battery started.

Solar Heat. *See figure 3–5, Solar Heat System. Solar energy* is a popular source for both heat and power. Solar heating has been in use for centuries. Buildings in ancient times were constructed to retain and absorb as much heat from the sun as possible in the same manner used in present-day construction. In addition, solar heating systems use a panel (or panels) to absorb the heat from the sun and convert the water in the panel tubes to a warm water supply. The warm water generated by the sun in these panels is transferred to a pre-heat or storage tank and connected with either a hot water heater (shown) or a heating system to reduce or eliminate the hot water or the hot water/steam heating systems from other sources. Such systems have been in use for many years in the southwestern regions of the United States.

Solar Power. *See figure 3–6, Solar Power. Solar power* is common for minimal electrical requirements for residential and some light commercial usage. The disadvantage to such a system is that it will only work steadily in regions where it is exposed to the sun some portion of each day for a great part of the year. Solar panels collect the energy (heat) of the sun, which in turn energize the electronic solar cells within the panels, converting the heat energy into electrical energy. The electrical energy, direct current (DC), is transmitted from the panels to storage batteries. Another electronic device, called a *converter,* changes the DC current into alternating current (AC) to be used in the same manner as the power supplied from a standard utility company system. The collectors are connected with one another to transport energy to

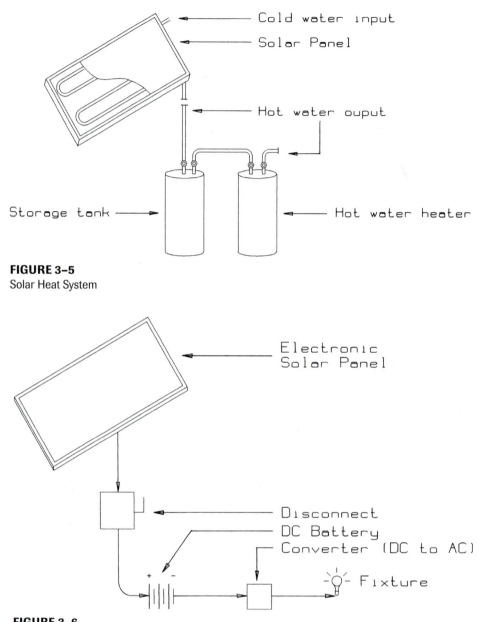

FIGURE 3–5
Solar Heat System

FIGURE 3–6
Solar Power

a transformer to increase the power output that can produce an electrical transmission system.

Wind Generation.   Wind generation is also being tested, with fields being constructed of hundreds of wind turbines in areas where winds are prevalent through most of the year. The fields are constructed of towers and/or poles with airplane-like propellers mounted on the top facing into the prevalent wind direction. The wind turns the propellers that in turn rotate electrical generators mounted at the base of the tower or pole. The combination of multiple generators, like the solar generation system, is also directed into transformers that can increase the power output and produce an electrical transmission system.

Other Services

There are at least two other utilities that are, or may be, involved in the site-improvement or off-site work. These are the telephone cable and the television cable services located along with the other major utilities. These services are frequently excluded from plot plan utilities locations since they are frequently installed in the same trench or underground areas along with the electrical service in separate conduit or cable and are also installed in accordance with the local utility requirements and local codes and ordinances.

In all cases of work being supplied laterally (underground), major caution is needed. Each trade (plumbing and electrical) must know the location of any and all underground conduits, pipes, and so on, prior to any trenching or excavating. A service has been established that supplies information to and from all utilities for protection of the underground services, and the personnel and equipment operating in and around them. No work is to be done until all utilities have been contacted and information returned to a contractor that the work is safe or that someone will be on the project to aid in the location and identification of any utility that may interfere, or be interfered with, during the construction. The telephone number of this service is readily available in every telephone directory and should be known by every contractor. The name given to the service varies from "Call Before You Dig" to "Joint Utility Location Information Exchange (J.U.L.I.E.)."

In the past, many underground utilities were "lost" because of various developers, building departments, and so on, having misplaced or destroyed the records of the installations. It is now required by code that a tracer wire (or wires) be placed in all utility trenches for the specific purpose of locating these underground utilities at a future date. This requirement introduces a safety factor never before available. When such future underground work is done, using the tracer check with the buried wire and electronic sensing equipment can prevent the destruction of existing equipment and injury or death to those working on the project.

CHAPTER EXERCISES

Completion

1. A _____ is an area located between a sidewalk and curb.

2. The underground electrical service is called a(n) _____.

3. Landscaping includes all trees, shrubs, ground cover, driveways and _____ where required.

4. A _____ system consisting of a tank and leach bed must be installed where sewer lines are not available to a property.

5. The general contractor is responsible for the installation of all _____ from utilities.

6. Site improvements include any work located _____ the property lines.

7. The Point of Beginning may be a datum point or a _____ marker.

8. An easement is the _____ that cut through a property.

9. An identification noted as N 30°22′10″ W is called a(n) _____.

10. A _____ is the measurement from a property line to the nearest point on a structure.

11. A footprint indicates the finish floor _____ of a structure on a site plan.

12. The site _____ is done by an engineering company.

13. _____ work includes all construction within the boundaries of the property normally to within 1.5 m of the structure.

14. Landscape plans may include a _____ system for watering the ground cover.

15. A(n) _____ is the direction noted in reference to true north.

Multiple Choice

_____   1. Off-sites include:
   a. Utilities construction
   b. Street improvements
   c. Curb, gutter, and sidewalk improvements
   d. All of the above

_____   2. Site improvements include:
   a. The foundation for the structure(s)
   b. The work from the property lines to the structure(s)
   c. Landscaping only
   d. The utility easement only

_____   3. The off-site work includes:
   a. Street, driveway, and berm improvements
   b. Work within the property not including the structure
   c. Work both on and off the property
   d. Utility construction

_____   4. The point of beginning should:
   a. Be a reference for all trades
   b. Be noted on both the site and plot plans
   c. Neither a nor b
   d. Both a and b

_____   5. The layout for a mass excavation uses:
   a. Taut string and batter boards
   b. Taut string, batter boards, and stakes
   c. Wire, batter board, and stakes
   d. Wire and batter boards

_____   6. Common plumbing pipe used for underground sewer may be:
   a. Type K, L, or M copper tubing
   b. Cast iron, ABS, or DWV pipe
   c. PVC or CPVC pipe
   d. All of the above

_____ 7. How many classifications of soil are there?
   a. No special classifications
   b. A minimum of two classifications
   c. A minimum of three classifications
   d. None of the above

_____ 8. A soils engineer is required for:
   a. Identifying the soils classifications
   b. Providing a soils report
   c. Neither a nor b
   d. Both a and b

_____ 9. A masonry retaining wall over 6'-0" (1.83 m) below the highest grade must:
   a. Have all $8 \times 8 \times 16$ (203.2 mm $\times$ 203.2 mm $\times$ 406.4 mm) structural CMU
   b. Have all $12 \times 8 \times 16$ (304.8 mm $\times$ 203.2 mm $\times$ 406.4 mm) structural CMU
   c. Meet local codes and ordinances
   d. None of the above

_____ 10. Modern technologies are now in use, or being tested, to provide electrical power. They include:
   a. Hydroelectric and nuclear power supply
   b. Solar and nuclear power supply
   c. Hydroelectric and wind-driven power supply
   d. Wind-driven and solar power supply

CHAPTER 4

Foundations and Below-Grade Construction (On-Site)

All work, both architectural and structural, described as the main structure, or within a maximum distance surrounding the structure as prescribed by codes and ordinances, are included in *on-site* construction. All trades are involved. This chapter discusses the below-grade construction material such as connections to all the utility services, concrete and/or masonry foundations, and below-grade moisture protection.

FOUNDATION CONSTRUCTION

The Frost Line

See figure 4–1, Average Footing Depths in the United States (Mainland Only). Weather conditions as well as local codes and ordinances determine the depth of concrete footings. There are similar maps found in many texts, specification pamphlets, and brochures from manufacturers. A study of the map shows that footings in the northern areas of the country must be 4'-6" (1.37 m) deep *or more*. The footings located in the southern and southwestern portions are from 1'-0" (0.30 m) to 1'-6" (0.46 m). Exception to the footing depths in these warmer climates is found in the higher altitudes (mountains). This is due to the weather conditions which are similar to those in the northern areas of the country. Because of the depth of the frost line in the northern sections of the country, basements (mass excavations to a minimum of 7'-0" [2.13 m] to the top of the foundation slab) are often constructed. In the mountainous areas of the southwestern United States, due to similar frost-line requirements, an owner or builder may construct either a full basement or under-floor *crawl space* to utilize the depth. A crawl space is an open area under the floor up to 3'-0" (0.61 m) or 4'-0" (1.22 m) deep, usually covering the same surface area as the structure above (to the foundation walls). Under-floor plumbing, piping, electrical, and HVAC installations may be found in these crawl spaces. Thermal protection for these items is also required in such spaces.

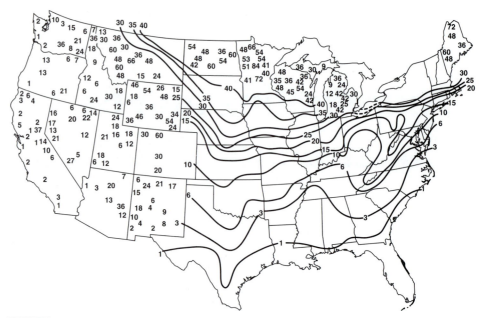

FIGURE 4–1
Average Footing Depths in the United States (Mainland Only)

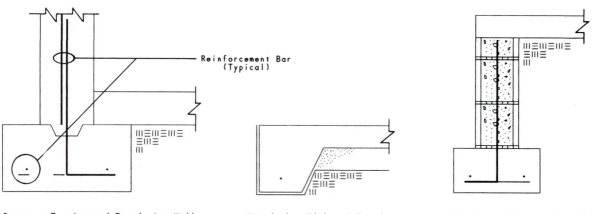

Concrete Footing and Foundation Wall   Monolithic Slab and Turndown   Footing w/Masonry Stem Wall and Concrete Slab

FIGURE 4–2
Foundations

Foundations

See figure 4–2, Foundations. To better understand the meaning of a *foundation* on a blueprint, one must understand the difference in the terminologies of a *footing,* a *foundation wall,* and a *slab.*

1. The footing is the *foundation support unit that must be sufficiently large and strong enough to support the structure built upon it.*

2. The foundation wall is the *exterior, below-grade bearing wall placed on a footing.* Foundation walls may also be referred to as *stem walls.*

3. The slab is the *base horizontal member that may be the support for the interior parts of a structure in conjunction with the footings.*
4. The term *foundation* includes *all of the above.*

CONCRETE

The following sections refer to concrete construction found in residential construction. More complex concrete construction common to commercial/industrial structures will be discussed in chapter 10.

Structural Classifications.   There are two major classifications given to concrete construction. The first classification is referred to as *structural concrete.* Structural concrete installations are controlled by rigid codes and regulations governing the mix and *compressive strength* of the concrete.

The second classification of concrete is referred to as *nonstructural concrete.* Items used for decorative purposes only and not considered structural support, such as arabesques, exterior window and door trim, balusters, railings, and fireplace trim, do not require the rigid standards of structural concrete. Some of these items may also be included in structural concrete, but most are of the nonstructural classification.

Compressive Strength.   *Compressive strength* of concrete is determined by how much weight or stress concrete can withstand before cracking or breaking. The compressive strength is determined by the quality of the *mixture* and *additives* that may be included in the concrete. These will be discussed in the following sections.

The compressive strength of many of the *nonstructural products* mentioned is 1000 psi (454.55 kg/cm^2), or less, depending upon the application. The minimum compressive strength for *residential construction* ranges between 2000 psi (909.1 kg/cm^2) and 2500 psi (1136.36 kg/cm^2), depending upon codes and ordinances.

Additives (Admixtures).   Chemicals or minerals added to the concrete that are capable of changing texture, controlling curing time or hardness, changing the color of the concrete, or increasing strength, are called *additives* or *admixtures.* A recent trend for strengthening concrete is the addition of a glass fiber or other strong fiber in the concrete mix, eliminating the necessity for welded wire fabric (see the following section at steel reinforcement). The mixture is referred to as *glass fiber-reinforced concrete* (GFRC) or *fiber-reinforced concrete* (FRC).

The location of the project and the time of year in which the project is under construction determine whether or not an additive is required to achieve the proper compressive strength and finish of concrete. Frost conditions require additives, such as an accelerator like *calcium chloride,* to assist in completing its cure without freezing, whereas desert regions may be more likely to use a retarder, such as *calcium lignosulfate,* to aid the curing process during the warmest periods. Care must be taken in the choice and/or quantity of additive so as not to harm the concrete (with too quick or too slow a curing time). Table 4–1 provides a partial list of other additives commonly used with concrete placement.

TABLE 4–1
Concrete Additives

Type	Use
Hardener and dustproofer	Increases the hardness of the concrete and aids in preventing the concrete from powdering when cured
Non-slip additive	Aids in preventing slippage when concrete is cured
Non-shrink additive	Reduces the shrinking in concrete during the curing process
Pozzolan (fly ash)	Aids in the curing time of concrete
Plasticizer	Stiffens the concrete mix
Fluidifier	Liquefies the mix for easier flow

TABLE 4–2
Cement Classifications

Type	Characteristics
Type I	For use when no special requirements are needed
Type IA	Air-entrained; for the same usage
Type II	Offers resistance to low soil and groundwater sulfates
Type IIA	Air-entrained; for the same usage
Type III	"High-early strength" to speed up curing time
Type IIIA	Air-entrained; for the same usage
Type IV	Produces less heat during cure. Used for large structural units such as dams, pilings, bridge abutments
Type V	Offers high resistance to soil and groundwater high sulfates

Concrete Mixtures.   The variation of the mixture of cement, sand, and aggregate (gravel or slag) also helps determine the compressive strength and curing time of concrete. A normal material mixture is identified as a 1:2:4 mix (one part cement, two parts sand, and four parts aggregate). The quantities determine the fluidity or stiffness of a mix. The type of cement used helps determine the quality of the mix. Table 4–2 identifies the types of cement common to concrete mixes.

The water-cement ratio also assists in the determination of the fluidity (how easily the mix will flow and settle), as well as the compressive strength of the mix in terms of the quantity of water (in gallons/liters) per bag of cement. The compressive strength of concrete is inversely proportionate to the water ratio. In other words, the more water used, the lower the compressive strength of the concrete.

Monolithic Concrete Placement.   *See Plan S-1, Garland Residence.* A monolithic placement is one in which a slab and footing are installed simultaneously. The footing and slab edges are formed as a single unit. The footing portions of the monolithic slab may include interior footings as well as the turndown at the perimeters. The size of the interior footing and turndown (width and height) varies with the size of the structure, the materials used for the structural walls, and the stability of the soil surrounding the structure. These are determined by the structural engineer.

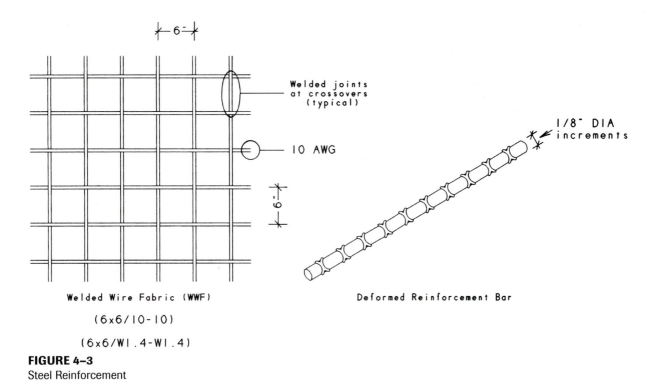

Welded joints
at crossovers
(typical)

10 AWG

1/8" DIA
increments

Welded Wire Fabric (WWF)

(6x6/10-10)

(6x6/W1.4-W1.4)

Deformed Reinforcement Bar

FIGURE 4–3
Steel Reinforcement

Steel Reinforcement. *See figure 4–3, Steel Reinforcement, and appendix III.* The most common steel reinforcing includes the installation of **reinforcement bar (rebar)** both smooth and deformed, and **welded wire fabric (WWF; mesh).** They are installed for the purpose of strengthening the concrete and to aid in preventing spalling (chipping) and cracking.

Rebar is manufactured in various sizes and is identified by the *diameter* of the bar in ⅛″ increments. #2 rebar (²⁄₈″ or ¼″ [6.35 mm] DIA) and #3 rebar (³⁄₈″ [9.53 mm] DIA), the smallest sizes, are normally smooth finished and are used to tie the heavier rebar in place until the concrete or masonry grout (a type of concrete) is installed. The #3 rebar may also be available as a deformed bar. All other sizes, #4 rebar (⁴⁄₈″ or ½″ [12.7 mm] DIA) and up, are deformed shapes only. The deformed shape is manufactured for the purpose of holding the steel in place in the concrete or grout after curing (setting and hardening of the concrete). Concrete shrinks while curing and can, therefore, release from the rebar. A smooth, straight section of rebar could be removed from the concrete as a result. The deformed rebar has various raised designs built into the bar that will prevent this from happening.

Rebar is also identified by its tensile strength. Tensile strength determines how much stress (stretch) the steel can resist before it breaks. The stress rating is given in kilo-pounds-per-square-inch (kpsi or kps), or classed as the grade of steel. The four commonly used strengths are 40 kpsi (40 grade), 60 kpsi (60 grade), 75 kpsi (75 grade), and 80 kpsi (80 grade).

See figure 4–4, Footing and Wall Reinforcement. There may be one, two, or more rebar installed horizontally in footings. This depends upon the structural requirements for the building that the footings support. The rebar is laid on chairs (small cementitious blocks to keep the rebar off the ground) before the concrete is placed. Rebar may also be necessary in both horizontal and vertical directions in concrete walls. Refer to figure 4–3. Installation of welded

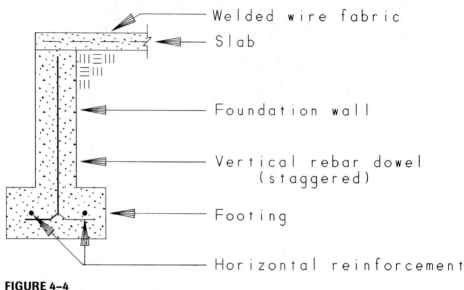

FIGURE 4-4
Footing and Wall Reinforcement

wire fabric (WWF) is regularly recommended in commercial construction for concrete slabs wherever there is continuous traffic weighing 3000 lbs (1363.64 kg) or more, or where heavy machinery (such as presses and stamping machines that can cause considerable vibration) is present.

Like rebar, welded wire fabric (WWF) is also manufactured in various sizes. The wire size and spacing are used to identify the material. For example, the smallest size is referred to as 6 × 6/10-10 or 6 × 6/W1.4-W1.4. The numbers on the left (6 × 6) indicate the spacing in perpendicular directions of 6″ (152.4 mm). The numbers on the right are the wire gauge (10 AWG—American Wire Gauge, or W1.4 mm, metric gauge). Many residential developers and architects also insist upon the use of this size in slab-on-grade construction.

Types of Concrete Foundations

Keyed Concrete Foundation. *See figure 4–5, Keyed Concrete Foundation. Placement* is the preferred term for the installation of wet concrete. Footings are normally placed independent of the foundation wall, that is, installed prior to the foundation wall. The footings may or may not be keyed to the foundation walls. The key is installed where seismic stability, freezing, or hydraulic (moisture pressure) control are required. Along with a moisture-resistant material (polyethylene or asphalt-impregnated), the key may also be used as a moisture barrier referred to as a *water stop.*

Dowels. Where rebar *dowels* are used, a key is unnecessary. A dowel is the connection between the footing and the foundation wall. It is usually made from #4 or #5 rebar in the shape of an "L" with the short length, called the "hook," installed into the footing. The "hook" may extend from 6″ (152.4 mm) to 9″ (228.6 mm) at a right angle to the vertical portion of the dowel. When used in conjunction with a foundation wall, the vertical part of the dowel extends a minimum of 2′-0″ (0.61 m) into the wall. The

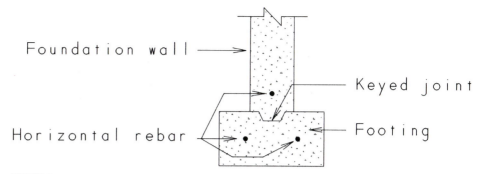

FIGURE 4–5
Keyed Concrete Foundation

angle is tied to the horizontal footing rebar so that the footing and wall are strengthened as a unit. Like the key, this system is also used where seismic stability is required.

The dowel may also be used horizontally in a slab. The horizontal slab dowel may extend up to 4'-0" (1.22 m) into the slab with the "hook" also extending from 6" (152.4 mm) to 9" (228.6 mm) into a foundation wall or footing.

Post-Tensioning.   A recent trend in residential concrete slab construction is the installation of reinforcement for *post-tensioning.* The reinforcement is placed in the slab by fastening one end of the *tendons* (steel rod, cable, or wire) to a plate (board or steel) along two sides of the foundation perimeter with the opposite ends exposed. The tendons are woven in a manner that resembles wire mesh. The concrete is placed, and *when fully cured,* plates are connected at the exposed ends and torsion is applied. The torsion is applied to strengthen the concrete slab. The system also protects against, or reduces, spalling and cracking of slabs when a structural load is placed upon it.

MASONRY

Brick, concrete masonry units (CMU), and *stone* are the three basic categories of masonry. The technology of recent years has improved on the old brick as well as having created new brick and concrete masonry units. Both brick and CMU are further categorized as *solid-core* or *hollow-core* units. Solid-core units contain 25% or less core (air) space. Hollow-core units contain from 25% to 75% core space. Solid-core units are used for trim or specialty work where reinforcement is unnecessary, such as for decorative finishes like corbels, for filling voids around other structural materials, as well as for veneers and pavers. Hollow-core brick and CMU are used where reinforcement and grout installations are required.

Masonry units are also identified by the **flexural measure (strength)** of the masonry unit. Flexural measure *(f'm)* is a combination of the measure of the compressive strength of a unit and its ability to withstand lateral and vertical stresses without breaking.

Another masonry term, which refers to the thickness of a wall, is the **wythe.** A single wythe wall is one unit thick; a double wythe wall is two units thick, and so on. *See figure 4–6, Double Wythe Masonry Wall.*

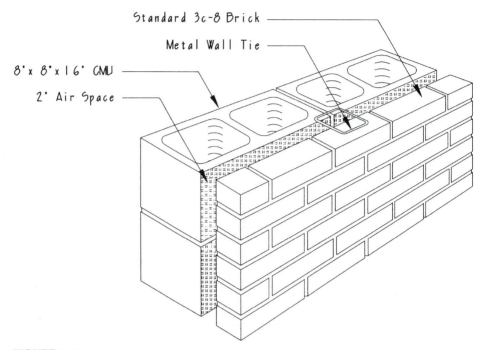

FIGURE 4–6
Double Wythe Masonry Wall

Concrete Masonry Units

See figure 4–7, Typical Concrete Masonry Units. CMU is made of concrete mixed with fine aggregates such as crushed rock, cinders, iron filings, or combinations of them, for strength and/or color (natural gray or tinted). They may also be classed as structural or non-structural depending upon usage. CMU is available in a variety of textures such as smooth-face, split-face, fluted, scored, raked, brushed, or glazed. CMU nominal sizes range from 2″ (50.8 cm) high to 12″ (304.8 mm) high, from 4″ (101.6 mm) wide to 16″ (406.4 mm) wide, and from 4″ (101.6 mm) long to 16″ (406.4 mm) long.

CMU is identified in size by width × height × length (W × H × L). The smaller CMU units (for example, 4″ × 2″ × 8″ [101.6 mm × 50.8 mm × 203.2 mm]) are usually solid-core bricklike concrete units. The larger sizes are usually of the hollow-core variety such as a nominal sized 8″ × 8″ × 16″ (203.2 mm × 203.2 mm × 406.4 mm) block. The actual size of this block is 7⅝″ × 7⅝″ × 15⅝″. The nominal size includes a ⅜″ (09.5 mm) thick mortar bed. The mortar is applied to the bottom and one end (head) of a unit to comply with the nominal measurements. (See the section on mortar and grout.)

Brick

See figure 4–8, Typical Brick Units. Clay brick, better known as "red brick," is the oldest and most common masonry unit in existence. Brick may be classed as solid- or hollow-core and is available in sizes ranging from 3¾″ (95.3 mm) to 6″ (152.4 mm) wide, 2¼″ (57.2 mm) to 5¼″ (133.4 mm) high, and 8″ (203.2 mm) to 12″ (304.8 mm) long. Brick is also identified in size by width, height, and

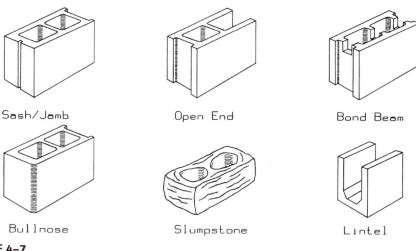

Precision/Smooth Face   Split Face   Fluted

Stretchers

Sash/Jamb   Open End   Bond Beam

Bullnose   Slumpstone   Lintel

FIGURE 4-7
Typical Concrete Masonry Units

length (W × H × L). The smaller, nominal size standard brick, 4″ × 2 ⅔″ × 8″ (101.6 mm × 67.8 mm × 203.2 mm), called a *3c-8 brick (3 courses = 8″ (203.2 mm))*, is usually a solid-core unit used mostly for veneers or pavers. Clay brick is available in many varieties of color from the standard red (terra cotta [clay] color) to variegated tinting and glazing. Brick, too, has a variety of textures such as cut, scored, scratched, broomed, or otherwise roughened surfaces.

See figure 4–9, Brick Positions. One of the advantages of brick over CMU is the ability to lay brick in various designs and positions more easily. The three most commonly used positions other than the stretcher course (standard position of a brick or block) shown in figure 4–9 are the header course, rowlock course, and the soldier course. The header course is most frequently seen as the cap brick on a brick wall, although it is used as a stabilizing unit in double wythe brick walls as well. The rowlock course is frequently used as the sloped-sill water table under exterior windows, or as the edge paver on steps and the like. The soldier course is used for decorative courses throughout a wall, or as the face brick on an arch along with a keystone masonry unit. The other brick positions are also used but are not seen quite as often as those mentioned.

Structural clay tile is classed as a brick although the sizes, shapes, and styles are more in the range of CMU. The difference between normal clay brick and structural clay tile is that standard brick is compressed into molds, whereas the tile brick is extruded (forced) under pressure through a machine

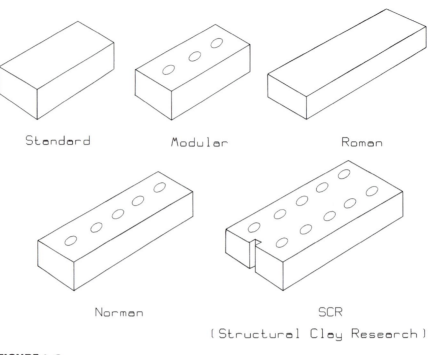

Standard   Modular   Roman

Norman   SCR
              (Structural Clay Research)

FIGURE 4–8
Typical Brick Units

mold. The extrusion process shapes the tile and compresses the mixture, thereby increasing the structural strength. The remaining manufacturing (kiln-drying) process is the same.

Stone

Granite, river rock, marble, slate, strata rock, limestone, and sandstone are all examples of natural stone used in masonry construction. Any of the stone types mentioned may be available in any area of the country. Stone may be a structural or nonstructural construction component. Stone may also be cut and set as a veneer over other masonry or frame wall construction.

Marble is primarily used as a facing over other materials, or as a tile, because it can be smoothed and polished into a fine aesthetic appearance. Slate and some strata rock can be obtained in flat sections that may be used for decks, plazas, patios, or entry floors, because of their structural strength and stability.

Limestone and sandstone are quarried and cut into shapes like brick. The most common treatment of limestone and sandstone is the Ashlar stone finish, which utilizes various pre-cut sizes of stone fitted together in a random design. They may also be sized in Roman and Norman brick sizes for standard bricklike applications. Because of the lack of strength in these materials they are used primarily as a veneer.

Cultured Stone is manufactured in panel form using a mix of variegated colored crushed rock and cement compressed and molded to look like natural stone. The panels vary in size from 2′ × 2′ (0.61 m × 0.61 m) to 4′ × 8′

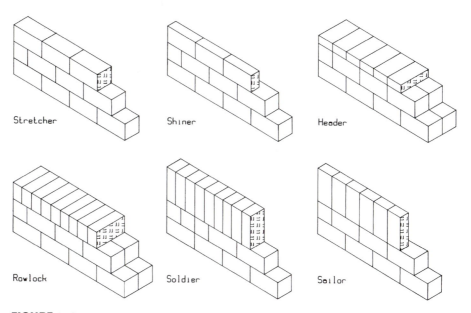

FIGURE 4–9
Brick Positions

(1.22 m × 2.44 m) and are approximately 1″ (2.54 cm) thick. The panels may be adhered to the back-up wall material (masonry or frame) by adhesives and/or masonry wall ties.

Masonry Wall Construction

See figure 4–10, Masonry Wall Construction. Structural masonry walls require a combination of concrete block or brick installed with mortar, grout, and reinforcement. The following sections identify and explain the use of these materials.

Mortar and Grout. A complete masonry installation includes mortar and grout used with the masonry units. *Mortar* is a concrete mix with a fine aggregate (sand) and may include a *fluidifier* additive to aid in binding the masonry units together. The need for the fluidifier depends upon weather conditions. Just as with concrete, hot, dry areas of the country may require its use while in more moderate and cooler temperatures it may not be necessary.

 Grout is also a concrete mix, similar to regular concrete, with a ⅜″ (0.95 cm) aggregate, with or without a *plasticizer* or other additive. Grout is used to fill the cavities of the hollow-core units containing reinforcement. When used in all wall cavities grout may increase the strength of the wall. The combination of an 8″ × 8″ × 16″ (20.32 cm × 20.32 cm × 40.64 cm) CMU structural unit (1535 to 1565 $f'm$ or better) and grout (2000 psi [909.1 kg/cm^2] or greater) can increase wall strength from a nominal strength of 1800 psi (818.18 kg/cm^2) to 3125 psi (1420.45 kg/cm^2) or more. A typical masonry foundation wall is filled solid with grout to strengthen the wall and to aid in moisture and fire resistance.

Reinforcement. Steel reinforcement used in masonry construction includes the rebar previously discussed in concrete and horizontal joint reinforcement. Horizontal joint reinforcement is a 9-gauge (AWG) wire system

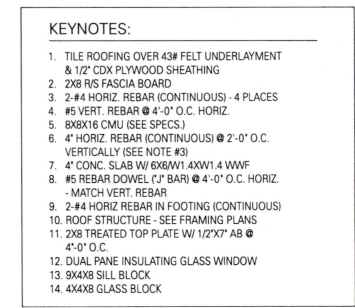

KEYNOTES:

1. TILE ROOFING OVER 43# FELT UNDERLAYMENT & 1/2" CDX PLYWOOD SHEATHING
2. 2X8 R/S FASCIA BOARD
3. 2-#4 HORIZ. REBAR (CONTINUOUS) - 4 PLACES
4. #5 VERT. REBAR @ 4'-0" O.C. HORIZ.
5. 8X8X16 CMU (SEE SPECS.)
6. 4" HORIZ. REBAR (CONTINUOUS) @ 2'-0" O.C. VERTICALLY (SEE NOTE #3)
7. 4" CONC. SLAB W/ 6X6/W1.4XW1.4 WWF
8. #5 REBAR DOWEL ("J" BAR) @ 4'-0" O.C. HORIZ. - MATCH VERT. REBAR
9. 2-#4 HORIZ REBAR IN FOOTING (CONTINUOUS)
10. ROOF STRUCTURE - SEE FRAMING PLANS
11. 2X8 TREATED TOP PLATE W/ 1/2"X7" AB @ 4'-0" O.C.
12. DUAL PANE INSULATING GLASS WINDOW
13. 9X4X8 SILL BLOCK
14. 4X4X8 GLASS BLOCK

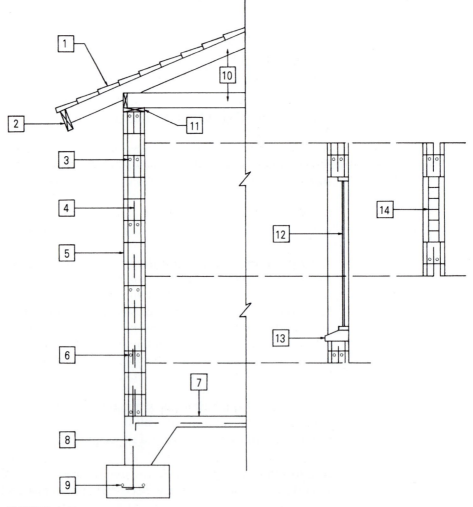

FIGURE 4–10
Masonry Wall Construction

formed in the shape of a ladder or an open-web truss in 10'-0" (3.05 m) to 20'-0" (6.1 m) lengths. The width of the material varies according to the width of the unit with which it is placed. Horizontal reinforcement is placed in the mortar bed every 16" (40.64 cm) vertically (every second course in an 8" (20.32 cm) high block or brick wall). It is placed every 12" (30.48 cm) vertically (every second course in a 6" (15.24 cm) high block or brick wall). Or it may be placed every 12" vertically (every third course in a 4" (10.16 cm) high block or brick wall). Horizontal reinforcement may reduce, or eliminate, the quantity of rebar required in a masonry wall. The elimination of rebar depends upon the type of structure, its geographic location, and local codes and ordinances.

Masonry Accessories.   There are two accessory classifications considered in masonry construction, masonry and non-masonry. Special formed masonry units such as lintels, sill block, keystones, or other non-standard block and brick are referred to as *masonry accessories*. *Non-masonry* accessories include all *embeds* such as rebar, horizontal joint reinforcement, wall ties, beam supports, anchor bolts, expansion bolts, and expansion (control) joint inserts. As in concrete installations, many embeds are supplied by others to be installed by the brick mason.

MOISTURE PROTECTION

Protection against water (moisture) and weather (moisture and thermal) are included under this heading. The title is correct in that the term *moisture protection* is preferred over the misnomers given to moisture protection, commonly called water*proofing* or damp*proofing,* because there is no product which will completely water*proof* or damp*proof.* Whether the protection is installed below grade or on the roof, the materials used to protect against moisture will only resist or retard penetration for extended periods. The longevity of any protection system depends upon the quality of the materials, proper installation procedures, and continued care and maintenance.

Asphaltic Moisture Protection.   *See figure 4–11, Asphaltic Below-Grade Moisture Protection.* Below-grade moisture protection is accomplished through the use of asphalt-based and coal tar-based materials, concrete additives, cementitious mixtures, and plastics (polyethylene, polyurethane, elastomeric polymers, acrylics or combinations of them). The products may be manufactured in sheet, roll, rigid board, or in a semi-viscous state for roll-on, brush-on, or spray-on applications. Asphalt-based and coal tar-based materials may be hot-mopped or cold-applied with a mop or brush.

Other Moisture Protection Materials.   Table 4–3 provides a list of other moisture-protective materials.
      Products such as gypsum or regular cement (not concrete), mixed with moisture-retardant additives and allowed to harden like concrete to reduce moisture penetration, are referred to as *cementitious* materials. Such products include both spray-on and hand-applied materials. Several of these products may be available for both moisture and thermal protection.

Hydrostatic Pressure in feet	Materials						Vertical wall protection (Layers)
	Cold Applied Emulsion			Hot Mop Asphalt and Base Sheet			
	Primer	Fabric	Emulsion	Primer	Base Sheet	Asphalt	
1	1	1	2	1	2	3	1
2	1	1	2	1	2	3	1
3	1	1	3	1	2	3	1
4	1	1	3	1	2	3	1
5	1	1	3	1	2	3	1
6	1	1	3	1	3	4	1
7	1	2	4	1	3	4	1
8	1	2	4	1	3	4	1
9	1	2	4	1	4	5	1
10	1	2	4	1	4	5	1
12	1	2	4	1	5	6	1
15	1	3	5	1	5	6	1
20	1	3	5	1	6	7	1
25	1	4	6	1	7	8	1
30	1	4	6	1	9	10	1

FIGURE 4–11
Asphaltic Below-Grade Moisture Protection

TABLE 4–3
Moisture Protection Materials

Type	Size	Use
Asphalt-impregnated rolls	1 sq, 3 sq, and 5 sq	Below-grade and on-grade moisture protection and roofing
Fiber-mesh sheets	"	"
Rubber-bed sheets	"	"
Polyethylene ("Visqueen")	Rolls to 20 lf × 100 lf	Horizontal slab protection
Polyurethane	Spray foam	Roofs and wall cavities
Elastomers	1 to 10 gal containers	Paint material
Acrylics	"	"
Composite boards	2′ × 4′ to 4′ × 8′	Moisture and thermal protection

CHAPTER EXERCISES

Multiple Choice

_____ 1. On-site construction includes:
   a. All work within the boundaries of the property
   b. All work within 5′-0″ (1.5 m) of the structure
   c. All work within the structure and for a distance of 5′-0″ (1.5 m) in all directions from the structure
   d. All of the above

_____ 2. The concrete contractor is responsible for:
   a. Excavation for all footings
   b. Supplying all the reinforcement for the concrete footings and stems
   c. Installing formwork where necessary for both the concrete and masonry work
   d. All of the above

_____ 3. All concrete mixes are:
   a. 1:2:4 ratio
   b. 1:2:6 ratio
   c. Made from a mixture of cement, sand, and aggregate
   d. 3500 psi (1587.6 kg/cm^2)

_____ 4. Footings may be:
   a. Placed over soil with less than 95% compaction
   b. Variable in size dependent upon the soil
   c. Variable in size dependent upon the soil and the structure above
   d. All of the above

_____ 5. The depth of the footings:
   a. Is a minimum 1′-6″ (457.2 mm)
   b. Is determined by the depth of the frost line
   c. Neither a nor b
   d. Both a and b

_____ 6. Masonry construction includes:
   a. The use of mortar and grout
   b. CMU or brick
   c. Stone
   d. All of the above

_____ 7. A measure of strength of a masonry unit includes:
   a. Its elasticity
   b. Its flexural strength
   c. Its impact resistance
   d. Its expandability

_____ 8. The purpose of reinforcement is:
   a. To make certain that the concrete or masonry properly cures
   b. To construct a heavier structure
   c. To add strength and rigidity to concrete or masonry
   d. None of the above

_____ 9. A monolithic placement of concrete:
   a. Is a slab and footing placed at the same time as a unit
   b. Is gigantic
   c. Requires separate placement of the turndown and slab
   d. Requires special concrete mixtures

_____ 10. The purpose of a key-cold, or keyed, concrete configuration is:
   a. The key aids in resistance to seismic pressure
   b. The key aids in resistance to moisture protection
   c. Neither a nor b
   d. Both a and b

True or False

T F   1. Divisions 1 through 16 are included in all on-site work.

T F   2. The masonry walls are all single wythe.

T F   3. The stem walls are constructed in concrete.

T F   4. Concrete slabs are to be a minimum 2000 psi (907.2 kg/cm^2).

T F   5. All masonry walls are solid grouted.

T F   6. The average frost-line footing depth for the state of Maine is 3'-6" (1.07 m).

T F   7. The term foundation refers to below-grade walls only.

T F   8. All brick is non-structural.

T F   9. The basic unit position of brick or block is the stretcher.

T F 10. Reinforcement bar is identified by its grade.

T F 11. The compressive strength of concrete is its ability to resist moisture.

T F 12. Concrete is classified for both structural strength and moisture resistance.

T F 13. Masonry includes brick and CMU only.

T F 14. A 1:2:4 mix in concrete equals one part sand, two parts aggregate, and four parts cement.

T F 15. Moisture protection for below-grade installations is necessary for both concrete and masonry walls.

Completion

1. The _____ course is the base course of masonry installations.

2. The size of an 8″ (203.2 mm) concrete masonry stretcher is _____″ × _____″ × _____″.

3. Concrete used for decorative purposes is normally classified as _____.

4. The abbreviation WWF stands for _____.

5. _____ of concrete can be accomplished by the installation of a special additive such as glass fiber reinforced (GFRC) concrete.

6. Moisture protection for any below-grade wall should have a _____ board.

7. On-site construction includes all work performed within a _____.

8. The _____ strength of masonry is its resistance to compressive and lateral stresses.

9. The frost line determines the _____ of a footing.

10. Moisture protection includes all materials required to protect a structure from below-grade _____ and weather.

CHAPTER 5

The Structure Above Grade (On-Site)

On-site construction refers to the main structure to be installed on a property. The construction of on- or above-grade concrete and masonry walls, rough framing, the roof structure and roofing, finishes, mechanical, plumbing, electrical, cabinetry, and appliances are all part of the on-site construction work.

ROUGH CARPENTRY (FRAMING)

Rough carpentry includes both wood and *light-gauge metal framing* necessary for the installation of the floor, walls, ceiling, and roof structure. Light-gauge metal framing is discussed later in this chapter.

See appendix III, Grade Designation for Dimension Lumber. The useful purpose of the framing member determines the classification and grade of the lumber, For example, a **stud** is classed as *stud* or *economy* grade while **joists** are classed as *select structural (SS)*, and *grades 1, 2,* or *3*. These levels are used for each of the lumber types that follow.

The *quality* classification of lumber is determined by the lumber grade. For example, Douglas fir-larch (DF-L) is the best grade of fir. The classification DF is one grade lower than the DF-larch. These classifications are common to the northwestern regions of the United States and western Canada. There is also DF-S, identifying the Douglas fir found in the southwestern regions (Nevada, Arizona). Hemlock fir (HF), also common to the western regions of the United States, is classified in the same manner as the Douglas fir.

Pine is a separate grade of lumber common to Idaho and the southeast (Alabama, Georgia, Tennessee). The pine lumber common to the southeast is referred to as the Southern Pine. As noted in the *Grade Designation for Dimension Lumber* in appendix III, the types of lumber are given various classes dependent upon usage.

One of the quality checks of lumber is the determination of the number of *knots* in 1'-0" (0.30 m) of board. The fewer the knots found, the higher the lumber classification. These lumber classifications were established by the Western Wood Products Association (WWPA).

Wood Framing Members

The wood framing members for all building construction necessary to rough carpentry installations includes **sill plates, sole (or bottom) plates, top plates, floor** and **ceiling joists, studs, rafters, subflooring (under-layment),** and **sheathing (siding and roof)** construction. Each of these materials carries one or more of the classifications mentioned in the appendix III. Any portion, or all, of the framing members discussed in the following sections may be a part of any one structure such as the Garland residence. *See figures 5–1 and 5–2, Architectural and Structural Sections, Garland Residence.*

Plates

Plates are the framing members to which floor, wall, and ceiling framing are attached. They are properly identified by their location and use, such as the sill plate, sole plate, and single or double top plate. Plate stock is usually ordered, shipped, and installed in random lengths (R/L), meaning that the lumber may

SECTION A-A

KEYNOTES:

1. Wood truss w/2x6 top chord
   and 2x4 bottom chord.

2. 6:12 hip. Wood shake roofing.

3. Vaulted ceiling w/1/2" GWB.

4. 1/2" GWB at all walls (UNO).

5. 6'-0" x 6'-8" cased opening.

6. 4040 FX dual-pane window
   (typical of 2).

7. 1668 FX dual-pane sidelite
   (typical of 2).

8. 3068 panel entry door
   w/entry latch and deadbolt.

9. 4" concrete slab and footing -
   see plans.

FIGURE 5–1
Architectural Section, Garland Residence

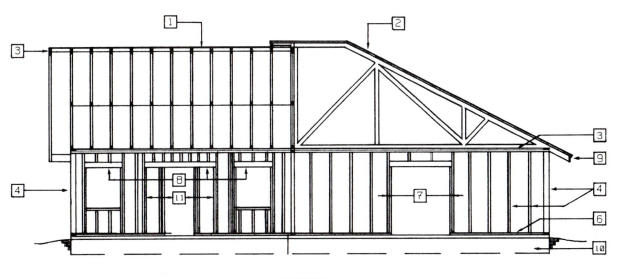

SECTION A-A

KEYNOTES:

1. 5:12 scissors truss @ 24" o.c.
   1/2" CDX plywood sheathing over.

2. 6:12 hip (half) truss @ 24" o.c.
   1/2" CDX plywood sheathing over.

3. 2x double top plate

4. 2x6 studs @ 16" o.c. - typical
   at all exterior walls.

5. 2x4 studs @ 24" o.c. - typical
   at all partitions UNO.

6. 2x6 mudsill

7. King stud - typical at all
   openings. Match wall framing.

8. 2x6 DF #2. or better. for all
   lintels (headers) UNO.

9. 2x8 R/S fascia (typical)

10. 3000 psi concrete foundation
    slab and footing - monolithic
    placement.

11. Trimmer stud - typical at all
    openings. Match wall framing.

FIGURE 5–2
Structural Section, Garland Residence

be shipped in varying lengths ranging from 8 lf (2.44 m) to 24 lf (7.32 m) mixed into a single load. The lumber may be longer, but for normal shipping by truck or rail car, these are the most economical lengths. For smaller work the carpentry contractor may use all 16 lf (4.88 m) to 20 lf (6.1 m) lengths.

Sill Plate. *See figure 5–3, Basic Framing Components.* Wherever wood framing meets a concrete or masonry substrate, a sill plate is required to protect the framing above from caustic deterioration from the alkaline content of the concrete or masonry. The sill plate is also used as a deterrent for insect and rodent infestation. The lumber used may be either redwood or pressure-treated wood, referred to as a *mudsill* installed for this protection. One of the treated lumber processes is called *Wolmanizing®*. The process utilizes a salt-based solution impregnated into units (bundles) of lumber under pressurized heat and moisture inside a tank. The lumber is then removed from the tank

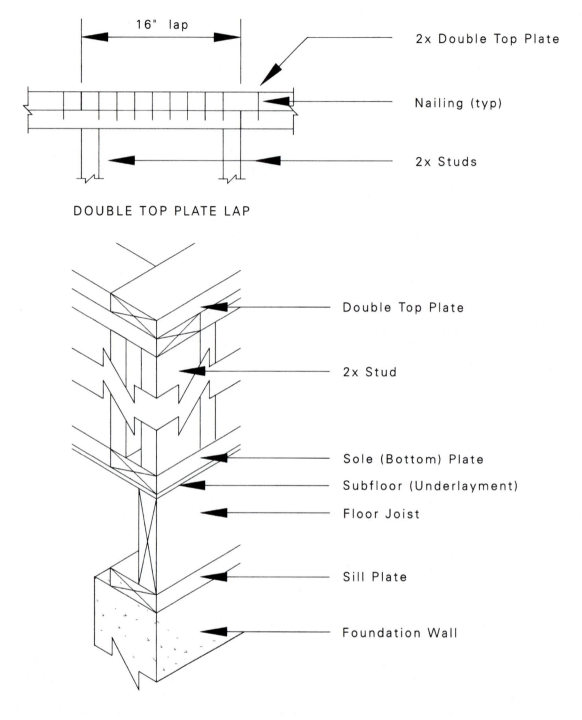

16" lap

2x Double Top Plate

Nailing (typ)

2x Studs

DOUBLE TOP PLATE LAP

Double Top Plate

2x Stud

Sole (Bottom) Plate

Subfloor (Underlayment)

Floor Joist

Sill Plate

Foundation Wall

WALL FRAMING

FIGURE 5–3
Basic Framing Components

and kiln-dried to remove as much moisture as possible to prevent warping. The treated wood is identified by the letters *PTMS* (*Pressure Treated MudSill*). Hemlock Fir (HF) #3 or Douglas Fir (DF) #3 is used for this process. Unless specified otherwise, treated members are required for the exterior bearing walls only. Where allowed by code, *untreated* HF #3 or DF #3 may be used as the sill plate on slabs for all interior walls.

Refer to figures 5–1 and 5–2, Architectural and Structural Sections, Garland Residence, and Sheet A-1, Floor Plan, Garland Residence. The size of the standard sill plate may range from a 2 × 4 (50.8 mm × 203.2 mm) up to a 2 × 12 (50.8 mm × 304.8 mm) to match the surface upon which it is installed such as a 12″ (304.8 mm) thick concrete foundation wall, or the framing above. The Garland residence requires the 2 × 6 (50.8 mm × 152.4 mm) treated sill plate for all exterior walls. The interior walls of the Garland residence are also constructed on the concrete slab. The sill plate may be either treated or untreated stock.

Sole and Top Plate.   *Refer to figure 5–3.* Frame walls placed on a wood base (beams, joists and subflooring) require a sole (bottom) plate. The top of a frame wall also requires a plate, called the top plate, which may be single or double thickness. The sole plate and top plate are cut from DF, common, or HF, utility stock. Exterior wall and interior bearing wall framing require a double top plate. Non-bearing partition walls may have a single top plate. The sole and top plates are normally the same size as the studs, *unless noted otherwise* (U.N.O.).

All the walls for the Garland residence are topped with a double top plate. Where the ends of the double top plate abut one another, the abutting joints must be staggered so there is a minimum of 16″ (406.4 mm) in each direction from the lapped joints. 8-10d or 8-16d nails are used to secure the plates. (*Refer to the top section cut in figure 5–3*).

FLOOR AND CEILING JOISTS

See tables 5–1, Floor Joists, and 5–2, Ceiling Joists. Both floor joists and ceiling joists are horizontal framing members installed to support some portion of the structure built above. Just as with plate stock, each member should be identified by its use and location on the construction site. For example, floor joists support the floor and all framing above to the top plate, as well as the roof structure. Ceiling joists support the floors above in multi-floor dwellings, as well as the roof structure.

Joists must meet the minimum standards for Douglas fir, Hemlock fir, and Southern Pine as found in the International Building Code. Joists are placed utilizing the shortest practical span from bearing point to bearing point due to the allowable bending (fiber) stress, *Fb*, and the modulus of elasticity, *E*, the ability of the lumber to stretch. All codebooks include the structural capabilities of each classification of lumber and the maximum span allowed for each. The information provided in tables 5–1 and 5–2 are excerpts from the International Code 2000 book.

The maximum span allowed depends upon the installed or anticipated load and the joist spacing. This depends upon the **live load** and **dead load** applied to the structure (as noted at the top of the tables). A *live load* is any load that is moveable, such as a person or furniture not affixed to the structure (chair, table, desk, and so on). A *dead load* is any load that is fixed to the structure such as cabinetry, plumbing fixtures or HVAC units as well as the weight of the structure itself.

TABLE 5–1

Allowable Floor Joist Spans

FLOOR JOIST SPANS FOR COMMON LUMBER SPECIES

(Residential Sleeping Areas, Live Load = 30 psf, L/Δ = 360)

DEAD LOAD = 20 psf

(2x8 @ 16″ O/C)

Species	Grade	Maximum floor joist span (ft-in)
Douglas Fir-Larch	SS	15′-0″ (4.57 m)
Douglas Fir-Larch	#1	13′-6″ (4.11 m)
Douglas Fir-Larch	#2	12′-7″ (3.83 m)
Douglas Fir-Larch	#3	9′-6″ (2.89 m)
Hem Fir (Hemlock)	SS	14′-2″ (4.32 m)
Hem Fir	#1	13′-1″ (3.99 m)
Hem Fir	#2	12′-5″ (3.79 m)
Hem Fir	#3	9′-6″ (2.89 m)
Southern Pine	SS	14′-8″ (4.47 m)
Southern Pine	#1	14′-5″ (4.40 m)
Southern Pine	#2	13′-6″ (4.11 m)
Southern Pine	#3	10′-3″ (3.12 m)
Spruce-Pine-Fir	SS	13′-10″ (4.22 m)
Spruce-Pine-Fir	#1	12′-7″ (3.83 m)
Spruce-Pine-Fir	#2	12′-7″ (3.83 m)
Spruce-Pine-Fir	#3	9′-6″ (2.89 m)

TABLE 5–2

Allowable Ceiling Joist Spans

CEILING JOIST SPANS FOR COMMON LUMBER SPECIES

(Uninhabitable Attics With Limited Storage, Live Load = 20 psf, L/Δ = 360)

DEAD LOAD = 20 psf

(2x8 @ 16″ O/C)

Species	Grade	Maximum floor joist span (ft-in)
Douglas Fir-Larch	SS	19′-7″ (5.97 m)
Douglas Fir-Larch	#1	17′-5″ (5.31 m)
Douglas Fir-Larch	#2	16′-3″ (4.95 m)
Douglas Fir-Larch	#3	12′-4″ (3.76 m)
Hem Fir (Hemlock)	SS	18′-6″ (5.64 m)
Hem Fir	#1	16′-10″ (5.13 m)
Hem Fir	#2	16′-0″ (4.88 m)
Hem Fir	#3	12′-4″ (3.76 m)
Southern Pine	SS	19′-3″ (5.87 m)
Southern Pine	#1	18′-11″ (5.77 m)
Southern Pine	#2	17′-5″ (5.33 m)
Southern Pine	#3	13′-3″ (4.04 m)
Spruce-Pine-Fir	SS	18′-1″ (5.51 m)
Spruce-Pine-Fir	#1	16′-3″ (4.95 m)
Spruce-Pine-Fir	#2	16′-3″ (4.95 m)
Spruce-Pine-Fir	#3	12′-4″ (3.76 m)

There is one additional load included in a roof structure, the **wind lift.** It deals with wind resistance. The engineer designing the structural roof support system must also include this where strong winds, such as gales and hurricanes, are of concern.

A double joist must be installed parallel to, and under, a bearing wall. Double joists must be installed perpendicular to walls running the other direction. For example, joists installed in a north-south direction for one room may change to an east-west direction at an adjoining room, requiring a double joist at the direction change. Additional joists may be required such as under kitchens and bathrooms where the load is greater than normal.

Header Joists.   The header joist, also known as the rim joist, is a continuing member the same size as the floor or ceiling joist extending end-to-end (or out-to-out) along the perimeter of a wall. It is placed on the sill or sole plate, or double top plate of a multi-story structure at the floor or ceiling joist, so the outside face of the header (rim joist) matches the outside edge of the sill, sole, or top plate. It is used to hide, protect, and stiffen the ends of the interior joists abutting it. The lengths of these members may be all the same or in random lengths.

Bridging.   *Refer to figure 5–4, Joist Framing.* Bridging may or may not be indicated on the plans. Most building code requirements state that bridging must be installed for all joists where the span is greater than 8 lf (2.44 m). The purpose of the bridging is to provide more strength and rigidity to the floor or ceiling structure, thus offering a shorter span upon which to apply load from above. The bridging may be a *solid* member (the same size as the joist) cut to fit between joists, 2 × (50.8 mm) wood cross bridging, or pre-fabricated metal cross bridging.

Structural Wood Beams

See figure 5–5, Beams and Joists. Alternates to the standard 2 × (50.8 mm) are pre-fabricated engineered products that are especially designed for beams and joists. Maximum sizes and lengths are prescribed by code in the same manner as the 2 × (50.8 mm) beam or joist members. The products described in this section are produced by Trus-Joist.

Micro-Lams®.   The Micro-Lam® beam/joist is manufactured from several layers of plywood, glued and compressed into a beam in sizes from 10″ (25.40 cm) to 12″ (30.48 cm) in width, 2″ (5.08 cm) to 6″ (15.24 cm) thick, and up to 20′-0″ (6.10 m) in length in regular lumber increments of 2′-0″ (0.61 m). They may also be ordered in specific lengths as required. The Micro-Lam® beam may be used for floor joists, ceiling joists, or lintel (header) beams over framed wall openings, such as a garage door header beam.

Parallams®.   One of the more recent beams to be manufactured is the Parallam® beam. This beam is manufactured from compressed and glued wood fragments and fibers to form beams for use as joists similar to the Micro-Lam® beam. They are exposed architectural and/or structural support beams or lintels (headers) over framed wall openings.

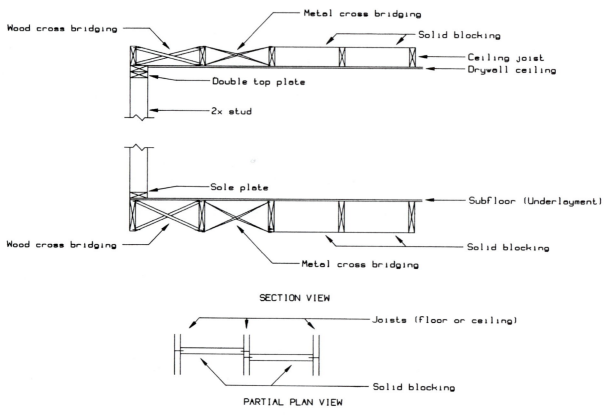

FIGURE 5-4
Joist Framing

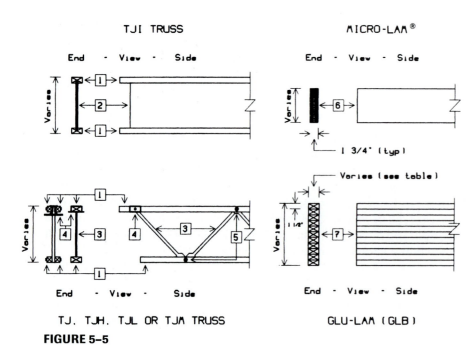

KEYNOTES:

1. 2x top and bottom chord - varies w/truss size
2. Structural I plywood web - varies w/truss size
3. Tubular steel web - varies w/truss size and type
4. Truss bearing plate variations
5. Thru bolt - size varies w/truss size and type
6. Micro-lam beam (see table Figure 9-1 for sizes)
7. Glu-lam beam (GLB) (see table Figure 9-2 for sizes)

FIGURE 5-5
Glue-Laminated Beams and Trusses

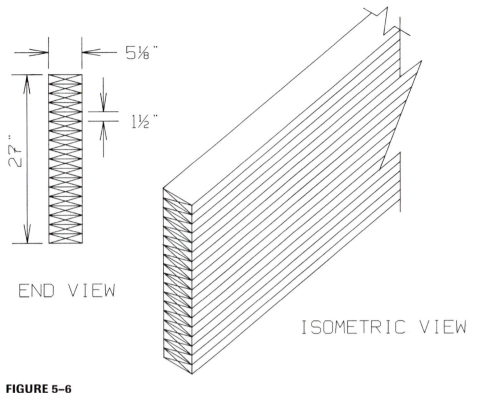

FIGURE 5–6
5⅛" x 27" Glue-Laminated Beam

Glue-Laminated Beams. *See figure 5–6, 5⅛" × 27" Glue-Laminated Beam.* Another more common and larger beam is known as the **glue-laminated beam** (glu-lam or GLB). Glu-lams may be used solely for architectural aesthetics, for structural support, or both. They may be used as a girder beam for floor support, as a hip or ridge beam for roof support, or as a buttress support for wall structures where both aesthetics and structural design criteria are desired (such as church construction). The architectural beam is finished with a varnish or paint for appearance. The structural beam is used where no finishing is necessary, or, in some cases, where a paint finish may be required.

The glu-lam is manufactured from multiple layers of milled select lumber. The lumber is glued on the wide side under compression and heat, milled for a smooth finish, and wrapped in plastic (heavy gauge polyethylene sheets) when totally dried. The milling reduces the size of the lumber even more than the original milling. The nominal 2 × 4 (50.8 mm × 101.6 mm) size is reduced to 1½" × 3⅛" (38.1 mm × 79.4 mm) and is ordered by its finish size. For example, the drawing in figure 5–6 shows a glu-lam beam produced from 2 × 6 (50.8 mm × 152.4 mm) lumber. The milled lumber is 1½" × 5⅛". The beam is 27" (685.8 mm) deep. The quantity of lumber necessary to make a 27" (685.8 mm) deep beam is determined as follows:

27" ÷ 1½" =
27" ÷ 1.5" = 18 pc

or, in metric calculation:

685.8 mm ÷ 38.1 mm = 18 pc

The beam is identified as a 5⅛″ × 27″ (130.2 mm × 685.8 mm) beam. GLB's are manufactured on special order and prepared in specific lengths as required.

The Truss Joist

Refer to figure 5–5. Truss joists are manufactured with one or two 2 × (50.8 mm) top and bottom *chords* and several layers of plywood fastened edgewise between, or they may be manufactured using tubular metal or 2 × (50.8 mm) wood webbing in diagonal design, extending the full length of the truss. As with glu-laminated beams, open-web trusses are prefabricated to prescribed lengths on special order.

Subflooring

Refer to figures 5–3 and 5–4. Subflooring, or underlayment, is normally installed by gluing and nailing ¾″ (19.1 mm) or 1″ (25.4 mm) CDX, 5-ply, 4′ × 8′ (1.22 m × 2.44 m) sheets over the floor joists. An alternate subfloor is the Oriented Strand Board® (OSB®) installed in the same manner as the plywood. OSB® is made from the same basic materials as the Parallam® beam. The compressed and glued chips and fragments are mixed with fibrous strands (vegetable and/or mineral) and formed into sheet sizes similar to plywood. The subfloor adds stability to the floor structure as well as backing for the finish floor materials.

The letters CDX identify the type of plywood to be used as established by the APA-The Engineered Wood Association. The letters *"C"* and *"D"* identify the exterior layers of plywood. *"C"* is a smooth, finished face with few knotholes. *"D"* is slightly less smooth with some knotholes exposed. The *5-ply* means that there are five layers of plywood. The grain of each layer is always at right angles to the previous layer and glued on both sides, except for the exposed layers, which are glued on one side only. Plywood is always produced in an odd number of layers (three and five layers). The *"X"* is the abbreviation for *"exterior grade."* Therefore, CDX is an exterior grade plywood with a layer of *"C"* and *"D"* classifications exposed. Subflooring is available with plain butts (straight ends), tongue-and-groove (T&G) joints, or shiplap joints. The T&G and shiplap board offers better control in the installation of the board.

Wall Framing

See figure 5–7, Miscellaneous Wall Framing—Wood. Wall framing includes top and bottom (sill or sole) plates, studs, and window or door lintels (headers). The walls may be either bearing walls or partition (non-bearing) walls. All exterior walls supporting the structure above are bearing walls. There may also be interior bearing walls installed as part of the structural support system. Exterior and interior bearing walls are normally framed with 2 × 6 (50.8 mm × 152.4 mm) studs at a maximum 16″ (406.4 mm) on center (O/C). Stud sizes equal to, or

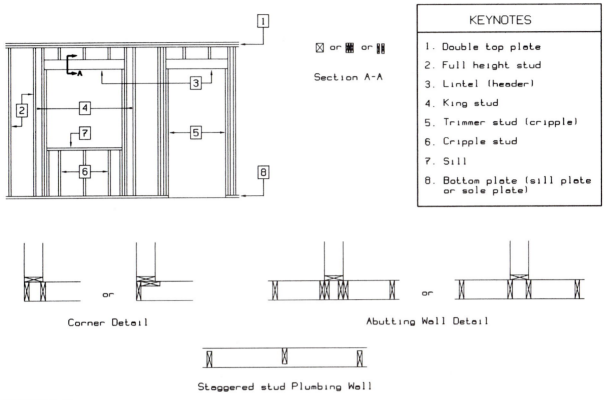

FIGURE 5–7
Miscellaneous Wall Framing—Wood

larger than, 2 × 6 (50.8 mm × 152.4 mm) such as 3 × 4 (76.2 mm × 101.6 mm), 2 × 8 (50.8 mm × 203.2 mm), 2 × 10 (50.8 mm × 254.0 mm), and so on, may be installed if necessary or desired. Studs larger than 2 × 6 (50.8 mm × 152.4 mm) may be spaced at 20″ (508.0 mm) or 24″ (609.6 mm) O/C, depending upon the structural load requirements. Some codes allow 2 × 4 (50.8 mm × 101.6 mm) studs at 16″ (406.4 mm) O/C for exterior and interior bearing walls in one-story residences. Interior plumbing walls are also normally framed with 2 × 6 (50.8 mm × 152.4 mm) studs at 24″ (609.6 mm) O/C and 2 × 6 (50.8 mm × 152.4 mm) plates. They may be installed with 2 × 4 (50.8 mm × 101.6 mm) studs staggered at 24″ (609.6 mm) O/C on 2 × 6 (50.8 mm × 152.4 mm) top and bottom plates. The remaining non-bearing, or partition, walls are usually framed with 2 × 4 (50.8 mm × 101.6 mm) studs at 24″ (609.6 mm) O/C.

Studs are graded as DF construction grade or HF #3 common. Both grades are available in pre-cut sizes of 92½″ (2.349 m) to 92⅜″ (2.35 m) for standard 8′-1″ (2.46 m) high walls, or can be obtained in even 2′-0″ (0.61 m) increments for shorter or longer wall heights. The standard wall height is identified from the pre-cut 92½″ (2.349 m) studs and the top and bottom plates (using actual thicknesses or lengths) as follows:

1½″ bottom plate + 92½″ stud + 3″(1½″ × 2) double top plate = 97″ or 8′-1″

In metric calculation, the stud is identified as follows:

0.0381 m bottom plate + 2.35 m stud + 0.0762 m double top plate = 2.46 m

Lintels (Headers).   *Refer to figure 5–7, Section A-A*. The lintel (header) is installed over an opening in the wall framing to replace the load support for the structure above the opening. It may be made from double or triple lengths of 2 × (50.8 mm) structural members, or a beam of the proper wall thickness. The lintel (header) gets larger by at least one size (length) as the opening gets wider. A rule of thumb for a structural member over a window or door opening states that the lintel (header) should be one size larger than the wall opening and at least 8″ (203.2 mm) longer than the opening (4″ [101.6 mm] on each end). For example, the member required for a 4′-0″ (1.22 m) wide opening in a 2 × 6 (50.8 mm × 152.4 mm) bearing wall should have a minimum of two 2 × 6 (50.8 mm × 152.4 mm) framing members placed on end flush with the exterior and interior faces of the stud wall, or three 2 × 6 (50.8 mm × 152.4 mm) framing members placed on end back-to-back, or a 6 × 6 (152.4 mm × 152.4 mm) framing member. The framing member should be DF #1 or #2, or equal.

Specifications may require even larger sizes depending upon the load the lintel (header) supports. For example, in a balloon frame wall 20′-0″ (6.10 m) to 24′-0″ (7.32 m) high, the member required over a 6′-0″ (1.83 m) window on the lower level may be as large as three 2 × 12 (50.8 mm × 304.8 mm) or a 6 × 12 (152.4 mm × 304.8 mm), DF #1. These spans are determined by code in the same manner as joists. Lintels (headers) over openings in non-bearing partitions may be flat single members the size of the stud, or a double framing member placed on end.

King and Trimmer Studs.   *Refer to figure 5–7*. Wherever an opening in a wall occurs there are usually two king studs, one on each side of the opening. The *king* stud is the full-height stud immediately adjacent to an opening and abutting the lintel (header) over the opening. There are two trimmer studs, one on each side of the opening. The trimmer stud, also referred to as a cripple stud, is cut to fit under both ends of the header for its support. The opening between the trimmers should not be less than ⅛″ (3.2 mm) nor more than ¼″ (6.4 mm) larger than the required opening for the door or window that is to be installed.

Cripple Walls.   *Refer to figure 5–7*. Wall framing above an opening is supported by the header and extends to the top plate above a door or window. This is called a cripple wall. A cripple wall also extends from the sole or sill plate to the sill frame below a window opening. The stud spacing of a cripple wall is the same as the full-height wall framing in which the opening exists.

Diagonal Bracing or Shear Wall.   *See figure 5–8, Diagonal Bracing and Shear Wall Construction*. The purpose of **diagonal bracing** or **shear paneling** is to give additional structural strength, seismic stability, and lateral wind load protection to a structure as well as to maintain a true and straight alignment of the walls. Local codes and ordinances are required.

Diagonal, or let-in, bracing may be 1 × 6 (25.4 mm × 152.4 mm), HF #3 or DF #3, notched into the studs and nailed to each stud in which the embedment is made. The standard metal let-in brace may be used instead of the wood let-in brace and should also be notched into the studs. A diagonal brace is installed in both directions at each exterior corner at an angle of 60° maximum from horizontal. Additional bracing is installed in the same manner at intervals of 25′-0″ (7.62 m) clear wall space (no openings) along any exterior wall.

Wind and seismic codes, to provide for lateral loads imposed by wind and violent vibration, respectively, require that a shear panel ⅜″ (9.5 mm), 3-ply, or ½″ (12.7 mm), 5-ply, plywood, or equivalent OSB®, be installed vertically from

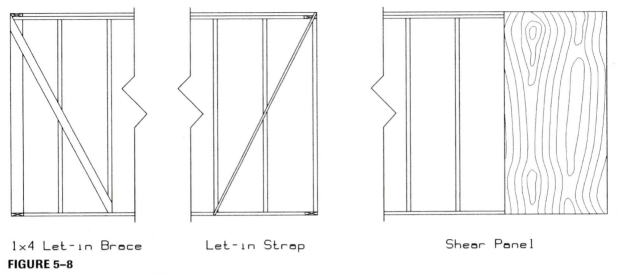

1x4 Let-in Brace   Let-in Strap   Shear Panel

FIGURE 5–8
Diagonal Bracing and Shear Wall Construction

bottom plate to top plate on both sides of the exterior corner in lieu of the let-in bracing. Code may require that the panels be installed both inside and outside of the exterior bearing walls. Such paneling may serve a dual purpose and be installed completely around the face of the structure as a back-up sheathing for exterior veneers or sidings as well as for shear wall.

Fireblocking or Fire-Stopping.   Building codes may require installation of fireblocking (horizontal framing components) at every 4'-0" (1.22 m) vertically between all exterior and interior bearing studs where the top plate is above 8'-0" (2.44 m). The purpose of the blocking is to reduce airspace through which a fire may spread within a wall. The same size and type of lumber used for the wall stud must be installed for fireblocking.

Platform Framing versus Balloon Framing

See figure 5–9, Platform vs. Balloon Framing. All previous sections discussed in this chapter refer to framing materials required for **platform,** or **western, framing,** the common framing system used today. This type of construction is more conducive to structural support requirements. The system is constructed using joists and subflooring between floors of a multistory structure. The first floor framing may include girders and joists over a foundation with a sill plate, subflooring, sole plate, wall framing, and double top plate. Where on-slab construction is performed, the girders, joists, and subflooring are eliminated. The upper floors use the same procedure up to the roof structure with the exception of the sill plate and girders. The walls are usually 8'-1" (2.46 m) high on all levels in tract or standard home construction. They may extend to 10'-0" (3.05 m) or 12'-0" (3.66 m) in some areas for larger custom residences and commercial office construction. Some variation of balloon framing may be incorporated into a platform frame pattern as explained in the following paragraphs.

Refer to figure 5–9. Wall framing extending continuously from the sill or sole plate at grade level to the roof structure in structures of more than one

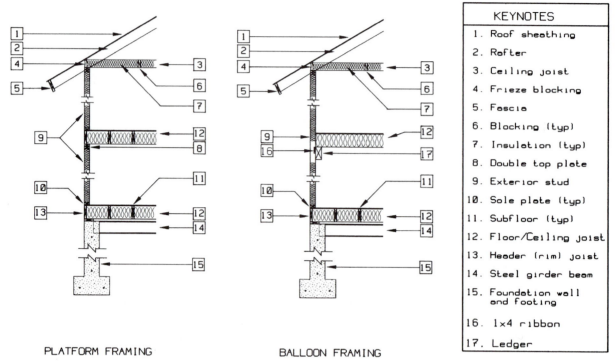

FIGURE 5–9
Platform vs. Balloon Framing

story is **balloon frame construction.** Balloon framing was used extensively in the eastern parts of the country. The practice has generally stopped because of code regulations regarding structural weaknesses in this type of framing.

The exterior, balloon-framed bearing walls for two-story structures may extend as high as 24'-0" (7.32 m) above finished floor (A.F.F.). These walls require a **ribbon** (a 1 × 4 or 1 × 6 [25.4 mm × 50.8 mm or 152.4 mm] notched perpendicular (horizontally) to the studs at a level just below the upper level floor joists. The ribbon is installed to help maintain rigidity in the walls in the same manner as a let-in brace is used for corner support. A **ledger** is a structural horizontal member installed on the interior side of the balloon framing to support the upper level floor joists. Interior partition walls may extend as high as 10'-0" (3.05 m) A.F.F.

See figure 5–10, Vaulted and Cathedral Ceilings. There is one area of framing still allowed by code similar to balloon framing. It is found mixed in with platform framing in today's construction where *vaulted* or *cathedral* ceilings are designed. A *vaulted* ceiling is one that slopes in only one direction. A *cathedral* ceiling is one that slopes in two directions forming a gable-like appearance on the interior of the residence. This type of construction is used to provide smaller rooms in a residence with the aesthetic feeling of larger, more spacious rooms. Where there is a custom vaulted or cathedral ceiling more than one story high, platform wall construction is used. A double plate matching the plate of the first level framing is placed over the wall framing. If the wall extends beyond the second plate level another double plate may be installed. The remaining wall above is then constructed as a gable-end framework. Where wall openings occur and the opening extends to plate level, the header over the opening may be used for the plate.

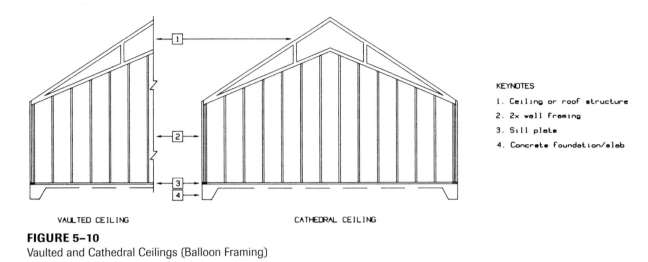

VAULTED CEILING   CATHEDRAL CEILING

FIGURE 5–10
Vaulted and Cathedral Ceilings (Balloon Framing)

Conventional Roof Framing

See figure 5–11, Roof Designs. As described in figure 5–11, there are a variety of roof shapes— flat, hip, gable, shed, and mansard, or combinations of them—common to residential construction. Each design requires special construction materials and structural requirements necessary for a properly constructed roof. For example, sloped roofs require construction of rafters, ridge beams, and, perhaps hip beams. In flat roof construction, the ceiling joists and rafters are often one and the same framing member when the slope is less than ½″ (12.7 mm) per lineal foot or less.

Ceiling Joists.   *Refer to figure 5–4. Ceiling joists* are horizontal framing members that may be considered part of the roof in sloped roof construction. Where there is more than one story to a structure, the floor joist for the floor above is also the ceiling joist for the lower floor. Most residential construction and light commercial construction has a minimum 2 × 4 (50.8 mm × 101.6 mm), DF #2, or better (one-story construction), or a 2 × 6 (50.8 mm × 152.4 mm), DF #2, or better, for a ceiling joist (multistory). The spacing of a ceiling joist is determined by the required structural support for the finished ceiling materials, the walls below, and the roof above. Spacing usually is at 16″ (406.4 mm) O/C or 24″ (609.6 mm) O/C, and like the floor joist, the shortest practical span is utilized. Bridging may also be required where spans exceed 8′-0″ (2.44 m). A rim joist or rim blocking may be installed at the exterior ends of the ceiling joists.

Frieze-Blocking.   Another system, called *frieze blocking,* or *vent blocking,* found in the southern and southwestern areas of the United States, is installed to aid with air circulation in attic spaces. If used, the number of spaces between the rafters determines the quantity. The block is usually installed in every second or third space between rafter tails and is used like rim joist blocking. A frieze-block may be manufactured in 1 × or 2 × (25.4 mm or 50.8 mm) thick common stock, OSB®, or 1″ (25.4 mm) plywood, with two or three screened holes cut into the member to allow for air circulation. The screens are placed over the openings to prevent insulation from falling from the attic space and to keep birds and rodents from nesting in the attic. Rim blocking is installed in the remaining spaces.

Rafters.   **Rafters** are the framing members that form the roof shapes shown in figure 5–11 and are also DF #2, or better. The live and dead load govern the

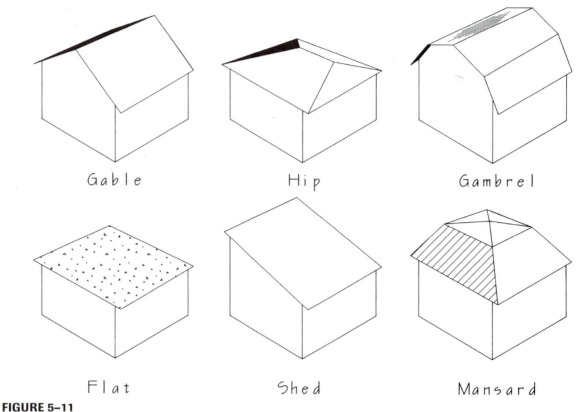

Gable   Hip   Gambrel

Flat   Shed   Mansard

FIGURE 5–11
Roof Designs

size, length, and spacing of the roof structure members. For example, a sloped roof using a tile roofing system requires more strength than one with composition shingles. In another example, the load applied to a flat roof (3"/lf [76.2 mm/0.305 m] or less slope) with several pieces of heavy air-handling equipment installed requires heavier and/or closer spaced rafters than one with only a small single air-handling unit. The loads are determined in the same way as those for joists—live load, dead load, and wind lift requirements.

See figure 5–12, Ridge-to-Rafter Connections and appendix III, Roof Slope Table. The drawing notes the comparative size of a ridge beam to a rafter connection in conventional roof framing. A practical rule of thumb is that a ridge beam should be at least 2" (50.8 mm) deeper than the rafter to be attached to it. As the slope in a pitched roof gets steeper, the size of the ridge beam must be larger to accommodate the end cut of the rafter. The drawing notes this necessity by indicating the ridge size comparisons. On the left side of the drawing the pitch and slope are indicated. The ridge and rafter drawings are horizontally aligned to match the left-hand symbols. For example, the ridge beam in the center drawing is a 2 × 6 (50.8 mm × 152.4 mm). This beam is wide enough to accommodate a 2 × 6 (50.8 mm × 152.4 mm) rafter at 3:12, but the ridge beam is too small for the cut of the 2 × 6 (50.8 mm × 152.4 mm) rafter at the 6:12 slope. The ridge beam for the 4:12 slope could be used, but it is also better to enlarge the ridge because of the depth of the rafter.

The two types of rafters installed in a sloped roof structure are the **common rafter** and the **jack rafter.** *A common rafter extends from the ridge to the top plate at the exterior bearing wall without interruption.* A rafter that is

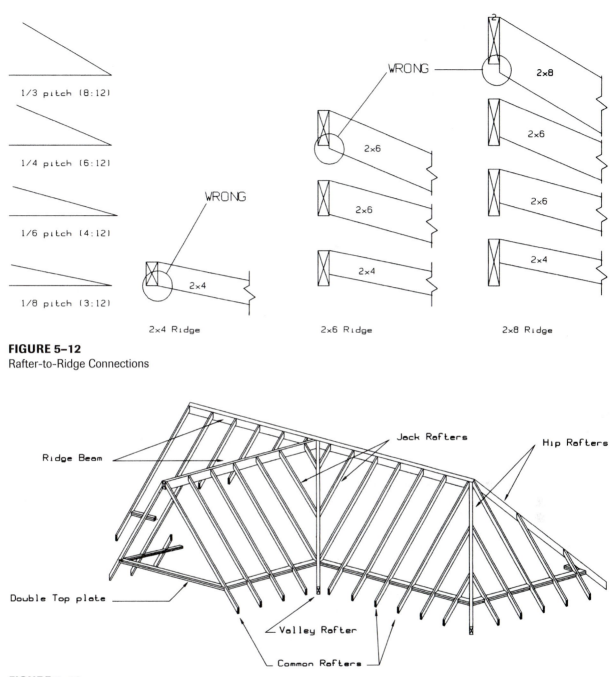

FIGURE 5–12
Rafter-to-Ridge Connections

FIGURE 5–13
Roof Structure

interrupted somewhere between the ridge and plate (for example, by a chimney, dormer, or hip beam) *is a jack rafter.*

Hip, Ridge, and Valley.   *See figure 5–13, Roof Structure.* The final portion of a conventional structural roof frame may include the hip beam, ridge beam, and valley. As previously mentioned, the hip and ridge are normally one size larger than the rafters. For example, a 2 × 6 (50.8 mm × 152.4 mm) raftered roof should have a single or double 2 × 8 (50.8 mm × 203.2 mm) or a single timber of similar size (ridge beam or hip beam). The ridge is the topmost horizontal framing member of all sloped roofs. A hip, if used, slopes from the ridge in any direction to a junction bearing point with the exterior bearing walls at the top plate. A valley is the inverse of a hip. For example, where a building is L-shaped with a sloped roof structure, the connecting members at the intersection of the two slopes are called the valley. The valley may be a single timber member or a double smaller member similar to the hip.

Additional Structural Roof Members and Accessories.   Additional members used to support the roof structure in conventional framing include, **king posts, purlins,** and **bracing.** King posts are structural members used to support the ridge and/or hip beam, placed directly under the beam, and spaced equidistant under them at a maximum 4'-0" (1.22 m) O/C. The king posts may be double- or triple-stacked studs or a single structural member, such as three 2×6 (three 50.8 mm $\times$ 152.4 mm), or a 6×6 (152.4 mm $\times$ 152.4 mm), large enough to support the roof structure above. *Vertical bracing* is centered between the king post and the top plate parallel to, and on both sides of, the ridge beam. Horizontal bracing, called a **collar tie,** is fastened to the rafters and the vertical bracing. Continuous horizontal members perpendicular to, and directly under, the collar ties and fastened to the vertical braces and collar ties are the purlins. Where such construction is required, the king posts are placed on double ceiling joists for support.

Other framing accessories include the installation of straps, clips, and hangers for strengthening and providing additional support to the framing members. The clips, referred to as *hurricane clips* (Simpson A34 or A35, or equal), are installed at the junction of the rafters and the ceiling joists. Hangers are used to tie the rafters, hips, valleys, and ridges together. Straps are used between floors to tie plates and joists together on multistory structures.

Roof Sheathing.   Roof sheathing is normally specified as a $4' \times 8' \times \frac{1}{2}''$ (1.22 m $\times$ 2.44 m $\times$ 12.7 mm) CDX, 5-ply, plywood. CCX may be used where the underside of the roof is exposed, such as along the eave line, for appearance and the CDX is installed on the remainder of the roof. An alternate to the plywood is the use of a minimum $\frac{7}{16}''$ (11.11 mm) OSB®.

Roof Trusses

Alternate installations use pre-fabricated trusses for sloped roof structures that replace the ceiling joists, roof raftering, and ridge beam. The most common trusses for residential construction use 2×4 (50.8 mm $\times$ 101.6 mm) *bottom chords* (the equivalent of the ceiling joists) and 2×6 (50.8 mm $\times$ 152.4 mm) *top chords* (the equivalent of the sloped rafters). The structural members that are built into them replace the conventional framing members mentioned above.

Fireplaces

See figure 5–14, Fireplace Construction. Fireplaces require special construction treatment. Fireplaces that are all masonry require specially constructed footing pads at least 1'-0" (304.8 mm) deep with reinforcement spaced at 8" (203.2 mm) to 12" (304.8 mm) O/C each way in the footing. The masonry required may be double wythe all brick or CMU interior and face brick exterior, or all CMU

FIGURE 5–14
Fireplace Construction

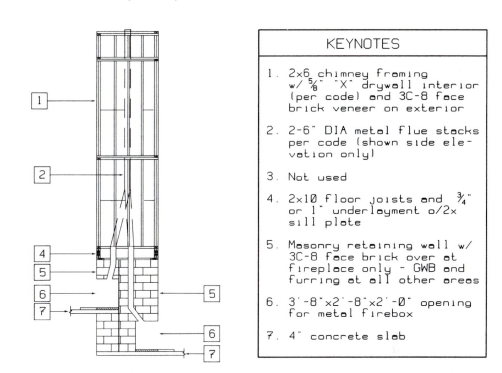

KEYNOTES

1. 2x6 chimney framing w/ ⅝" "X" drywall interior (per code) and 3C-8 face brick veneer on exterior

2. 2-6" DIA metal flue stacks per code (shown side elevation only)

3. Not used

4. 2x10 floor joists and ¾" or 1" underlayment o/2x sill plate

5. Masonry retaining wall w/ 3C-8 face brick over at fireplace only - GWB and furring at all other areas

6. 3'-8"x2'-8"x2'-0" opening for metal firebox

7. 4" concrete slab

exposed in single wythe. Inside the masonry exterior, a terra cotta flue liner and steel damper must be installed. A firebrick floor and walls must be installed for exposed wood or gas burning fireboxes. A clean-out pit must also be included and located at the lowest possible point on the structure.

The more common fireplace installed today is the pre-fabricated firebox unit. Fireplaces constructed for metal firebox modules may be all wood frame. The extra-deep footing is not required although an additional 4" (50.8 mm) to 8" (101.6 mm) concrete pad depth may be placed under the firebox area. The framing is installed using 2 × 6 (50.8 mm × 152.4 mm) lumber with single or double ⅝" (16.0 mm) "X" (fire-retardant) drywall on the inside and outside. The flue is made in sections of 4" (50.8 mm) or 6" (152.4 mm) DIA galvanized sheet iron (GI). A minimum 26-gauge (ga) GI fire stop must be installed completely surrounding the flue and framing inside the chimney stack at maximum 8'-0" (2.44 m) intervals.

Carpentry Accessories

All framing requires special connectors to assist in keeping a building structurally sound. Some accessories have been mentioned in the previous paragraphs but most have not been discussed. The accessories include:

Anchor bolts: ½" (1.3 cm) or ⅝" (1.6 cm) bent bolts placed in concrete with the threaded end exposed for anchoring steel or wood members to the concrete.

Hold-down anchors: A formed galvanized iron (GI) metal anchor fastened to the bottom plate and studs and anchored into the concrete.

Powder actuated shot-and-pin: Used in lieu of anchor bolts, to hold any framing member to concrete, masonry, or steel. A special gun is used that fires pins (similar to nails) into concrete, steel, or wood for fastening materials together. Shot-and-pin is not recommended for masonry.

Rafter and joist anchor clips: Installed to aid in maintaining proper spacing and support to the framing member when fastened at the plate. Commonly used with truss installations.

Joist and rafter hangers: GI formed metal units in the widths and thickness of standard lumber—2 × 6, 2 × 8, 2 × 10 (50.8 mm × 152.4 mm, 50.8 mm × 202.3 mm, 50.8 mm × 254.0 mm), or larger—into which the joist or rafter is inserted and fastened. The hangers may be straight, sloped, or skewed (twisted) to fit horizontal, vertical, and angled positions.

Galvanized iron (GI) straps: For supplying additional rigidity and strength between lower and upper levels of a structure. Installed vertically from lower level top plate to upper level bottom plate.

THERMAL INSULATION

Thermal protection includes products offering resistance to heat, such as mineral wool (a by-product of soft coal/coke), fibrous materials (paper and wood), minerals (perlite and vermiculite), fiberglass, cementitious mixtures, and plastics such as polystyrene, polyester, or combinations of some of these products. The insulation materials may be formed into rigid board, foam, loose fill, batt, and blanket products.

The thermal insulation rating for resistance to heat and cold is called the **R-factor.** The most commonly installed insulations are rated at R-7, R-9, R-11, R-13, R-19 and R-30. Energy requirements in most areas of the country include R-19 in exterior walls and under floors, and R-30 in ceilings or on the roofs. The thickness of the insulation helps to determine the R-value. For example, a 4″ (101.6 mm) thick fiberglass batt or blanket is designated as an R-11 or R-13, and a 6″ (152.4 mm) thick batt or blanket is rated as an R-19.

Batt and Blanket Insulation

Batts and *blankets* are types of thermal insulation used for wall, ceiling and roof installations. They may be unfaced or faced and made from fiberglass or similar insulating materials. Insulation combined with building paper, kraft paper, or foil backing is classed as faced insulation. The two types may be applied directly to, or between, studs. Insulation used horizontally in the floor or ceiling joists is normally the unfaced type.

Batts are sheets 8′-0″ (2.44 m) long and blankets are in rolls 24′-0″ (7.32 m) long or more. They are both available in 16″ (406.4 mm) or 24″ (609.6 mm) widths.

Loose Fill Insulation

The four types of loose-fill insulation are *perlite*, *vermiculite*, *cellulose*, and *mineral wool*. Loose-fill insulations are available in bags and may be blown under pressure or poured into wall or ceiling cavities. These materials are best used for horizontal installations, such as ceilings, in lieu of batt insulation. It is not uncommon to find perlite and vermiculite in masonry walls in some areas of the southwest.

Rigid Insulation

Insulation manufactured into board-like shapes is referred to as rigid insulation. The boards are combinations of any of the previously mentioned insulating materials that may be mixed together, compressed, and covered with surfacing materials. The most commonly used are materials manufactured of fiberglass, polystyrene, and composite boards. The composite boards are made from cement or other cementitious materials mixed with perlite or vermiculite with a covering to help protect from, or aid in, the installation of various roofing materials over them. The covering usually is a bituminous material that may be sprayed or applied in sheets.

Polyurethane Foam

This material is used for insulating existing and new roof applications as well as for masonry wall cavities. The foam is applied in a liquefied state under pressure. The cured foam, when used for roofing, must be coated with an acrylic elastomer for moisture and ultra-violet ray protection.

ROOFING

Roofing refers to the finish materials used for moisture protection of any roof structure. Sloped roofs include composition asphalt shingle, wood shingle, wood shake, tile (clay, concrete, and combinations of cement-based and organic or inorganic materials), panelized and pre-formed metal, standing seam, and corrugated cold-rolled steel. Roofs upon which these materials may be used must have a minimum 3:12 slope ($\frac{1}{8}$ [3.20 mm] pitch). Slopes of 3:12 that are to have any of the above materials installed must include a built-up roof (BUR) underlayment. A roof with a 3:12, or less, slope is considered a flat roof and requires some form of bituminous material for protection. *See Roof Slopes, appendix III.*

Built-Up Roofing (BUR)

Many varieties of roofing felts and procedures are found in BUR. Asphalt felts, the most commonly used BUR for residential construction, are made from rag, paper, fiberglass, or other fibrous materials, which are mixed with asphalt or coal-tar pitch, and compressed into a single ply. They are manufactured into one-square (9.29 m^2) rolls (approximately 33'-0" [10.05 m]), three-square (18.58 m^2) rolls (approximately 90'-0" [42.5 m]), and 5-square (46.45 m^2) rolls (approximately 165'-0" [50.29 m]). The standard 3-ply or 5-ply BUR is installed with 3 to 5 layers with a coating of asphalt or coal tar applied between each layer and a cover sheet or asphalt/coal-tar coating over.

LIGHT-GAUGE METAL FRAMING

See figure 5–15, Miscellaneous Wall Framing—Metal, and appendix III, Light Metal Studs and Joists. Wherever wood frame construction is installed, alternate *structural light gauge* and *light-gauge metal framing* may be substituted. Structural light-gauge metal framing includes both studs and joists in 18 gauge to 12 gauge cold-rolled steel forms used primarily for exterior and interior bearing walls, floor and ceiling joists, and roof rafters. Most structural studs and joists are unpunched (no prefabricated holes in their lengths) and coated with rust resistant primer baked into the stud.

Standard structural studs and joists have a C-shaped cross-section. There are several other varieties of structural studs available for special construction. Included are E-shaped, H-shaped, and L-shaped studs used for installations such as elevator shafts, where rigidity and soundproofing are desired. These special studs may be installed with both drywall and rigid insulation as integral parts of the construction. Structural light-gauge metal framing requires the use of *stiffeners* at all connections. The stiffeners are angles similar to angle iron clips, but of the same gauge as, or slightly heavier than, the framing being installed. The stiffeners may be connected to the framing with screws, but all connections are always welded.

Light gauge metal framing is available as studs only in 20 gauge, 22 gauge, and 25 gauge galvanize-coated cold-rolled steel. The 20-gauge stud may be used in residential one-story, or light commercial construction for bearing walls. The lighter studs are used for interior non-bearing partitions or other non-structural framing. The studs have either C-shaped or channel shaped cross-sections. The C-shaped stud offers more rigidity than the channel shapes. Light-gauge metal framing and accessories do not require stiffeners or

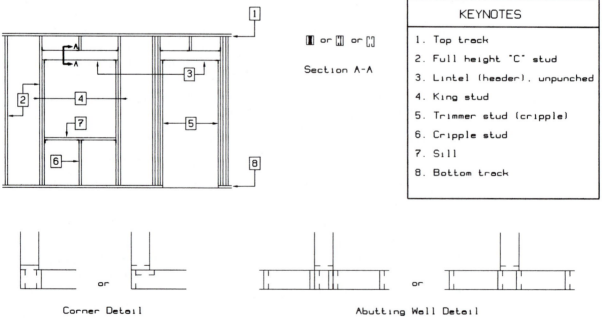

FIGURE 5–15
Miscellaneous Wall Framing—Metal

welding. All connections are screwed together with ¾" (19.05 mm) to 1¼" (31.75 mm) long case hardened metal screws known as "Tek" screws.

An unpunched channel shaped metal member, called a *track,* is used in lieu of the top, bottom, and sill plates for all metal stud framing. The gauge of the track is usually the same as, or heavier than, the stud gauge. A wood sill plate, although rarely required, may be necessary under certain circumstances beneath the bottom track when framing is installed below grade.

Accessory forms used for metal soffit or suspended ceiling installations include a light-gauge angle iron (steel or structural aluminum), called "black metal" because of the black anodized finish applied to it, and ¾"(19.05 mm) to 1¼" (31.75 mm) wide channel, called *hat channel,* for finish applications such as drywall attachment at furred-down or suspended ceilings. Like the light-gauge metal frame, these materials are screwed together at all connections.

It must be cautioned that metal stud framing and wood framing cannot be applied within the same wall.

CHAPTER EXERCISES

True or False

T F   1. The geographical location of the source of lumber determines its quality classification.

T F   2. The sill plate is the horizontal framing member used to protect other framing members from termite infestation.

T F   3. The sill plate and the sole plate are one and the same.

T F   4. A platform frame includes a ribbon and a ledger in the wall construction.

T F   5. The top plate may be either single or double thickness.

T F   6. A rafter is the horizontal member of a roof support system.

T F   7. A joist header is the framing member used to support a structure above a door or window opening.

T F   8. Sheathing may be used both for shear panel construction and as a roof underlayment.

T F   9. Three major concerns of a structural engineer include the necessity of determining dead load, live load, and wind lift.

T F 10. Conventional sloped roof framing is installed using prefabricated trusses.

T F 11. The material installed over the floor joists is called the subfloor, or underlayment.

T F 12. The trimmer stud is used to support the lintel (header) over a wall opening.

T F 13. A king post is the same as a king stud.

T F 14. Purlins are the vertical support members of a conventional roof structure.

T F 15. Studs are graded as DF, construction grade, or HF, structural grade #3.

T F 16. All framing members are available in increments of 2'-0" (0.61 m) unless special ordered.

T F 17. The structural classification for rafters and joists determines the allowable span for the framing members.

T F 18. The term *laminated beam* includes glue-laminated 2 × members as well as glue-laminated plywood for use as beams and trusses.

T F 19. Wall framing requires additional support at the corners using diagonal bracing or shear panels.

T F 20. The term *header* is used for a perimeter joist and is also referred to as a *rim joist*.

Completion

1. The lowest framing member for exterior walls is called the _____ plate.

2. The connectors used for rafter and ceiling joist connections are referred to as _____ fasteners.

3. The symbol *E* is a notation referring to the _____ of a framing member.

4. Most bearing walls in wood frame construction require a(n) _____ top plate.

5. The standard precut stud measures _____".

6. The work involving the structure itself is called the _____ work.

7. There is a bottom and top _____ used in light-gauge metal framing of a wall.

8. The vertical framing member, called a(n) _____, of a sloped roof structure is used to support the ridge.

9. The walls over and under wall openings are referred to as _____ walls.

10. The lumber classifications are determined by the location of the _____ from a log.

11. Structural light-gauge framing includes cold-rolled steel from 18 gauge to _____ gauge.

12. The standard classification for a horizontal support member is _____ #2, or better.

13. Balloon framing is in use today only for _____ or cathedral ceiling installations.

14. Balloon framing, when used, may extend to _____' above finish floor (A.F.F.).

15. Western framing is also referred to as _____.

16. In wood frame floor construction, the _____ plate is installed over the subflooring.

17. Underlayment used for floor construction may be 4′ × 8′ (1.22 m × 2.44 m) plywood sheets butted together, or may have tongue and groove (T&G), or _____ edges.

18. Nailing of double top plates where they lap at other than corners calls for _____ 10d or 16d nails.

19. The sections for the Garland residence (figures 5–1 and 5–2) note that the trusses used over the living room area are called _____ trusses.

20. The header over a 6″ (152.4 mm) wide bearing wall opening - better than 4′-0″ (1.22 m) long may be a double 2 × 6 (50.8 mm × 152.4 mm), triple 2 × 6 (50.8 mm × 152.4 mm), or a(n) _____ member.

21. A glue-laminated beam, identified as a 5⅛″ × 27″ (130.2 mm × 685.8 mm) beam, is produced from re-milled _____ lumber and requires _____ pieces.

22. Insulation may be used for both thermal and _____ protection.

23. Non-bearing partitions are usually placed at _____″ O/C.

24. The symbol *Fb* refers to the _____ of a structural member.

25. Wood frame fireplaces require a fire shield spaced at a maximum _____′ apart, vertically.

Multiple Choice

_____   1. The lower member of a wood frame floor is:
    a. The sole plate
    b. The double top plate
    c. The sill plate
    d. None of the above

_____   2. The floor joists are:
    a. Larger in size than the ceiling joists in multistory structures at all times
    b. Smaller in size than the ceiling joists in single story structures
    c. Larger than the ceiling joists in single story structures
    d. Are interchangeable with the ceiling joists

_____   3. A conventionally framed roof structure includes:
    a. Rafters, purlins, braces, and king posts
    b. Ceiling joists and sheathing
    c. None of the above
    d. All of the above

_____   4. Thermal protection is provided by:
    a. Batt insulation, rigid insulation, or foam insulation
    b. Batt insulation and rigid insulation only
    c. Rigid insulation and foam insulation only
    d. Batt insulation only

_____ 5. Light-gauge metal framing is:
     a. 25 gauge to 16 gauge cold-rolled steel forms
     b. 18 gauge to 12 gauge cold-rolled steel forms
     c. 25 gauge to 12 gauge cold-rolled steel forms
     d. 25 gauge to 20 gauge cold-rolled steel forms

_____ 6. The track for light-gauge metal framing is:
     a. The same gauge steel
     b. The same or heavier gauge steel
     c. Lighter gauge steel
     d. The same or lighter gauge steel

_____ 7. The bearing wall stud spacing for light-gauge metal framing:
     a. Is always the same as that for wood framing
     b. May be spaced at 24″ (60.96 cm) O/C for 6″ bearing studs
     c. Must be spaced at 24″ (60.96 cm) O/C for 6″ bearing studs
     d. None of the above

_____ 8. The difference between structural light-gauge and light-gauge metal stud framing is:
     a. The finish used on the cold-rolled metal
     b. The structural light-gauge metal is from 18 gauge to 12 gauge metal
     c. There is no difference
     d. Light-gauge metal framing is used for bearing walls only

_____ 9. In conventional roof framing, a roof rafter:
     a. Is larger than the ridge or hip beams
     b. Is normally at least one size smaller than the ridge or hip beams
     c. It makes no difference in the sizes, it depends only on span requirements
     d. None of the above

_____ 10. The subfloor is:
     a. Referred to as an underlayment
     b. Usually ¾″ (19.05 mm) or 1″ (25.4 mm), 5-ply, plywood or equivalent OSB®
     c. Both a and b
     d. Neither a nor b

_____ 11. Shear paneling or diagonal bracing:
     a. May be required at all exterior wall construction corners
     b. Is required where lateral wind pressure is a major problem
     c. Is required for seismic stability
     d. All of the above

_____ 12. The perimeter joist used to protect the butt end of interior joists is called a:
     a. Lintel
     b. King stud
     c. Trimmer
     d. Header (rim) joist

_____ 13. A 6″ (152.4 mm) wide lumber, or larger, used for structural joists, is classified as:
     a. Select structural   c. #1, #2, #3, or economy
     b. Stud grade   d. Utility or common

_____ 14. (Refer to appendix III). The milled finish of lumber is also classified. A piece of lumber that is smoothed on all sides is classified as:
   a. S1S
   b. R/S
   c. S4S
   d. S4S2E

_____ 15. The typical roof sheathing is referred to as CDX plywood. The meaning of the classification is:
   a. Special exterior grade, structural II, glued
   b. Marine grade, structural I, glued
   c. Neither a nor b
   d. Both a and b

Matching

_____ 1. Truss

_____ 2. Sill plate

_____ 3. Balloon frame

_____ 4. Joist

_____ 5. Header

_____ 6. Frieze block

_____ 7. Sheathing

_____ 8. Trim

_____ 9. Sill frame

_____ 10. Trimmer

_____ 11. King post

_____ 12. Rafter

_____ 13. Conventional frame

_____ 14. Platform frame

_____ 15. Sole plate

_____ 16. King stud

_____ 17. Hip

_____ 18. Cripple

_____ 19. Top plate

_____ 20. Ridge

a. Blocking between rafter tails at top plate

b. System using ceiling joists and rafters

c. Support post for ridge beam

d. Framing member on concrete or masonry

e. Western framing system

f. Made with top and bottom chords

g. Full-height stud next to wall opening

h. A structural horizontal roof member

i. Bottom plate of wood frame structure

j. Horizontal structural wall member

k. Main sloped structural roof member

l. Stud framing system continuous from foundation to roof structure

m. Horizontal floor or ceiling structural member

n. Structural floor, wall, or roof cover of plywood

o. Double or single member at top of wall frame

p. Stud above or below wall opening

q. Sloped member of a roof structure

r. Bottom member of window opening

s. Finish framing material

t. Stud used to support lintel (header)

1. *Match the following wall components with the identifying numbers in figure 5–16.*

a. Concrete wall   ———   i. Rigid Insulation   ———
b. Combination wall   ———   j. Threshold   ———
c. Bi-fold door   ———   k. Brick veneer   ———
d. FX GL window   ———   l. Door Opening   ———
e. Sliding Glass door   ———   m. Exterior plaster   ———
f. CMU wall   ———   n. Drywall (GWB)   ———
g. 2 × 6 exterior wall   ———   o. 2 × 4 interior wall   ———
h. Cased opening   ———

FIGURE 5–16
Wall Components

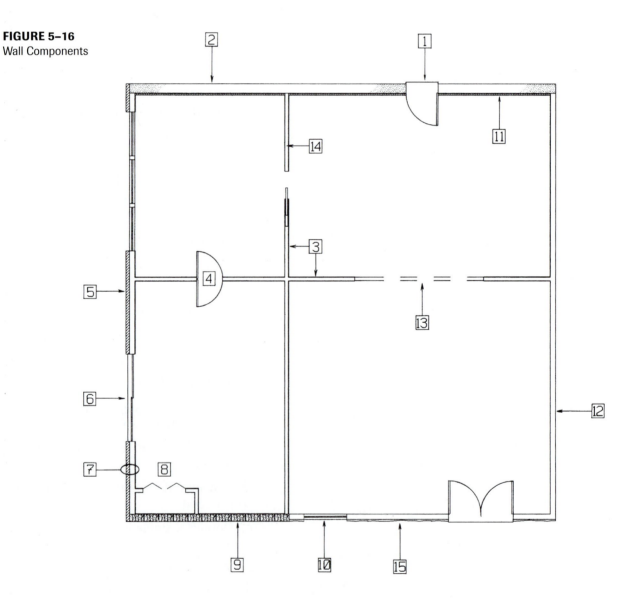

2. Identify the materials called out below with the wall section in *figure 5–17*.

a. Rafter   ————   n. Foundation wall   ————
b. Stud   ————   o. Sill plate   ————
c. Double top plate   ————   p. Footing   ————
d. Ceiling joist   ————   q. Drywall   ————
e. Sheathing (roof)   ————   r. Subfloor   ————
f. Sole plate   ————   s. Lintel (Header)   ————
g. Floor joist   ————   t. Window   ————
h. Beam   ————   u. GI screed   ————
i. Tile roofing   ————   v. R19 insulation   ————
j. Fascia board   ————   w. Rigid insulation   ————
k. Window trim   ————   x. Baseboard   ————
l. R-30 insulation   ————   y. Siding   ————
m. Cold key   ————   z. Concrete slab   ————

FIGURE 5–17
Wall Section

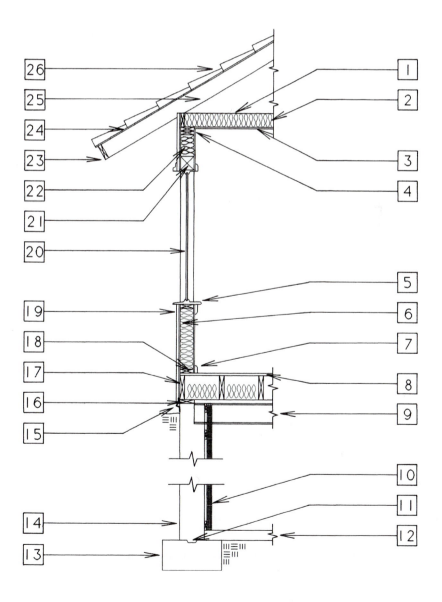

CHAPTER 6

The Structure (Continued)

Once the rough-in construction work is completed—foundation, framing, rough-in plumbing, and rough-in electrical—the trades used for the purpose of covering or completing the work, or installations necessary to provide an aesthetic appearance for a structure, are called upon. These include finish carpentry, a section of Division 6; door and window installations, Division 8; and those trades referred to as *Finishes*, Division 9, of the CSI MasterFormat. Division 9 includes lath and other metal support systems, such as suspended ceilings and soffits, and light-gauge metal framing (discussed in chapter 5); exterior and interior cement plaster, and interior gypsum plaster; drywall (GWB—gypsum wall board); quarry and ceramic floor and wall tile; floor coverings such as carpeting, vinyl resilient floor covering (sheet and tile), and special wood flooring (parquet and the like); acoustical treatments, such as spray-on acoustical, acoustical directly adhered tiles, and suspended acoustical systems; painting and wall coverings.

See figure 6–1, Finish Schedule, Garland Residence. All of the finish installations are identified and located on the finish schedule. The finish schedule indicates the location (room, office, and so on) as well as the materials or finishes to be installed to the floor, wall base, wall, and ceiling. The information on a finish schedule must be adhered to in the same way as the *specifications*. The schedule is normally included in the drawings, or it may be in the specifications found in a project manual accompanying the set of plans, or both. A *specification* is additional information on a specific project that cannot be placed in the plans but requires further description.

THE GARLAND RESIDENCE

See Sheets A-1 and A-2, Architectural Plans for the Garland residence. The floor plan of the Garland residence provides several symbols that are used for identification of rooms, walls, and fixtures, as well as doors and windows. The following sections are written to supply general information regarding use of these symbols and schedules, which are an important part of a well-organized set of plans.

FINISH SCHEDULE						
LOCATION	FLOOR	BASE	WALLS (N S E W)	CEILING	REMARKS	
Living Room	1	1	a · a · a (b · b · b)	1	vaulted ceiling	
Dining Room	1	1	a · a · a (b · b · b)	1	8'-0" ceiling	
Kitchen	2	2	a · a · a (a · a · a)	1	8'-0" ceiling	
Bedroom	1	1	a · a · a (b · b · b)	1	vaulted ceiling	
Study	1	1	a · a · a (b · b · b)	1	8'-0" ceiling	
Laundry	3	3	a · a · a (a · a · a)	1	8'-0" ceiling	
Bathroom	2	2	b · a · b (a · a · a)	1	8'-0" ceiling	
Garage	4	-	a · c · a	2	8'-0" ceiling	

KEYNOTES:

FLOOR:
1. Carpet w/pad
2. Quarry tile – 12" square
3. VCT – 8" square
4. Exposed concrete

BASE:
1. 4" oak base
2. Tile coving to match floor tile
3. VCT coving to match floor tile

WALLS:
a. 1/2" GWB orange peel texture
b. Flat latex paint – 2 coats
c. 5/8" "X" GWB both sides of wall. Textured one side only. Firetaped to underside of roof on garage side.

CEILINGS:
1. 1/2" GWB w/acoustical texture

FIGURE 6–1
Finish Schedule, Garland Residence

FINISH CARPENTRY

Finish carpentry includes installation of all wood, plastic, and light-gauge metal finish materials used for both interior and exterior decorative trim. The same contractor may be involved with both the rough and finish carpentry as well as all doors and windows. Cabinetry, both mass-produced (manufactured) and custom made, is also a part of finish carpentry. The manufacturer or representative of the cabinet supplier normally install manufactured cabinets, whereas custom cabinetry is produced and installed by the custom cabinetmaker.

Interior Trim

Wood stairs, stair railings and newel posts, architectural woodwork (built-in book cases and the like), cabinetry, interior window and door trim (not a part of the window or door package), baseboard, and moldings are all a part of the interior finish carpentry. Where no trim is included in the door and window package, the plans or finish schedule must indicate it, and where such trim is to be installed. The areas that are of interest to the finish carpenter are all the finishes, including pre-manufactured packages.

Exterior Trim

The amount and variety of materials necessary for exterior trim may also be noted in the finish schedule. Normally these materials are indicated on the exterior elevations or in the keynotes for the exterior elevations that are a part of the drawings. Exterior trim includes items such as siding, plant-ons, and exterior window and door trim not a part of the window or door package. The trim may be installed prior to, or after, the installation of the finish work is completed. When exterior trim is installed after the exterior finish work is completed, it is considered a plant-on because it is installed ("planted") over the exterior finish. Many windows and doors may be purchased that have no trim other than the jambs, therefore, the owner must select a trim to be added.

PLASTICS

The most common structural plastic fabrications include molded and laminated-surface countertops and molded fiberglass countertops, both used for kitchen and bath cabinet surfaces. Other structural plastics considered in finish construction are impact-resistant decorative items such as room divider screen walls, posts, shelving, atrium and patio roof covers, and plastic (vinyl) sheets and panels used for roofs and siding.

Also included in this category are some non-structural fabrications such as items made for decorative use in lieu of wood or concrete. These plastics are included with carpentry since, again, the carpenter or cabinet installer is usually responsible for the installations of siding, cabinetry, and roofing. Some of the plastics may be rigid molded units or may be Styrofoam units used as forms for the decorative impressions or plant-ons.

DOORS AND WINDOWS

Doors

See figure 6–2, Door and Window Schedules, Garland Residence. Door and window schedules may be included in the drawings, in the specifications in a project manual accompanying the set of plans, or both. An identification number or letter on the floor plan identifies the door or window to be found on the schedule, referred to as the *mark*. When a number is used for the door mark, a letter is used for the window mark. The same number or letter is found in the first column of the schedule(s). In addition to the mark, door and window schedule formats have columns identifying the size of the unit, the style of unit, the finish, and any other information necessary (remarks).

See figure 6–3, Door Types. Doors are identified by the style of the unit. The door size may be indicated in either of two ways, the normal measurement given in feet and inches (3'-0" × 6'-8" [0.91 m × 2.03 m]), or by the numbers without foot and inch notations (3068). Both methods are in common use.

There are two main classifications of door styles, *panel* and *flush* (slab). All doors are fabricated in these two styles or combinations of them. They are manufactured from steel or wood, a combination of structural light gauge, cold-rolled steel formed over wood, or a structural plastic molded over wood. Combination metal-and-wood doors are referred to as *metal-clad wood* doors. Wood-and-plastic door combinations are called *vinyl-clad wood* doors.

Many other designations, as shown in the schedule, are necessary to supply the proper door for the purpose and location desired. For example, exterior doors are 1¾" (44.5 mm) thick while interior doors are 1⅜" (34.9 mm) thick. The

DOOR SCHEDULE

MK	SIZE	TYPE	MATERIAL	QA	REMARKS
1	3´-0˝ x 6´-8˝	3-panel s/c	metal-clad	1	hdwre selected by owner
2	3´-0˝ x 6´-8˝	Flush. s/c	birch	1	self-closer stain finish
3	3´-0˝ x 6´-8˝	Flush. h/c	birch	1	stain finish
4	2´-6˝ x 6´-8˝	Flush. h/c	luan	2	paint finish by owner
5	6´-0˝ x 6´-8˝	Sliding glass	aluminum frame	1	anodizied bronze finish
6	10´-0˝x 7´-0˝	garage door	steel	2	white baked enamel finish
7	8´-0˝ x 6´-8˝			1	cased opening
8	4´-0˝ x 6´-8˝			1	cased opening

WINDOW SCHEDULE

MK	SIZE	TYPE	MATERIAL	QA	REMARKS
A	1´-6˝x6´-8˝	sidelites	plastic	2	Wood frame – custom
B	4´-0˝x4´-0˝	Fixed	insulating	2	˝ ˝ ˝
C	4´-0˝x4´-0˝	single hung	insulating	6	˝ ˝ ˝
D	6´-0˝x4´-0˝	Fixed	insulating	3	˝ ˝ ˝

FIGURE 6–2
Door and Window Schedules, Garland Residence

exterior flush doors may be solid-core (*s/c*), units filled with wood blocking for strength and insulating material for sound attenuation, or panelized doors of hardwood materials, with or without glazing. Interior doors may also be panelized or flush doors. Flush doors are normally hollow-core (*h/c*), lighter in weight, and have little additional strengthening materials added. Insulating materials such as corrugated cardboard sound barriers are installed within the door.

Panel doors are designed and manufactured in a variety of combinations. The doors may have a minimum of just one panel to as many as ten panels.

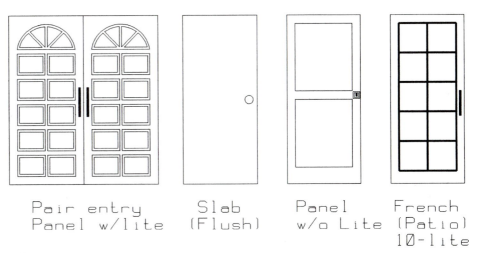

Pair entry
Panel w/lite

Slab
(Flush)

Panel
w/o Lite

French
(Patio)
10-lite

FIGURE 6–3
Door Types

They may have glass (*lites*) installed, for example, a single lite, a half-moon lite, or multi-lites (the French door), or may be a solid glass lite with just the headers and stiles for support.

Doors are further designated as:

1. *Inside swing:* The door opens into the structure or room.
2. *Outside swing:* The door opens outward to a hall or the outdoors.
3. *Right-hand swing:* The door is hinged on the right when facing the door from the inside of a room.
4. *Reverse right-hand swing:* The same as the right-hand swing, except it swings outward; used for exterior commercial or institutional installations.
5. *Left-hand swing:* The door is hinged on the left when facing the door from the inside of a room.
6. *Reverse left-hand swing:* The same as the left-hand swing, except it swings outward; used for exterior commercial or institutional installations.
7. *Double-swing:* A door hinged to swing both inward and outward, such as the connecting door to a restaurant kitchen and dining room.
8. *Gate (Dutch):* The door is halved in the middle so that the upper or lower sections can be opened separately; hinged in the same manner as a left-hand or right-hand swing; can also be latched together to be opened as a regular full door.
9. *Sliding:* A single or double door that moves horizontally on a track; such doors may be glass exterior doors or mirrored for closet doors.
10. *Bi-fold:* A double-leaf door hinged between leaves and at the attachment to the jamb; used primarily for multi-purpose room construction in hotels and schools; also used for closet doors; may or may not include latches.
11. *Accordion:* This door has smaller leaves for folding together more tightly; also common in multi-purpose room construction in hotels and schools; smaller versions may be used for closet doors.

Windows

See figure 6–4, Window Types. Windows, like doors, are also available in a variety of materials—steel, aluminum, metal-clad wood, vinyl-clad wood, and wood. The steel and aluminum windows are normally manufactured without casings or jambs. They are installed in the walls and trimmed over with drywall and trims to be selected by the owner. The other styles, like the doors, are available in complete packages including the casings, frames, and jambs.

    Refer to figure 6–2. Schedules are also provided for windows. The window schedule is designed in the same format as the door using the mark, size, description, and remarks. There may be a section drawing for the windows included with the pictorials of the window sizes and types matching the schedule. The window sizes are often identified in the same way as the doors: a window may be sized as a 4'-0" × 4'-0" (1.22 m × 1.22 m), or as a 4040. As with doors, there are classifications for windows, which include the following:

1. *Fixed glass (FX):*   Cannot be opened such as used for picture windows.
2. *Sliding glass (OX or XO):*   Opens horizontally on a track assembly; the "X" identifies the fixed portion of the slider.
3. *Single-hung sash (SH):*   In two sections, one above the other; only the bottom half opens vertically.
4. *Double-hung sash (DH):*   Similar to single-hung; both halves may be opened vertically.
5. *Awning (AW):*   A top-hinged window that swings outward.
6. *Hopper (HO):*   A bottom-hinged window that swings inward.
7. *Casement:*   A single or double window that swings outward horizontally using a crank or lever to open.

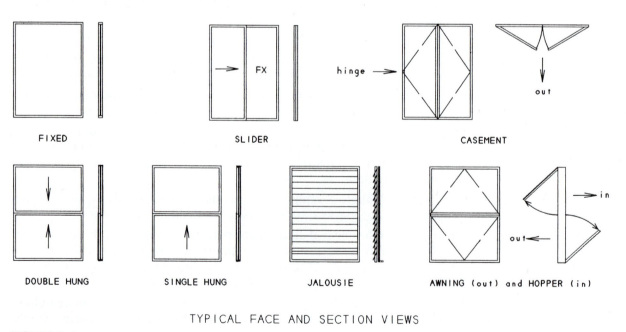

FIXED   SLIDER   CASEMENT

DOUBLE HUNG   SINGLE HUNG   JALOUSIE   AWNING (out) and HOPPER (in)

TYPICAL FACE AND SECTION VIEWS

FIGURE 6–4
Window Types

8. *Jalousie:*   Used primarily for enclosed porch doors, windows, and screens and on mobile homes, motor homes, and trailers; is actually a multi-paneled awning operated by crank or lever.

Metal Doors and Door and Window Frames

Doors and door and window frames made of heavy-gauge (16 or 14 gauge) steel, with matching steel frames and casings, known as *hollow-metal (HM)*. They are manufactured in standard sizes, but special customized construction is available on special order. Such doors and frames are used primarily for commercial and institutional construction because of their strength and resistance to fire and vandalism.

A second type of steel frame, used for installations with wood, metal-clad wood, vinyl-clad doors, and plastic doors, is called a *knock-down hollow-metal (KDHM),* which is manufactured from 18 gauge or 16 gauge cold-rolled steel. The KDHM frame provides damage protection and requires minimal maintenance. They are used in exterior and interior door construction for multi-family housing, such as apartments, and for interior door installations for hotels, offices, and other commercial or institutional construction.

HARDWARE

All plans and/or specifications also have a hardware schedule included. The schedule may be included in the door and window schedules, as a separate schedule, or included as part of the specifications governing the plans. The hardware is identified by the manufacturer, style, and type of door handles, latches, deadbolts, and hinges (butts). Other special door and window hardware may include *no special knowledge* door fasteners, kick plates, non-latching handles, and emergency locks.

Hinges are identified by the number required to be installed on a door. The quantity may be designated for two hinges as *2 hinges* or *1 pair of butts*. A door with three hinges may be designated as *3 hinges* or *1½ pair of butts*.

FINISHES

Plaster

The general term plaster includes both *cement plaster,* used primarily as an exterior wall covering, and *gypsum plaster,* applied on interior walls for a hard, smooth finish.

Exterior Cement Plaster.   Cement plaster, also known as *stucco,* is a smooth concrete mix in a semi-liquid state that can be sprayed or troweled and textured on a surface. Cement plaster may be used as a surface coating for new structures or for rehabilitation of the exteriors of existing structures. The textures most commonly used for this type of treatment include a sand (smooth) finish, a lace texture (slightly roughened), or a rough antique Spanish finish.

Plaster is often pigmented (colored) to give a permanent color to the finish, eliminating the necessity for paint over the plaster.

Cement plaster may be etched or stamped to look like brick or stone. Many of the finishes found on the buildings in some of the major amusement parks—for example, the Disneyland and Disney World Main Street building facades—use a hard-coat cement plaster that is designed to look like brick or stone in lieu of real materials because it is more cost efficient, both in the materials required, and the labor necessary for a completed finished product, and maintenance.

Cement plaster is applied in one, two, or three coats. The exterior elevations in a set of plans would note the exterior finish to be applied. If a project manual is available with the drawings, a specification would be given in Division 9 stating the proper application. The standard application procedures are as follows:

1. *One-coat system:*   The base for this method is a polystyrene foam board with 1″-20 gauge (25.4 mm-20 gauge) wire lath. A fine clay-sand, hydrated lime, and cement mix is applied to the lath approximately ⅜″ (9.5 mm) thick. When properly cured, a finish coat using a white (silicone) sand and cement, with or without integral color, is applied approximately ⅛″ (3.2 mm) thick. This system is in common usage today in residential construction, particularly throughout the west and southwest areas of the country.

2. *Two-coat system:*   This system is applied over masonry walls, primarily CMU, to provide aesthetic finish as desired. The application is exactly the same as the one-coat system without the lath.

3. *Three-coat system:*   Although this is the more common exterior plaster system, it is losing popularity in some areas of the country because of its weight requirements and tendency toward feathering and cracking as it cures and ages. The system uses the same base lath as the one-coat system with a base coat referred to as the scratch coat, a coarse clay-sand and cement mix, applied approximately ⅜″ (9.5 mm) thick over which the other two coats used in systems 1 and 2, above, are applied after curing.

Exterior Insulation and Finish System (EIFS).   *See figure 6–5, Exterior Insulation and Finish System.* A more recent trend in exterior plastering is the installation of the EIFS procedure. This system also uses an insulation board base the same as the one-coat system, but there the similarity ceases. A fiber mesh, such as nylon or polyester, is applied over the polystyrene foam board with an adhesive. A skim coating of cement plaster (⅛″ [3.2 mm] thick) is applied over the fiber mesh. When cured, an acrylic color coating (20 to 60 mil thick) is applied, over which an elastomeric coating (60 mil thick) is installed. One mil equals 0.001″ (¹⁄₁₀₀₀″). This system is especially popular in the desert areas of the country because it is both insulating and a weather protection.

Gypsum Plaster.   Gypsum plaster was primarily used as an interior plaster system prior to the introduction of drywall (GWB). The original lath was made from rough-sawn (R/S) 1 × 2, 1 × 3 or 1 × 4 (25.4 mm × 50.8 mm, 76.2 mm, or 101.6 mm) common or utility grade lumber spaced ½″ (12.7 mm) apart. Upon the introduction of metal lath products, expanded metal lath became

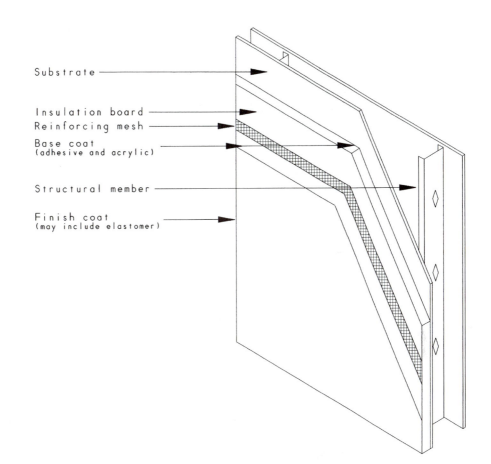

Substrate

Insulation board
Reinforcing mesh
Base coat
(adhesive and acrylic)

Structural member

Finish coat
(may include elastomer)

FIGURE 6–5
Exterior Insulation and Finish System

popular and replaced the wood. Later, a gypsum board called Sheetrock®, a product of United States Gypsum Corporation (USG), became popular and replaced metal lath in many applications. Sheetrock® is still available in lengths from 4'-0" (1.22 m) to 8'-0" (2.44 m) long by 2'-0" (0.61 m). Originally, spackle (plaster of Paris) mixed with water was used with Sheetrock® for the plaster.

Gypsum plaster is still in use as a fine, smooth wall finish in more expensive residential construction, especially custom homes, and commercial construction (offices and hotels, in particular). The cost is greater than a drywall and texture installation but is much more durable than drywall. Gypsum plaster is rarely, if ever, sprayed. It is hand applied with trowels and sanded smooth or textured as desired similar to cement plaster.

Lath.   Included with both cement and gypsum plaster is the lath which is applied as a base for the plaster. Exterior lath applications may be installed using a *wire mesh,* classified as 1"-17 gauge or 1"-20 gauge (25.4 mm-17 gauge or -20 gauge) wire mesh, available in rolls up to 100 lf × 3 lf (30.48 m × 0.91 m). There are two types of 26 gauge galvanized iron (GI) or aluminum lath: *expanded metal lath* and *hi-rib lath.* Both types are available in sheets from 8'-0" to 10'-0" by 3'-0" (2.44 m to 3.05 m by 0.91 m). The 1"-17 or 1"-20 gauge (25.4 mm-17 gauge or -20 gauge) wire mesh, similar in appearance to "chicken wire" fencing, is recommended for application on vertical wall surfaces only.

Expanded metal lath is smooth finished with punched holes similar to a grillwork or grating. This lath is also used primarily for wall applications. There are some applications where expanded metal lath may be used for horizontal surfaces in the same manner as hi-rib lath.

Hi-rib lath is similar in appearance and thickness to the expanded metal lath. The difference is that hi-rib lath has ribs (small circular rods) fastened in a staggered pattern throughout the lath to give it more rigidity and to aid in gripping the plaster surrounding the holes. Hi-rib lath is primarily used for horizontal applications such as ceilings and soffits.

Lath is available without a moisture barrier such as building-paper, or with the moisture barrier as an integral part of the lath. Where moisture protection already exists, or sheathing has already been applied over a moisture barrier, the lath without the moisture barrier is used.

Gypsum Wall Board

Gypsum wall board (GWB), better known as **drywall,** is a product that is already finished to look like a smooth gypsum plastered wall. It has replaced most interior plaster systems because of its economy. The material needs no lath and is, therefore, applied directly to the rough framing. It is available in sizes from 4' × 8' to 4' × 12' (1.22 m × 2.44 m to 1.22 m × 3.66 m) sheets. GWB is also available in several thicknesses and fire-rated categories. *See figure 6–6, Gypsum Wall Board (GWB) Sizes and Types.*

Drywall may be applied to any surface, wood or metal frame, and masonry or concrete. Drywall is nailed or screwed to framing, directly adhered (glued) to masonry or concrete, or applied over special insulating wall systems. In all instances a pre-mix compound (prepared mix) or spackle must be applied to the drywall joints and over the nail or screw indentations. The joints must be taped with a paper or self-adhering nylon mesh tape, with the compound or spackle sanded smooth and, if necessary, taped, coated, and sanded again to give a complete smooth wall finish.

Drywall may remain smooth to appear as plaster or may be textured. The most common textures are the "orange peel," a light roughened finish, usually sprayed on the wall or ceiling; "lace," hand-troweled and similar in appearance to the exterior plaster finish; or "knock-down," also hand-troweled to attain the look similar to the rough antique Spanish exterior plaster. The pre-mixed compound used for taping is also used to achieve these textures.

Other Special Drywall Applications

Specialty drywall products manufactured for purposes other than just a covering for rough framing, concrete, or masonry systems are used for *moisture protection, thermal insulation, sound insulation, radiation shielding,* and *fire protection.* See the section on acoustical treatment for sound insulation.

BOARD THICKNESS	BOARD SIZE				BOARD TYPES				
	8´	9´	10´	12´	Reg	MR**	WR***	"c"**	"x"**
1/4" GWB	×			×	×				
3/8" GWB	×			×	×	×	×		
1/2" GWB	×	×	×	×	×	×	×	×	×
5/8" GWB	×	×	×	×	×	×	×	×	×

REMARKS:

* Fire-resistant Gypsum Board - 1/2" "C" - 3/4 hr rating
5/8" "X" - 1 hr rating
** MR Board - Moisture-resistant for exterior use.
*** WR Board - Water-resistant for interior wet area use.

Standard sizes available as indicated.
Other sizes may be obtained upon special order.

FIGURE 6–6
Gypsum Wall Board (GWB) Sizes and Types

Moisture Protection. Drywall especially made for use around water areas such as bathtubs and showers is referred to as water resistant (WR) board. Drywall that is prepared for exterior use, such as the base for an EIFS system or exterior soffits, is called moisture resistant (MR) board. The boards are available in the same sizes as regular drywall.

Thermal Insulation. The thermal insulation referred to here is separate from the others mentioned previously only because it is a part of the drywall installation. One of the thermal insulation systems is called the "Styrostud" system, using either 26 gauge aluminum, or GI cold-rolled steel framing, and polystyrene board insulation. The studs are 1½" (38.1 mm) or 2" (50.8 mm) deep Z-shaped and are available in lengths of 8'-0", 9'-0", or 10'-0" (2.44 m, 2.74 m, or 3.05 m). They are screwed, nailed, or shot-and-pinned into the wall. The polystyrene boards are 2'-0" (0.61 m) wide, and 1½" (38.1 mm) or 2" (50.8 mm) thick to match the stud being used. The board slips into the stud and is adhered to the wall with panel glue. The studs are used as the backing for fastening the drywall over the insulation system.

A similar system using 26 gauge aluminum or GI cold-rolled steel channel-shaped studs is placed over the polystyrene panels. The panels have grooves cut into the insulating board matching the end return depth and width of the channel. The studs are available in the same sizes as the "Styrostud." The panels are adhered to the wall and the studs are fastened in the same manner as the Z-shaped studs. The studs for this system are also the backing for fastening the drywall over the insulation system.

A third system, a wood furring, may include 1×2 (25.4 mm $\times$ 50.8 mm) or 1×4 (25.4 mm $\times$ 101.6 mm) wood strips in lieu of the metal-stud systems noted earlier. The system has a horizontal strip installed along the bottom and top of the wall, and vertical strips placed at 2'-0" (0.61 m) O/C along the whole wall. The strips are also fastened with nails, screws, or shot-and-pin. The insulation may be either batt insulation or polystyrene board adhered to the wall between the furring strips. The drywall is then placed over the insulating system and fastened in the same manner as indicated for the metal-stud system.

Radiation Protection.   Another product, radiation shielding drywall, includes a leaded layer from ¹⁄₃₂" (0.8 mm) to ⅛" (3.2 mm) thick added to the GWB and installed as a single unit to prevent and/or reduce radiation exposure to other areas. This product is for use in X-ray and radiation laboratories, hospitals, other clinical applications, and in locations such as nuclear reactor control centers.

Fire Protection.   Fire protection may require special applications such as those used for elevator, hoist, and dumbwaiter shafts. Firewalls are constructed within residential and commercial structures to aid in the reduction of the spread of fire. These walls may be required to extend to the underside of the roof structure on one or both sides of a separation wall. In commercial construction such a wall is located between several areas. This depends upon the size of the project.

In many areas of the United States, residential construction requires a firewall partition between an attached garage and the residence, extending the full width of the garage and to the underside of the roof structure. The wall is constructed with ⅝" "X" (15.9 mm), GWB on both sides of the frame wall. The drywall extends to ceiling height on the residence side. On the garage side, it continues to the underside of the roof structure. Any installations, such as pipe or conduit, that pass through a firewall must have fire-insulating wrap. This means that the wall must be sealed to maintain the fire resistant rating and to meet the requirements of local and national fire codes. This type of installation is classified as a one-hour fire-rated drywall system.

Tile

Quarry Tile.   Quarry tile, used primarily for floor covering, is a kiln-dried, clay-based (terra cotta) material available in sizes from 8" to 12" (101.6 mm to 304.8 mm) square. The tiles are normally installed in a bed of thinset cement approximately ½" (12.7 mm) thick with a maximum 1" (25.4 mm) wide gap between the tiles and grouted between the tiles to the level of the edge of the tile so as to seal the joints for moisture protection. These tiles may also be vitrified and glazed to increase the moisture protection and improve appearance.

Ceramic Tile.   Ceramic tile is a glazed, vitreous tile that may be used for either floor or wall tiles. The tiles may be clay-based or cement-based and are available in a variety of baked enamel plain colors or colorful designs. The sizes range from 1″ (25.4 mm) square tiles (called mosaic tiles), 1″ (25.4 mm) squares adhered to a 12″ (304.8 mm) square base sheet, to larger tiles from 4″ to 12″ (50.8 mm to 304.8 mm) square. The same application procedures are used for ceramic tiles as for quarry tiles. It may be necessary to install the tile with thinset mortar and grout over a lath when applied on walls for moisture protection.

Terrazzo. Terrazzo pavers may be made from combinations of crushed seashells, nutshells, and/or glass and mixed with concrete and formed into various sizes and designs. The tiles are then polished for a smooth finish.

Acoustical Treatment

Direct-adhered acoustical treatment includes either of two systems. One is a pre-mixed compound and the other is a *direct-adhered acoustical tile*. The pre-mixed compound is more commonly used for residential, light commercial, and some office construction. Its appearance is similar to the pre-mixed drywall compound with loose-grain perlite, vermiculite, or fiberglass, combined with moistened powdered gypsum and sprayed on the ceilings.

Direct-adhered acoustical tiles are manufactured from the same materials as used for composite board or fiberglass insulations but are compressed and formed into 8″ to 12″ (203.2 mm to 304.8 mm) squares from ⅛″ to ½″ (3.2 mm to 6.4 mm) thick. They may require an adhesive base or may be self-adhering. In either case, they are pressed directly onto walls and ceilings. These tiles are most commonly used in small areas where sound attenuation is required, such as the enclosures surrounding public telephones. Direct-adhered tiles may have the same appearance and texture as suspended acoustical tiles.

Suspended Acoustical Tile.   *See figure 6–7, Acoustical Ceiling Tile (ACT) System.* Although not common to residential construction, suspended acoustical ceiling tile (ACT) systems may be found in some locations such as kitchens, bathrooms, or garages. The system is installed by suspending tie wires from the roof or ceiling structure above that are fastened to a track (called a runner) at the opposite end. The runners are flanged T-shapes that are used to support acoustical ceiling tiles. The track is spaced so as to form square or rectangular 2′ × 2′ (0.61 m × 0.61 m) or 2′ × 4′ (0.61 m × 1.22 m) open areas into which the tile is placed. The track is fastened to an angle iron of the same gauge at all wall junctures. The depth of the suspension system depends upon the height above the finish floor (A.F.F.) desired and the distance to the structure above. The tiles are composite fiberboard with smooth or fissured faces. A fissured face is one with indentations or grooves throughout. Acoustical tiles may also have a fire-rated classification of 1-hour resistance to fire.

Sound Insulation.   This section may be considered a part of the acoustical treatment or drywall treatment. There are two classifications of sound insulations—*sound attenuation* and *sound enhancement.*

Sound attenuation.   Sound attenuation is the *reduction of the sound level* between areas or within a room. There are two types of sound attenuation systems applied in which GWB is included. One is the pre-fabricated sound attenuation panel with integral wall coverings, padding, and connection fittings affixed to wall framing. Many office complexes (especially for conference

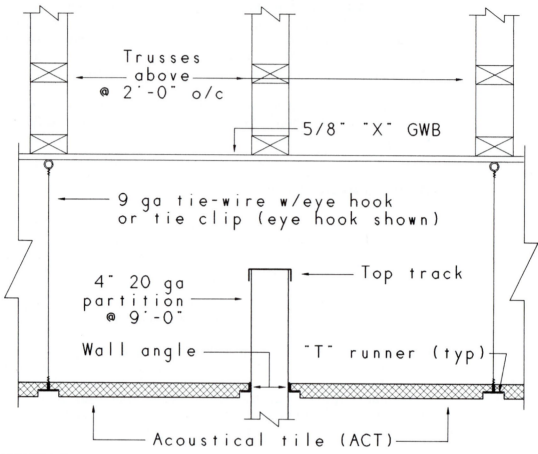

FIGURE 6–7
Acoustical Ceiling Tile (ACT) System

rooms) and schools (for music and rehearsal rooms) frequently use these panel systems.

See figure 6–8, Sound Wall Insulation System. The system commonly installed in multifamily (such as apartments and hotels) and commercial construction (such as offices or public restrooms) uses drywall with batt or board sound insulation built into the wall between units.

Noise levels developed within a room, the building, or from external sources may have a sound level of 60 decibels (60dB) or more. Where such conditions exist, and the sound is to be retarded, special walls or panels are constructed to prevent this level of sound from penetrating to other areas. One system, using drywall in combination with insulating materials, provides this control. The increase or reduction of sound from one area to another is identified as the *sound transmission class (STC).* The STC states the decibel count in a specific room or area.

Sound enhancement. Where it may be necessary to *maintain or increase the sound level* such as in concert halls, theaters, opera houses, and the like, the sound may be increased by what is termed sound enhancement. Special wall and ceiling panels provide this ability to make and control the volume change and echo reduction.

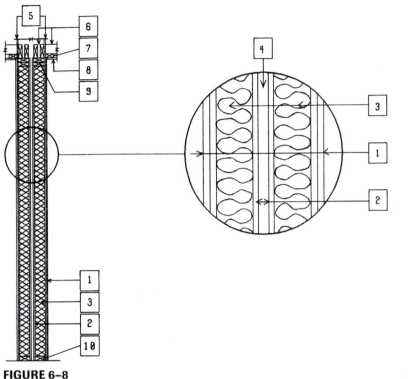

KEYNOTES:

1. Dbl 5/8" "X" GWB o/2x or steel frame
2. 1/2" sound (fiber) board.
3. Alternate batt imsulation.
4. 1" air space
5. 5/8" "X" GWB to underside of roof.
6. Ceiling joists.
7. Furring.
8. 5/8" "X" GWB on furring @ ceiling.
9. Dbl top plate.
10. Sole (bottom) or sill plate.

FIGURE 6–8
Sound Wall Insulation System

Finish Flooring and Floor Coverings

Finish flooring materials include wood plank, parquet, and special elastomeric and polymeric mixtures. The wood flooring may be installed over a subfloor-ing or adhered directly to a concrete slab and can be set in many aesthetic designs. Oak, walnut, cherry wood, and other hardwoods are used for such installations because of their durability and appearance.

Special materials and coatings such as asphalt planking (similar to roof pads), plastic laminated floor coverings, and epoxy-based semi-liquid mixes (such as crushed gravel mixed with elastomeric or resin-based coatings) are especially popular for use as a finish for decks, exterior balconies, and arcades. These polymers are applied by spray, roll, or brush over a moisture barrier (asphalt felts polyester sheets, or polyethylene sheets). Asphalt planking is installed over the same type moisture barrier but uses a hot-mop application (hot bitumen) or cold-applied emulsion-based adhesive.

Floor coverings also include *resilient vinyl composition sheet, vinyl composition tile (VCT),* and *carpeting* for interiors. Resilient vinyl sheet and vinyl tile floor coverings are manufactured with pre-printed design (for example, floral or symmetric) in combination with bitumen-based mixtures and epoxy cements compressed in a calender mill under heat and moisture, and slowly dried. The vinyl sheet material is obtained in 12'-0" (3.66 m) wide rolls up to 100'-0" (30.48 m) in length.

The vinyl composition tiles (VCT) are compressed even more than the sheet materials. The process makes them more rigid than the sheet materials. Having completed the pass through the calender, they are passed through a shear mill and cut into the sizes desired. The sizes normally range from 8″ to 12″ (203.2 mm to 304.8 mm) square. These floor coverings are applied with a base adhesive.

Carpeting is classified as a floor covering that is installed from wall to wall in all directions. The materials are available in residential or commercial quality and with many textures and designs. The complete carpeting system includes padding, a rubber-based mixture with fine scraps of carpeting for softness, that is partially adhered to the substrate (underlayment or slab), webbing (a nylon or other cloth-like mesh available in rolls 4″ [101.6 mm] to 6″ [152.4 mm] long) for joining carpet edges, and tack strips for use along the perimeter of a room. Rugs and mats are not considered carpeting. They are classified as specialty items included in Division 12, Furnishings.

Painting and Wall Coverings

Paints are coatings such as epoxies, acrylics, latexes, lacquers, varnishes, and stains used for exterior and interior finishes for walls, ceilings, exposed wood, or other back-up material specified to be weather protected or to have added aesthetic coloring and design. Paints are installed in two-coat or three-coat applications, using a base paint, or a sealer, with the finish coats in oil-based or latex mixtures. Both types may be used for interior or exterior applications. Oil-based paints include a linseed oil base, while latex paints are produced from a rubber or synthetic rubber base mixed with polymers or acrylics. Paints may be applied over concrete, masonry, steel, wood, or drywall. Lacquers, varnishes, and stains are applied to wood surfaces only for appearance and/or durable gloss finish. Epoxies are a synthetic resin used to produce a hard and durable surface. Such applications may include marine deck or concrete slab construction.

Any material applied to interior walls other than plaster or paint is considered a wall covering. *Wallpaper* includes *paper, vinyl, cloth,* or *other woven materials,* applied directly to the wall surface. Wall coverings also include *decorative wood* and *paneling*. In new construction, where wall coverings are applied, the drywall backing must be smooth and clean for wallpaper applications. The applicator cleans and prepares the wall with *sizing* when making preparations for the wallpaper installation. The material (paper, cloth, or vinyl) is applied using a water-soluble paste mixture. Other wall coverings are applied using glue and/or nails or screws. Most wall covering, other than wallpaper, is applied by the finish carpenter.

Sealants

Sealants are materials made from rubber or synthetic rubber used for closure of control joints in concrete and masonry installations. The sealants vary in thickness from ⅛″ (3.2 mm) DIA to 1″ (25.4 mm) DIA and are available in cartons or in rolls of up to 500′-0″ (152.4 m). The sealant is pressed into the control joints and allowed to cure. They may be epoxy painted, cemented, or covered with a metal joint strip connected to siding, and the like, or exposed, as with concrete slabs.

CHAPTER EXERCISES

The following questions refer to the Garland residence.

Multiple Choice

_____ 1. The main entry door is:
   a. Metal-clad wood
   b. A panel door with "half moon" lites
   c. Two 3'-0" × 6'-8" (0.91 m × 2.03 m) doors
   d. All of the above

_____ 2. The windows are:
   a. All custom made
   b. All metal frame
   c. Neither a nor b
   d. Both a and b

_____ 3. The door and window trim:
   a. Match the baseboard
   b. Is customized and packaged with the doors and windows
   c. May not be a part of the door and window package
   d. Is pre-stained

_____ 4. Exterior trim includes:
   a. All window and door trim and fascia board
   b. Door trim only
   c. Window trim only
   d. Fascia trim only

_____ 5. The exterior finish is:
   a. CMU and shiplap wood siding
   b. Concrete plaster and exposed CMU
   c. Brick veneer, exposed CMU, and metal siding
   d. Exterior Insulation and Finish System

_____ 6. The sheathing for the roof underlayment:
   a. Is ⅜" (9.5 mm) Masonite panel
   b. Is either ⅝" (15.8 mm) OSB® or ½" (12.7 mm) CDX
   c. Includes ⅜" (9.5 mm) CDX shear panels over the sheathing
   d. Is used with 43 lb (15.45 kg) building paper

_____ 7. The roofing is:
   a. A one-piece S tile application
   b. A wood shake roofing material
   c. Asphalt composition shingles
   d. A panelized metal roof system

_____ 8. All roof penetrations shall include:
   a. No protection
   b. Galvanized iron or aluminum flashings
   c. Galvanized iron or aluminum flashings with collar
   d. None of the above

_____ 9. The roof slopes are:
   a. 4:12 and 8:12
   b. 5:12 and 8:12
   c. 5:12 and 6:12
   d. 4:12 and 6:12

General Information

_____ 10. The materials included in Finishes, Division 9, are:
   a. Painting and wall coverings
   b. Floor coverings and lath and plaster
   c. Both a and b
   d. Neither a nor b

_____ 11. Gypsum wallboard is available:
   a. In 5′ × 10′ (1.52 m × 3.05 m) sheets
   b. In ¾″ (19.05 mm) thickness
   c. As Sheetrock or fire-coded
   d. With finish compound and tape already attached

_____ 12. Cement plaster:
   a. Is installed in one-coat, two-coat, and three-coat applications
   b. Is a synthetic system
   c. Does not require a moisture barrier
   d. Must be trowel-applied only

_____ 13. Quarry tile:
   a. Is available in sizes from 8″ (203.2 mm) to 12″ (304.8 mm) square
   b. Is used for wall tiles
   c. Must be self-adhering
   d. Is produced from quarry stone

_____ 14. Ceramic tiles:
   a. May be used only on kitchen floors
   b. Are non-breakable
   c. May be used for both floor and wall finishes
   d. None of the above

_____ 15. Resilient flooring:
   a. Is produced in the same manner as vitreous tile
   b. Is always adhered with a cement-based material
   c. Is tacked to the substrate
   d. Is available in sheets and tiles

_____ 16. Painting includes:
   a. Wall coverings and sealants
   b. Integral coloring of cement plaster
   c. Latex, lacquer, varnish, epoxy, and oil-based materials used for covering interior and exterior surfaces
   d. Plastic coatings for below-grade moisture protection

_____ 17. Exterior plaster systems include:
   a. Metal lath with moisture barrier
   b. Cement-based and gypsum-based plaster materials
   c. Synthetic plaster systems with nylon or polyester mesh for lath
   d. All of the above

_____ 18. Lath for plaster coatings:
   a. May be 1"-20 gauge (25.4 mm-20 gauge) wire mesh, expanded metal, or hi-rib metal lath
   b. May require a foam board backing
   c. Neither a nor b
   d. Both a and b

_____ 19. Drywall classifications include:
   a. Moisture resistant (MR) and water-resistant (WR) sheets
   b. A finish plaster requirement for all surfaces
   c. Only fire-resistant material
   d. None of the above

_____ 20. Sealants are used for:
   a. Painting surfaces
   b. Mixing with plaster
   c. Sealing control joints
   d. All of the above

True or False

T F   1. Lath is used for drywall applications.

T F   2. Light-gauge metal stud framing is installed in much the same manner as wood stud framing.

T F   3. Suspended ceiling systems for plaster or drywall finishes are similarly installed.

T F   4. Acoustical ceiling tile (ACT) systems include track and angle iron.

T F   5. A three-coat cement plaster is applied with two brown coats and a scratch coat.

T F   6. A synthetic plaster system may be a panelized system applied over a polystyrene foam board.

T F   7. Carpeting normally includes the edge track strips, padding, webbing, and carpet.

T F   8. Latex paint may be used for both interior and exterior surfaces.

T F   9. When used for exterior surfaces, the paint specifications require a primer.

T F 10. Floor tile is made only from quarry tile.

T F 11. Tiles may be glazed and vitrified with designs and multiple colors.

T F 12. All tiles are made from cement-base material.

T F 13. Tiles may be applied with a self-adhering adhesive base or a thin-set concrete base.

T F 14. Acoustical treatment infers the installation of a suspended ACT ceiling only.

T F 15. Special lead-backed drywall sheets are used for radiation protection.

T F 16. Hi-rib lath, when used, is applied on the underside of any area, often referred to as a *lid,* such as soffits, overhangs, or ceilings.

T F 17. GWB is available in ¼", ⅜", ½", and ⅝" (6.4 mm, 9.5 mm, 12.7 mm, and 15.9 mm) thicknesses.

T F 18. Sloped roof systems may include only composition shingle or tile.

T F 19. Tile roof systems include an asphaltic or pitch felt underlayment.

T F 20. Wood-framed chimney construction requires ⅝" × (15.88 mm) GWB installed completely around the interior and exterior framing.

Completion

1. The _____ wire mesh is the cheapest and most common lath used for cement plaster.

2. A(n) _____ application is most common for cement plaster over a masonry surface.

3. Synthetic plaster systems use a(n) _____ surface material over cement plaster and polystyrene foam board.

4. _____ protection is required under all exterior plaster systems.

5. A ⅞" (22.2 mm), 3-coat cement plaster system requires a ⅜" (9.5 mm) scratch coat, a _____" (_____ mm) brown coat, and a ⅛" (3.2 mm) finish coat.

6. Drywall, when installed for a fire-rated wall system, is usually a single or double layer of _____" (_____ mm) type "X" board.

7. To complete a drywall system screws or nails, _____, and tape are required.

8. _____ may be used for patching existing gypsum plaster or drywall.

9. A(n) _____ system may be required in lieu of wood framing in any structure.

10. The _____ contractor is responsible for all trim work.

Refer to the schedules for the Garland residence to answer the following questions.

11. Window type, mark "D," is a _____ (_____) window.

12. Door type, mark _____", is a 3'-0" × 6'-8" (3068 [0.91 m × 2.03 m]) door.

13. The exterior walls have _____" (_____cm) wide R-19 insulation.

14. A(n) _____ felt underlayment is installed over the ½" (12.7 mm) CDX plywood roof sheathing for moisture protection.

15. 26 gauge galvanized iron, aluminum, or _____, may be used for flashings at pipe penetrations.

CHAPTER 7

Plumbing, Mechanical, and Electrical (On-Site)

As with off-sites and site improvements, all on-site work for the mechanical, plumbing, and electrical work must be coordinated with all of the other trades. The rough-in work of these trades includes any sleeving, pipe, and/or conduit, that must be installed prior to, or during, the placement of concrete or masonry so that the **stub-outs** are in the proper locations. A stub-out is the exposed end of plumbing, piping, or electrical conduit installed from the off-sites extending into the structure. The ends are exposed above the concrete slab, wood floor, or walls so that future crews can complete the construction as the work progresses.

Coordination must continue between trades because the same contractors who installed the rough-in plumbing, mechanical, and electrical also install all of the finish plumbing, mechanical, and electrical work. This includes finished plumbing fixtures and connections; HVAC units, grilles, and registers; and electrical fixtures, switches, outlets, and protective covers. The water and waste pipes, and gas lines with appropriate **angle stops** (a shut-off valve at a fixture), and/or electrical outlets must also be in place for the cabinet and appliance installers.

Other common installations included in on-site plumbing are fire-protection systems such as fire-sprinkler systems; automatic chemical spray systems (foam or CO_2); gas and fuel-oil heating systems; and liquid-transfer heating and cooling systems associated with HVAC. All information, regulations, and codes are based upon the recommendations of the American National Specifications Institute (ANSI) and/or the National Fire Protection Association (NFPA). There are some areas now requiring a sprinkler system installed as part of the standard residential, as well as commercial, codes and ordinances.

PLUMBING AND PIPING

See figure 7–1, Isometric Piping Diagram, and figure 7–2, Pictorial Plumbing Section, Garland Residence. An isometric plan or pictorial section of the plumbing and piping installations may be used for residential or small commercial structures. The isometric diagram is used for most commercial construction projects. The drawings include a layout of the materials necessary for a complete installation

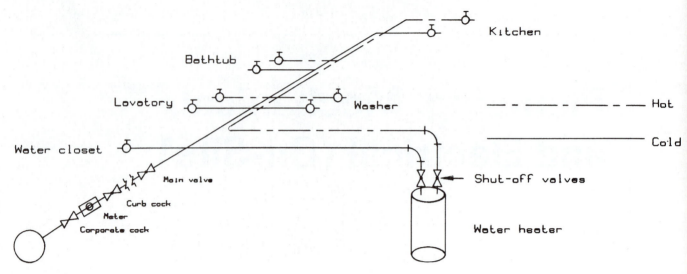

FIGURE 7–1
Isometric Piping Diagram, Garland Residence

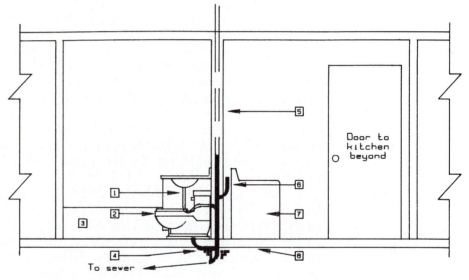

KEYNOTES:

1. 1½" waste pipe and P-trap @ lavatory

2. Water closet

3. Bathtub beyond

4. 2" water closet waste pipe

5. 4" waste pipe and vent –
   Vent through roof

6. 1½" washer drain

7. Washer

8. 4" thick concrete slab

FIGURE 7–2
Pictorial Plumbing Section, Garland Residence

with the exception of the fixtures. The fixtures are indicated on the architectural floor plan or on the floor plan layout within the plumbing drawings. Where there are specifications, they include the material and installation procedures so that all codes are noted and properly followed. Plumbing, mechanical, and electrical schedules are used to indicate the fixtures required, the manufacturer of the fixture, and the fixture manufacturer's identification code.

One or all of the above must note the material types to be used. If no information exists, the contractor must get engineering requirements provided so that the system is installed in accordance with all codes and ordinances and the work is done to the standards of the trade.

MECHANICAL

Mechanical specifications and drawings include all *Heating*, *Ventilation* and *Air-Conditioning* (HVAC). All pertinent information found in the schedule of materials in a set of plans identifies the type of unit required, such as:

1. A combination furnace/air-conditioner
2. Roof-top air-conditioner
3. Gas-fired or oil-fired furnace
4. Heat pump
5. Accessories
    a. Piping—water and steam, fuel
    b. Ductwork—flexible or rigid galvanized steel
    c. Supply registers—diffusers
    d. Return grilles

Heating and air-conditioning units are rated in British thermal units (Btu). *A Btu is the amount of heat—1 calorie—required to raise the temperature of one pound of water one degree (1°) Fahrenheit.* This rate is determined on the basis of the maximum density of water at 39° Fahrenheit or 22° Centigrade/Celsius. There is more energy expended for cooling, therefore, the amount of Btu's required for cooling is greater than for heating. It is for this reason that furnaces, used in areas where heating more than cooling is necessary, are designated at a lower Btu rating than are air-conditioners. In addition, air-conditioning units are rated in "tons of cooling" capacity, where one ton is equal to 12,000 Btu.

Where space is available, such as a basement or utility room, either an air-conditioning unit or furnace may be used. Furnace systems include forced air heating, hot water heating, or steam heating. The supply system for heating is installed utilizing the most efficient placement of the ducts or plumbing to maximize the output.

Hot water and steam heating systems include circulating pumps to force the water or steam through the supply piping as quickly as possible. These systems are less efficient than forced air because a return is piped back to the boiler from each radiator or radiant heater supplied, by-passing the heating supply lines. The units farthest from the heating unit will receive less heat as a result. Forced-air systems have a circulating motor and fan which forces the air to the areas supplied as efficiently as possible. There are fewer return lines since the cooled air can be drawn directly from a general area (more than one room) back to the furnace for reheating.

The warmer climates making use of air-conditioning will normally install combination units, heat pumps or air-conditioning units, and/or swamp coolers. A swamp cooler is an exterior-mounted device that is connected to a water supply. The water is regulated to allow so much flow into the base of the unit. A fan circulates air over the water for a cooling effect and blows the cooled air into an area within the structure (room, factory, warehouse).

The rule of thumb for sizing an air-conditioning unit is one (1) ton (12,000 Btu) per every 400 sq ft to 500 sq ft area. Therefore, the average residence of 1,800 sq ft to 2,000 sq ft usually requires no more than a four- or five-ton unit. Unless a combination unit is installed, utility space is unnecessary. Self-contained units are frequently placed on roofs or in attic spaces. A split unit where the compressor is separated from the heating/cooling unit may be placed in an attic space or garage with the compressor placed outdoors on a concrete pad next to the structure in the vicinity of the unit. For larger structures (2,500 square feet or more), it is necessary to install larger units, such as five- to ten-ton sizes, or multiple units equaling the same capacity.

See figure 7–3, HVAC Reflected Ceiling Plan, Apartment. HVAC piping or ductwork installations are divided into two categories, *supply* and *return*. *Supply* includes all parts of an installation, excluding the unit, required for the heating or cooling to the structure. The supply materials include fiberglass or vinyl-coated flexible tubing connected to the unit and extending to all the supply registers. There are variations in the size of a duct. Where one duct may be used to supply several areas, branches from the duct are connected to extend to the register. These ducts are smaller in size and are connected with a unit called the **transition piece** (a special reducing coupling). The transition piece may be in the form of a tee (T) or a straight reducer used to change the size of the ductwork.

Registers are noted on a mechanical ceiling plan with a number and letters. These identifications denote the size required for the supply duct and register. For example, a supply register identified with *120 CFM* calls for the register to be capable of supplying 120 cubic feet of air per minute. This requirement will also give information as to the size of the duct. The more air required, the larger the duct size. Most mechanical reflected ceiling plans include this information.

Return includes all parts, excluding the unit, used to remove the heating or cooling from the piping or the air, and re-circulate it to the unit for re-heating or re-cooling. The operation of the unit draws the used air back into it to be re-circulated. The return air may also be ductwork or an **air plenum.** A plenum is the air space in unexposed areas of a building, such as in suspended ceiling areas. A plenum may also be a part of the unit where return air can be drawn directly into the unit. This area is usually directly under an HVAC unit that is installed within a utility area in a dwelling or commercial structure.

The unit is the third part of the system and is separated from the supply and return definitions since it is involved with both the supply and re-circulation.

The unit installed for the apartment in figure 7–3 is a three-ton unit, or the equivalent of 36,000 Btu. The reflected ceiling plan identifies the locations of all HVAC *supply* and *return* equipment. A schedule is supplied with a set of HVAC plans showing the size of the unit, the sizes of the supply ducts, the supply registers (diffusers), and the return grilles and ducts. The units for each apartment are placed on the apartment roof for convenience of maintenance and protection from vandalism. The duct used may be flexible insulated duct common to residential installations, or sheet-metal insulated ductwork more commonly used for commercial/industrial applications. All supply and return

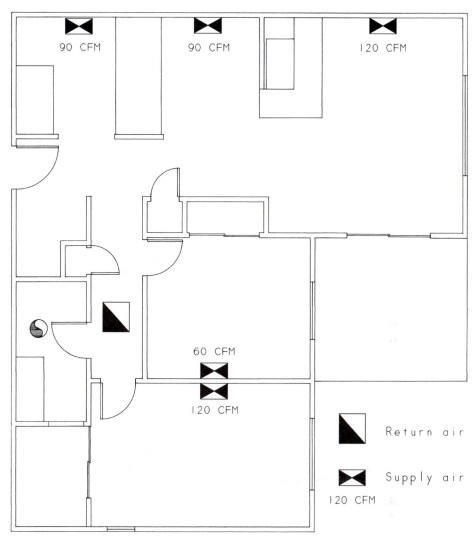

FIGURE 7–3
HVAC Reflected Ceiling Plan, Apartment

ducts may be installed in the walls of the structure (as they are in the apartment), or in an attic space to and from the unit supplying the apartment.

THE HVAC AND ELECTRICAL TRADES RELATIONSHIP

There are times when the mechanical and electrical contractors may be required to interact. An agreement is normally included in the structural general notes in a set of plans. In most instances the agreement is specified in a manner similar to the following instructions:

1. The installation and maintenance of all wiring and conduit from the main power supply to the disconnect controlling the HVAC unit is the responsibility of the electrical contractor.

2. The conduit installation for the thermostat cable is the responsibility of the electrical contractor.

3. The supply, installation, and maintenance of the units and internal controls and wiring, including the thermostat cable from the unit, are the responsibility of the HVAC contractor.

ELECTRICAL

See figure 7–4, Electrical Service Entrance Systems, Residential. Electrical systems include all materials and equipment installed, from the power source to the smallest outlets within a structure. The on-site construction includes everything from the service entrance equipment (residential) or switchgear equipment (commercial/industrial) to the finished interior product, excluding appliances (unless they are included in the contract). The service entrance equipment includes the meter, main circuit breaker (CB), and branch circuit breakers (CB) located in a metal enclosure on the exterior of a single-family residence (garage, utility, or basement wall).

The power source is a step-down transformer located near or on the property. This transformer may be located on a pole with connections to the structure (*refer to figure 7–4*) or may be an underground connection from a transformer located at street level or underground. The pole-mounted connections are called an *overhead*. They connect to a *pothead* fitting at the top of a conduit extending from the service entrance to 2'-0" (1.22 m) above the roof line. An overhead connection requires minimum heights from 10'-0" (3.05 m) in open areas to as high as 18'-0" (5.49 m) in traffic areas (streets, sidewalks, driveways).

The underground connection is called a *lateral*. This may be exposed electrical cable buried underground or in a conduit and is connected to the bottom of the service entrance. The minimum depth of a lateral is 18" (457.2 mm) in open areas to 4'-0" (2.44 m) deep in traffic areas (streets, sidewalks, driveways).

For commercial and industrial installations, a small substation may be installed to supply the power necessary to run machinery. The power is supplied

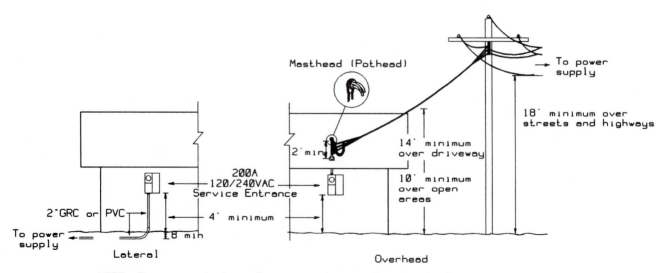

FIGURE 7–4
Electrical Service Entrance Systems, Residential

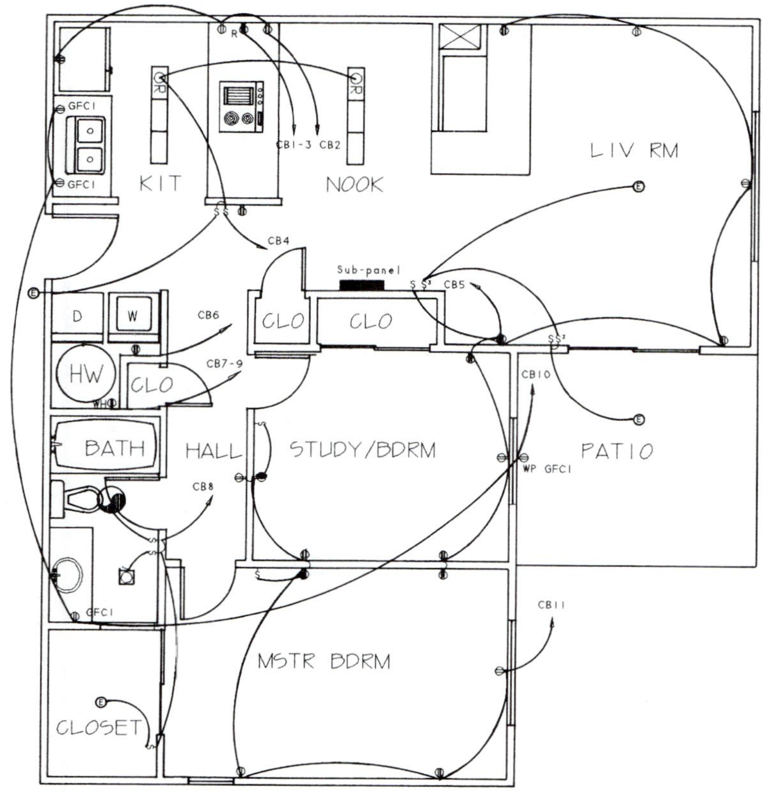

FIGURE 7-5
General Power/Lighting, Apartment

SUB-PANEL

Main CB 150A

CB1	Range/oven	-50A
CB3		
CB5	Liv Rm Recept	-20A
CB7	Water heater	-30A
CB9		
CB11	Bdrm Recept	-20A

CB2	Kitchen appliance circuit	-20A
CB4	Kitchen/Nook lighting	-15A
CB6	Washer/Dryer circuit	-20A
CB8	Bath lighting/fan	-15A
CB10	GFCI circuit	-20A
CB12		
CB14	Air conditioner (not shown)	-30A

from the transformer to *switchgear* equipment located in an enclosure next to the exterior wall or within the substation established for security around the equipment. The power for such supply is referred to as the voltage (V), and alternating current (AC) supply usually reduced from 4160VAC to 480VAC, 240VAC or 208VAC, and 120VAC. Residential service entrances are normally rated as a 120/240VAC service. The switches and receptacles (convenience outlets) are also rated for either 120VAC or 240VAC. For example, the standard duplex receptacle is rated at a maximum 240VAC and 20A, whereas a standard light switch is normally rated at a maximum 125VAC and 15A.

An electrical engineer determines the electrical requirements in much the same manner as the mechanical engineer prepares the plumbing and mechanical requirements. Once the requirements are known, the electrical contractor determines the size of the service entrance equipment to a residence or the switchgear requirements for a commercial or industrial project. The National Electric Code (NEC) establishes the minimum requirements for all these calculations and for the materials to be used within a structure.

See figure 7–5, General Power/Lighting, Apartment. The general power and lighting layout for the apartment shows the placement of the convenience outlets, light switches, lights, and circuitry. The apartment has its own individual service equipment (sub-panel) supplied from a central source. A schedule is also provided showing the circuit breakdown for the unit.

CHAPTER EXERCISES

True or False

T F   1. The plumbing vent pipe in figure 7–2 is 6" (152.4 mm) DIA.

T F   2. Plumbing, in the general meaning, refers to all water, sewer, and gas work.

T F   3. Normally, the electrician is responsible for maintaining all wiring to, and including, the HVAC unit.

T F   4. There are eight water connections within the Garland residence.

T F   5. The HVAC compressor is always located on a pad outside of a structure.

T F   6. All supply-air ducts are to have grilles installed.

T F   7. The air output capacity of an HVAC system is referred to as the CFM.

T F   8. The normal service entrance equipment for a residence is rated at 120/240VAC.

T F   9. There is a combination ceiling fan/light in the apartment living room.

T F   10. The apartment bathroom has a combination heat/vent/light in the ceiling.

Multiple Choice

_____   1. A stub-out is:
   a. The end of a pipe or conduit installed in the concrete slab or wood floor
   b. A short fixture connection
   c. The same as a cleanout
   d. Any framing member cut longer than necessary

_____ 2. The electrical and mechanical contractors normally contract:
   a. For the electrical power supply to be installed by the electrical contractor
   b. For the mechanical contractor to install the power supply
   c. For the electrical contractor to maintain the complete unit
   d. None of the above

_____ 3. The type of air-conditioning/heating duct installed in the apartment is:
   a. 20 gauge galvanized prefabricated metal duct
   b. Flexible insulated fiber and plastic duct
   c. Flexible non-insulated fiber and plastic duct
   d. 26 gauge prefabricated metal duct

_____ 4. The plumbers' responsibility includes:
   a. Installation of all piping and plumbing including the fixtures
   b. Installation of natural gas supply from the meter to the appliances
   c. Installation of the hot water heater and its controls
   d. All of the above

_____ 5. The cold and hot water piping to be installed in the Garland residence is:
   a. Copper $^1/_2''$ (12.7 mm) ID and $^3/_4''$ (19.1 mm) ID
   b. $^1/_2''$ (12.7 mm) ID and $^3/_4''$ (19.1 mm) ID PVC cold and CPVC hot water
   c. Both a and b
   d. Neither a nor b

Completion

1. The electrician is responsible for connections to the _____ for the air-conditioning unit U.N.O.

2. The mechanical contractor installs the _____ for regulating heating and cooling.

3. The installation of materials and equipment that are a part of the potable water supply is called _____.

4. The _____ engineer is responsible for the design of all plumbing and heating/cooling equipment installations.

5. The electric service for the apartment has a maximum capacity of _____ A.

6. The is (are) _____ convenience outlet(s) installed on the exterior of the apartment.

7. A telephone jack is located in the _____.

8. The Btu rating for the apartment A/C unit is _____.

9. The hot water heater is connected to the _____ service in the Garland residence.

10. The closet lights are operated with a _____ switch.

CHAPTER 8

The Lee Residence Plans and Specifications

The owner may take the responsibility to become an *owner-builder* where the law allows, or where no regulations govern such actions. The owner-builder is responsible for all construction from the building permit application to the certificate of occupancy, and liability falls directly on the owner. The owner may hire crews directly.

Most contracts in residential construction may be negotiated between the owner and a contractor. An alternative is that the owner may request competitive bids from contractors by advertising in local construction periodicals or the local newspaper. If the owner chooses to hire a contractor to build the structure, the contractor may share liability for the application of permits and other certifications. Contract documents, such as those found in commercial negotiations, are used sparingly.

GENERAL INFORMATION

Residential plans may have specifications indicated in one or more ways. Most pertinent information is included on the individual drawings or in additional sheets in the set of plans referred to as general architectural and/or structural notes. The materials to be used may be specified as follows:

1. Directly on the plans (floor plan, elevation, section, or detail) by use of abbreviations, symbols, and keynotes.
2. By a combination of a Description of Materials (*see figure 8–1*) and the plans.
3. By a combination of plans and a simplified specification for the CSI divisions in paragraph form offering very basic information included in the plans.

DESCRIPTION OF MATERIALS

Documents, such as those found in commercial construction contracts, are not usually used in residential construction. The basic contract documents in

125

residential construction include a Description of Materials form, supplied by banks, and a proposal/contract.

See figure 8–1, Description of Materials, Lee Residence. The Description of Materials is a combination specification and estimate initially filed for the purpose of determining costs of a residential project to enable the owner to apply for a construction loan.

SPECIFICATIONS

See figure 8–2, Typical General Notes Plan Sheet. The general notes sheet shown in figure 8–2 is for the Lee residence. As stated, the specifications given are minimum statements for the work to be performed and the procedures to be followed. The specifications are written in this manner on the premise that the owner's representative and/or the contractors will follow them. As repeated previously, these inference statements are stated as follows:

1. "in accordance with the best standards of the trade."
2. "shall include, but not be limited to the information in the specifications."
3. "and all materials, labor, and/or equipment necessary to produce a complete installation."
4. "the installations shall be in accordance with all local codes and ordinances."

These and similar statements alert the contractor that all requirements must be met without going into the details of materials, equipment, or installation procedures to complete the work. There may be no specifications whatsoever if the dwelling is constructed under the owner-builder concept. In this case, all the work is in accordance with all of the above statements without any details.

CODES AND ORDINANCES

A specific set of rules is established in most areas of construction. These rules and regulations are *codes*. Some codes include such regulations as established by the National Electric Code (NEC), the American National Standards Institute (ANSI), the American Fire Protection Agency (AFPA), the Office of Safety and Health Administration (OSHA), the American Society of Heating, Refrigeration, and Air-Conditioning Engineers (ASHRAE), and others. A list of many of the organizations enlisted to help establish the codes are found in the Project Manual, appendix IV, for the construction of a commercial building called the Frontier Manufacturing Company.

The regional codes are established by several building code organizations known as the Building Officials and Code Administrators International (BOCA), the Southern Building Codes Council International (SBCCI), and the International Conference of Building Officials (ICBO). These organizations have coordinated information from each location and formed the International Code Council (ICC) organization. The ICC has established the International Building Code (IBC). The *IBC Code 2000* combines requirements from the three member organizations into a single construction code reference.

NORTH RIVER BANK

DESCRIPTION OF MATERIALS

☑ Proposed Construction   No. 101030
☐ Under Construction
Property Address _____ 900 South Mary Street _____ City _____ Roanoke _____ State _____ Virginia _____
Borrower _____ Mr. And Mrs. L.C. Lee _____ Address _____ 101 State Street, Roanoke, Virginia _____
Contractor or Builder_____ ABC General Contracting _____ Address _____ 4500 East 21st Street, Roanoke, Va. _____

Legal Description
        Lots 36 through 39, Tract 1, Mountain Township, County of _____, State of Virginia.

1. EXCAVATION:
   Bearing soil type: _____ Clayey Loam _____

2. FOUNDATION:
   Footings: Concrete Mix _____ 1:2:5 _____ Strength (psi)_____ 3000 _____ Reinforcing _____ rebar _____
   Foundation Wall: Material ____ 8×8×16 precision CMU ____ Strength (psi)_____ 2000 _____ Reinforcing_____ rebar _____
   Interior Foundation Wall: Material _____ same _____ Party Foundation Wall_____ n/a _____
   Columns: Material and Size _____ n/a _____ Pliers: Material and Reinforcing_____ n/a _____
   Girders: Material and Size _____ n/a _____ Sills: Material_____ 2×8 PTMS mudsill top of walls _____
   Basement: Entrance Areaway _____ n/a _____ Window Areaways_____ n/a _____
   Waterproofing _____ bituthene w/protection board _____ Footing Drains_____ yes – 2" perforated terra cotta pipe _____
   Termite Protection_____ yes – standard per code _____
   Basement-less space: Ground cover_____ n/a _____ Insulation_____ n/a _____ Foundation vents_____ n/a _____
   Special Foundations:_____ fireplace mats and patio monolithic slab _____

3. CHIMNEYS:
   Material: _____ masonry and wood frame; brick veneer _____ Prefabricated *(make and size)* _____ n/a _____
   Flue Lining: Material ____ metal flue lining ____ Heater flue size _____ 4" GI _____ Fireplace flue size _____ 6" GI _____
   Vents: Material and size: Gas or oil heater _____ 4" hot water heater vent (GI) _____

4. FIREPLACES:
   Type: ☐ Solid fuel; ☐ gas burning; ☐ circulator *(make and size)* _____ n/a _____ Ash dump and cleanout _____ yes _____
   Fireplace: Facing ____ brick veneer ____ ; Lining ____ metal box ____ ; Hearth ____ brick veneer ____ ; Mantle ____ n/a ____

5. EXTERIOR WALLS: Tyvek
   Wood Frame: Grade and Species __ stud grade; DF #2 or better __ ; ☐ Corner bracing _yes_ ; ☐ Building paper; weight __lb
   Sub-sheathing: __n/a__ ; thickness: __n/a__ ; width: __n/a__ ; ☐ Solid; ☐ spaced __n/a__ "o\c; diagonal __n/a__
   Siding: __n/a__ ; grade: __n/a__ ; type: __n/a__ ; size: __n/a__ ; exposure: __n/a__ ; fastening: __n/a__
   Shingles: __n/a__ ; grade: __n/a__ ; type: __n/a__ ; size: __n/a__ ; exposure: __n/a__ ; fastening: __n/a__
   Masonry: Solid: __no__ ; facing: __CMU precision__ ; thickness: __8"__ ; type bond __running (common)__
   Door sills _____ n/a _____ ; Window sills _____ n/a _____ ; Lintels _____ n/a _____

FIGURE 8–1
Description of Materials—Lee Residence

NORTH RIVER BANK

DESCRIPTION OF MATERIALS
(Continued)

5. EXTERIOR WALLS (continued):

Interior surfaces: Dampproofing, coats of ____1-parging____; Furring ____1 × 4 or 2 × 4 @ basement drywall____

Masonry veneer: ____n/a____; Sills ____n/a____; Lintels ____n/a____

Exterior Painting: Material ____exterior latex (walls); Olympic Stain (trim)____; No. of coats ____1 + 2____

Gable Wall Construction: ☐ ____same as main walls____; ☐ Other ____n/a____

6. FLOORING:

Concrete Slab: ☐ Basement floor; ☐ First floor; ☐ Ground supported; ☐ Self-supported; Mix ___1:2:5___; Thickness ___4″___

Reinforcing: ____rebar and WWF____; Insulation ____n/a____; Membrane ____20-mil Polyethylene____

Fill Under Slab: Material: ____type II____, thickness ____4″____

____fill compacted to 95% over virgin soil____

FLOOR FRAMING:

Joists-Wood: Grade and Species ___DF #2 or better___; Other ___n/a___; Bridging ___metal cross___; anchors ___n/a___

7. SUBFLOORING: (*describe under-flooring for special floors in section 22*)

Material: Grade and Species ____CDX or OSB®____; size ____¾″____; type ____exterior grade____

Laid: ☐ First floor; ☐ Second floor; ☐ attic ____sq ft; ☐ diagonal; ☐ right angles____

8. FINISH FLOORING: (*Describe kitchen and bath(s) under item 22*)

Location	Material	Size	Thickness	Area	Grade	Building paper	Underlayment
Basement	carpet			1024 sq ft	#1		concrete
Main Floor	carpet			789 sq ft	#1		concrete
Upper Floor	carpet			756 sq ft	#1		¾″ CDX or OSB®

9. PARTITION FRAMING:

Studs-Wood; grade and species ___HF construction___; Size and spacing ___2 × 4 @ 24″ O/C___; Other ___2 × 6 plumbing walls___

10. CEILING FRAMING:

Joists-Wood: Grade and Species ___n/a___; Other ___n/a___; Bridging ___n/a___; anchors ___n/a___

11. ROOF FRAMING:

Rafters: Wood, grade and species ___2 × 6 #2 or better___; Roof Trusses - Type ___TJ___; grade and species ___see plans___

12. ROOFING:

Sheathing: grade and species ___St #2 CDX___; size ___4′ × 8′ × ½″___; type ___5-ply___; ☐ Solid ☐ spaced ___16″ O/C___

Roofing: ___S-tile___; grade ___n/a___; weight and thickness ___88 #/sq ft___; size ___n/a___; fastening ___wire tie___

Stain or Paint: ____n/a____; underlayment ____43# fiberglass felt____

Built-up Roofing: ___n/a___; number of plies ___n/a___; surfacing material ___n/a___

Flashing: Material ___lead/aluminum___; gauge or weight ___3# or 26 ga___; gravel stop ☐ snow guards

FIGURE 8–1

Continued

NORTH RIVER BANK

DESCRIPTION OF MATERIALS
(Continued)

13. GUTTERS AND DOWNSPOUTS:

Gutters: Material_____PVC_____; gauge or weight_____schedule 80_____; size___3″___; shape___"U"___

Downspout: Material___PVC___; gauge or weight_____schedule 80_____; size___3″__; shape___round__; number___4___

Downspouts connected to: ☐ storm sewer ☐ sanitary sewer ☐ dry well ☐ splash block ☐ material and size_2 × 4 conc

14. LATH AND PLASTER:

Lath ☐ Walls ☐ Ceilings ☐: Material_____n/a_____; weight or thickness_____n/a_____

Cement Plaster: Type (1-2-3 coat)_____n/a_____; finish_____n/a_____

Exterior Insulation and Finish System (EIFS): Manufacturer_____Drivit, Sto, Synergy, or equal_____

15. DRYWALL (GWB):

Drywall: ☐ Walls ☐ Ceilings:_USG or equal_; thickness__½″ (UNO)__; finish__orange peel__; joint treatment_tape_

16. DECORATING: (*Paint, wallpaper, etc.*)

Room	Wall Finish Material and Application	Celling Material and Application
Kitchen	semi-gloss latex–2 coats	same as walls
Bath	semi-gloss paint/tile	semi-gloss paint – match walls
Other: Bedrooms	wallpaper	acoustical spray finish
Living Room	paint – flat latex	same as bedroom
Family Room	same as living room	same as bedroom
Dining Room	wallpaper	same as bedroom

17. INTERIOR DOORS AND TRIM:

Doors: Type_____flush_____; material_____luan_____; thickness_____1⅜″_____

Door trim: Type_____package_____; material____select pine____

Finish: Doors_____oak stain_____; trim____oak veneer____

Base: Type_____Slimline_____; material_____pine w/oak veneer_____; size___2″___

Other trim (item, type, and location)_____n/a_____

18. WINDOWS:

Windows: Type____vary____; make_____custom_____; Material_____select pine_____; sash thickness____½″____

Glass: Grade_____see plans_____; ☐ sash weights ☐ balances; type_____n/a_____; head flashing_____yes_____

Trim: Type_____match door trim_____; material_____select pine_____; paint : type and number of coats_____n/a_____

Weather-stripping: Type_____⅜″ self-adhering_____; material_____rubber_____; storm sash – number_____n/a_____

Screens: ☐ Full ☐ Half: Type_____aluminum frame_____; number____see plans____; screen material_____polyester_____

Basement Windows:_____fixed_____; material_____dual insulated wood frame_____; ☐ screens: number___see plans___;

storm sash – number_____n/a_____

Special Windows_____

FIGURE 8–1
Continued

NORTH RIVER BANK

DESCRIPTION OF MATERIALS

(Continued)

19. ENTRANCES AND EXTERIOR DETAIL:

Main Entrance Door: Material __oak__ ; width _6_ ; thickness _1¾"_ ; frame material __oak__ ; thickness ____½"____

Other Entrance Door: Material __birch__ ; width _3'_ ; thickness _1¾"_ ; frame material __oak__ ; thickness ____½"____

Head flashing: ____aluminum____ ; weather-stripping; type ____self-adhering rubber____ ; saddles ____n/a____

Screen doors: Thickness ____n/a____ ; number ____n/a____ ; Screen material ____n/a____ ; louvers ____n/a____

Combination storm and screen doors: Thickness ____n/a____ ; number ____n/a____ ; screen material ____n/a____

Shutter: □ hinged □ fixed: railings _____n/a_____ ; louvers _____n/a_____

Exterior millwork: Grade and species _____n/a_____ ; paint – type and number of coats ____n/a____

20. CABINETS AND INTERIOR DETAIL:

Kitchen Cabinets: Wall units: Material _____oak_____ ; linear feet – shelves _20_ ; shelf width ____12"____

Base units: Materials _____oak_____ ; countertop _____Corian_____ ; edging _____round_____

Back-splash □: end-splash □: cabinet finish _____varnish or lacquer_____ ; number of coats ____2____

Medicine Cabinets: Make _____to be selected by owner_____ ; number ____3____

Other Cabinets and built-in Furnishings: _____storage and wet bar – oak/corian/58'_____

21. STAIRS:

Stair	Treads		Risers		Stringers		Handrail		Baluster	
	Material	Thickness	Material	Thickness	Material	Size	Material	Size	Material	Size
Basement	select pine	1"	select pine	1"			oak	2 × 4		
Main	select pine	1"	select pine	1"	DF #2	2 × 14	oak	2 × 4	wrought iron	see plans
Attic										

Disappearing: Make and model _____n/a_____

22. SPECIAL FLOORS AND WAINSCOT:

FLOORS:

Location	Material, Color, Border, Size, Gauge, etc.	Threshold	Base	Underlayment
Kitchen	quarry title, 12" – to be selected	metal	coved	as required
Bath	resilient vinyl titles, 8" – to be selected	metal	coved	as required

WAINSCOT:

Bath	ceramic tile, 4" – variegated – to 6' A.F.F. – full height at tub and shower

PLUMBING:

Fixture	Number	Location	Make	Mfr. Fixture ID #	Size	Color
Sink	1	kitchen	Elkay (double)	8K42D	42"	stainless
Lavatory	3	powder room/baths	custom		18"	marble
Bathtub	2	1 each bath	custom		5'-0"	polished brass
Shower o/tub*	1	Bath #2	custom			polished brass
Stall shower**	1	master bath	cusotm		3'-0"	custom
Laundry trays	1	utility room	Elkay	EKLY 3020	30"	stainless
Wet bar	1	family room	Elkay	EKWB 2020	20"	stainless

*□ Curtain Rod **□ Door _____

FIGURE 8–1
Continued

NORTH RIVER BANK

DESCRIPTION OF MATERIALS
(Continued)

23. PLUMBING (continued):

Water supply: ☑ public; ☐ community system; ☐ individual (private) system *_____

Sewage disposal: ☑ public; ☐ community system; ☐ individual (private) system *_____

*** Show and describe individual system in complete detail in separate drawings and specifications according to requirements.**

House drain (inside): ☐ cast iron; ☐ tile; ☑ ABS; ☐ other _____

House drain (outside): ☐ cast iron; ☐ tile; ☑ ABS; ☐ other _____

Water piping: ☐ galvanized; ☑ Copper; ☑ PVC; ☐ other _____ ; sill cocks; quantity _____2_____

Domestic water heater: Type _____electric_____ ; make and model _____Ruud GL50_____

Recovery ____10____ gph; 100° rise. Storage tank; material ____glass____ ; capacity ____50____ gallons

Gas service: ☐ utility company; ☐ liquid petroleum gas (LPG); Other _____ ; gas piping; ☐ cooking; ☐ heating

Footing drains connected to: ☐ storm sewer; ☐ sanitary sewer; ☐ dry well; ☐ sump pump; ☐ other ___splash block___

24. HEATING:

☐ Hot water; ☐ steam; ☐ vapor; ☐ one-pipe system; ☐ two-pipe system

☐ radiators; ☐ convectors; ☐ baseboard radiation: Make and model _____n/a_____

Radiant panel: ☐ floor; ☐ wall; ☐ ceiling. Panel coil: Material _____n/a_____

☐ Circulator; ☐ return pump: Make and model _____n/a_____ ; capacity _____n/a_____ gpm

Boiler: Make and model ____n/a____ ; output ____n/a____ Btuh; net rating ____n/a____ Btuh

Warm air: ☐ gravity; ☑ forced air. Type and system: _____self-contained w/humidifier_____

Duct material: supply __flexible__ ; return __plenum__ ; insulation __yes__ ; thickness __standard__ ; ☐ outside air intake

Furnace: Make and model: _____Lennox # ———_____ ; input __18000__ Btuh; output __18000__ Btuh

☐ space heater; ☐ floor furnace; ☐ wall heater: Input __n/a__ Btuh; output __n/a__ Btuh; number of units __n/a__

Make and model; _____n/a_____

Controls: Make and type _____Honeywell – energy saver – thermostat (manual and automatic)_____

Fuel: ☐ coal; ☐ oil; ☑ natural gas; ☐ liquid petroleum gas (LPG); ☐ electric; ☐ other ____ ; storage capacity __n/a__

Firing equipment furnished separately _____n/a_____

☐ gas burner – conversion type; ☐ stoker; ☐ hopper feed; ☐ bin feed; ☐ oil burner; ☐ pressure atomizing; ☐ vaporizing

Make and model _____n/a_____ ; control _____n/a_____

Electric heating system: type __n/a__ ; input __n/a__ watts; @ __n/a__ volts; output __n/a__ Btuh

Ventilating equipment: type: Attic fan: make and model _____n/a_____ ; capacity ____n/a____ CFM

Kitchen exhaust fan: make and model ____Braun____ ; capacity ____n/a____ CFM

Other heating, ventilating, or cooling equipment_____n/a_____

FIGURE 8–1
Continued

NORTH RIVER BANK

DESCRIPTION OF MATERIALS
(Continued)

25. ELECTRIC WIRING:

Service: □ overhead; ☑ underground (lateral) _____ 1/0 USE – 3-wire w/ground _____

Panel: □ fuse box; ☑ circuit breaker _____ 120/240 VAC 200A _____ ; number of circuits _____ 30 available _____

Wiring: ☑ conduit; □ armoured cable; ☑ non-metallic cable; □ knob-and-tube; □ other _____

Special outlets: ☑ range; ☑ water heater; other _____ wall oven, furnace/A/C unit, isolated computer circuit _____

□ door bell; ☑ chimes; push-button location _____ front entry _____

26. LIGHTING FIXTURES:

Total number of fixture ____ 24 ____ ; Total allowance for fixtures, typical installation _____ $2500.00 _____

"   "   "   " , non-typical installation _____ $ 750.00 _____

27. INSULATION:

Location	Thickness	Material: Type and Method of Installation	Vapor Barrier
Roof	2″	Owen-Corning rigid fiberglass – screw and mop	43# underlayment
Ceiling	R-30	batt – 16″ and 24″ wide as required	n/a
Wall	R-19	batt – 16″ exterior; 24″ interior (UNO)	n/a
Floor	R-11	batt – 16″ and 24″ wide as required	n/a

28. MISCELLANEOUS:

(Describe any main dwelling materials, equipment, or construction items not shown elsewhere)

_____ Exterior deck – 2 × 4 self-spaced with matching railing, stairs and stringers – redwood or weather-treated construction grade DF or HF #3 _____

29. HARDWARE: *(makes, material and finish)* _____ Schlage – antique brass for all windows, doors, and cabinetry _____

30. SPECIAL EQUIPMENT:

☑ Built-in range: make _____ Thermador _____ ; model _____ to be selected _____

☑ Built-in oven: make _____ Thermador _____ ; model _____ to be selected _____

☑ Dishwasher: make _____ Maytag _____ ; model _____ to be selected _____

☑ Hood and Fan: make _____ Thermador _____ ; model _____ to be selected _____

□ Drop-in range and oven: make _____ ; model _____

☑ Garbage disposal unit: make ____ Kitchen-Aid ____ ; model _____ to be selected _____

□ Barbeque: make _____ ; model _____

□ Other: make _____ ; model _____

FIGURE 8–1
Continued

NORTH RIVER BANK

DESCRIPTION OF MATERIALS
(Continued)

31. PORCHES:
_____
_____
_____
_____

32. TERRACES:
_____
_____
_____
_____

33. GARAGES:
_____Attached – 2-car, Drywall w/5/8″ X firecode all walls and ceiling_____
_____Fire-wall of same material to be installed at wall adjoining residence per code____
_____
_____
_____

34. WALKS AND DRIVEWAYS:
Driveway width:___20′__; base material___sand__; thickness__10″__; surfacing material___concrete___; thickness___4″___
Front walk: width____3′____; material_____concrete_____; thickness__4″_____
Steps: material_____concrete w/stone pavers_____; tread___3___; risers___3___; cheek walls_____n/a_____
Service walks: width_____n/a_____; material_____n/a_____; thickness_____n/a_____

35. OTHER SITE IMPROVEMENTS:
(Specify all exterior improvements not described elsewhere, including items such as unusual grading, drainage, structures, retaining walls, fence, railings, and accessory structures.)
12′-0″ long by 8′-2″ high retaining walls both sides of residence w/16″ × 8″ concrete stepped footing and $8 \times 8 \times 16$ precision CMU and concrete slab cap. Specific grading to match._____
_____
_____

36. LANDSCAPING, PLANTING, AND FINISH GRADING:
Topsoil____4″___; ☑ front yard; ☑ side yard; ☑ rear yard to____feet behind main building_____full property_____
Lawns (seeded) ☑ *front yard;* ☑ *side yard;* ☑ *rear yard*_____26,563 sq ft (total)_____

Date _____   Borrower_____
                                               Borrower_____
                                               Builder_____

FIGURE 8–1
Continued

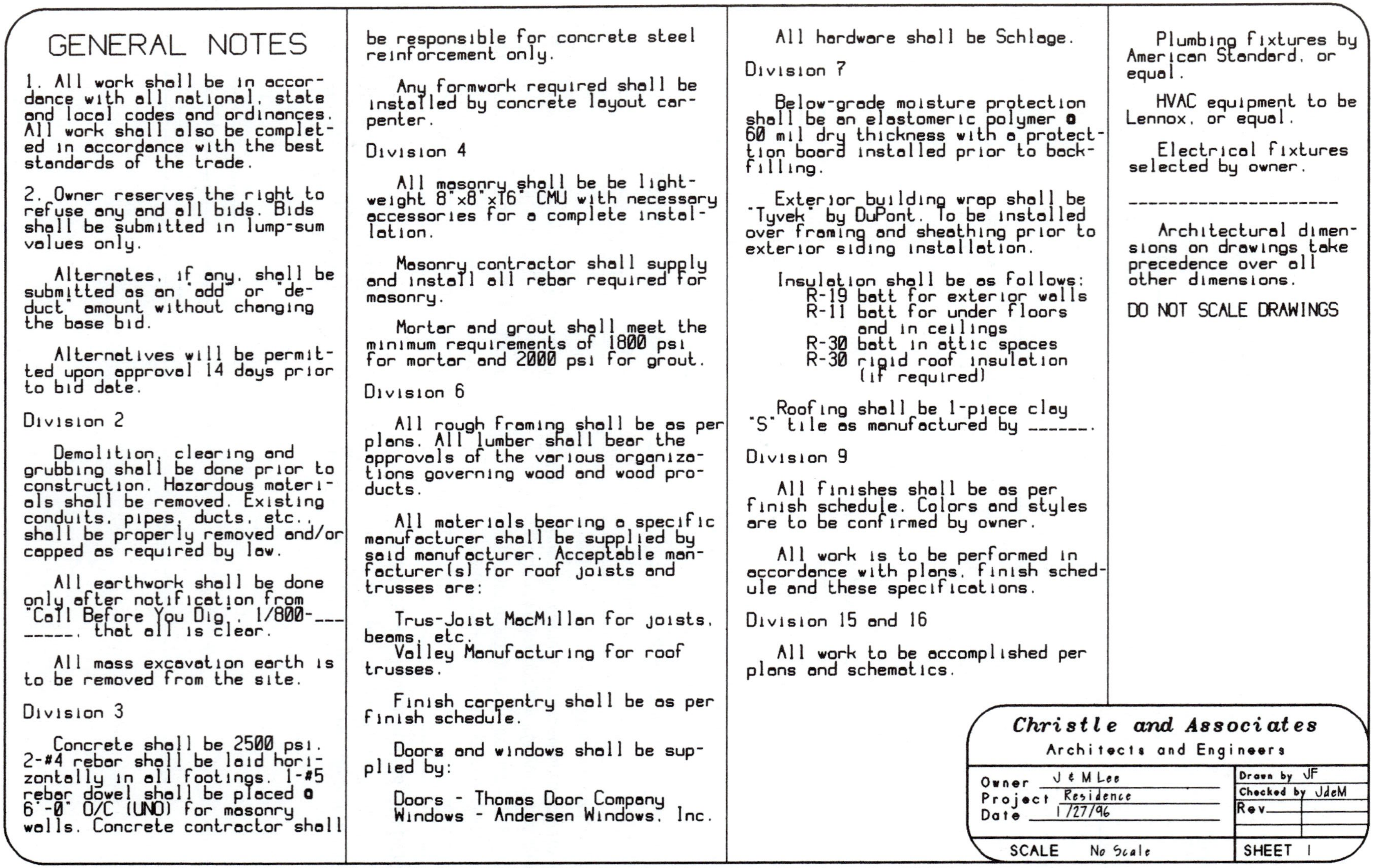

GENERAL NOTES

1. All work shall be in accordance with all national, state and local codes and ordinances. All work shall also be completed in accordance with the best standards of the trade.

2. Owner reserves the right to refuse any and all bids. Bids shall be submitted in lump-sum values only.

Alternates, if any, shall be submitted as an add or deduct amount without changing the base bid.

Alternatives will be permitted upon approval 14 days prior to bid date.

Division 2

Demolition, clearing and grubbing shall be done prior to construction. Hazardous materials shall be removed. Existing conduits, pipes, ducts, etc. shall be properly removed and/or capped as required by law.

All earthwork shall be done only after notification from "Call Before You Dig" at 1/800-____ that all is clear.

All mass excavation earth is to be removed from the site.

Division 3

Concrete shall be 2500 psi. 2-#4 rebar shall be laid horizontally in all footings. 1-#5 rebar dowel shall be placed @ 6'-0" O/C (UNO) for masonry walls. Concrete contractor shall be responsible for concrete steel reinforcement only.

Any formwork required shall be installed by concrete layout carpenter.

Division 4

All masonry shall be be lightweight 8"x8"x16" CMU with necessary accessories for a complete installation.

Masonry contractor shall supply and install all rebar required for masonry.

Mortar and grout shall meet the minimum requirements of 1800 psi for mortar and 2000 psi for grout.

Division 6

All rough framing shall be as per plans. All lumber shall bear the approvals of the various organizations governing wood and wood products.

All materials bearing a specific manufacturer shall be supplied by said manufacturer. Acceptable manufacturer(s) for roof joists and trusses are:

Trus-Joist MacMillan for joists, beams, etc.
Valley Manufacturing for roof trusses.

Finish carpentry shall be as per finish schedule.

Doors and windows shall be supplied by:

Doors - Thomas Door Company
Windows - Andersen Windows, Inc.

All hardware shall be Schlage.

Division 7

Below-grade moisture protection shall be an elastomeric polymer @ 60 mil dry thickness with a protection board installed prior to backfilling.

Exterior building wrap shall be "Tyvek" by DuPont. To be installed over framing and sheathing prior to exterior siding installation.

Insulation shall be as follows:
R-19 batt for exterior walls
R-11 batt for under floors and in ceilings
R-30 batt in attic spaces
R-30 rigid roof insulation (if required)

"Roofing shall be 1-piece clay "S" tile as manufactured by ____.

Division 9

All finishes shall be as per finish schedule. Colors and styles are to be confirmed by owner.

All work is to be performed in accordance with plans. Finish schedule and these specifications.

Division 15 and 16

All work to be accomplished per plans and schematics.

Plumbing fixtures by American Standard, or equal.

HVAC equipment to be Lennox, or equal.

Electrical fixtures selected by owner.

Architectural dimensions on drawings take precedence over all other dimensions.

DO NOT SCALE DRAWINGS

Christle and Associates
Architects and Engineers

Owner J & M Lee
Project Residence
Date 1/27/96

Drawn by JF
Checked by J&M
Rev

SCALE No Scale   SHEET 1

FIGURE 8-2
Typical General Notes Plan Sheet

Many city, county, and rural areas also have established rules and regulations, referred to as *local codes* and *ordinances*. Manufacturers also provide specifications for the products they make for construction. Where such codes and regulations exist, although not defined in a specification, they are often included by inference.

SCHEDULES

See figures 8–3, Finish Schedules, Lee Residence; 8–4, Door Schedule; and 8–5, Window Schedule. Schedules, like abbreviations, symbols, and keynotes, are used to assist in detailing information of importance without cluttering the plans. Schedules may also be noted in the specifications or general notes. The schedules for doors, windows, and finishes (see chapter 5) are examples of the types of schedules typically found in a set of plans. Other schedules, such as for identifying plumbing and electrical fixtures, may also be located on plans or in the specifications. One or more schedules may be included for each of the six major plan groups (see chapter 9). The schedules may include the following:

1. Civil schedules:
   a. Types of earth required for the areas of excavating or grading
   b. Grade elevations

Room	Floors				Walls			Ceilings				Remarks
	Exposed Concrete	Tile	Carpet	Base	GWB 1/2	GWB 5/8	Wall Finish	GWB 1/2	GWB 5/8	Paint	Acoustical Treatment	
Dining Room			+	2	+		3	+			+	Vaulted ceiling
Kitchen		+		1	+		2	+		+		Ceiling 7'-0" A.F.F. Paint to match walls
Mstr Bedroom			+	2	+		1	+			+	Ceiling 8'-0"
Mstr Bath		+		3	+		4/2	+		+		Ceiling 8'-0" Finish 2 Tile to 6'-0"
Mstr Closet			+	2	+		2	+			+	Ceiling 8'-0"
Living Room			+	2	+		3	+			+	Vaulted ceiling
Den			+	2			5	+			+	Install book shelves w/ paneling. Ceiling 8'-0"
Foyer		+		3			2	+			+	Vaulted ceiling
Pwdr Rm/Clo		+		3	+		1/3	+		+		Ceiling 8'-0" Finish 2
Family Room			+	2	+		3	+			+	Ceiling 8'-0"
Bedroom #1			+	2	+		1	+			+	Ceiling 8'-0"
Bdrm #1 Clo			+	2	+		1	+			+	Ceiling 8'-0"
Bedroom #2			+	2	+		1	+			+	Ceiling 8'-0"
Bdrm #2 Clo			+	2	+		1	+			+	Ceiling 8'-0"
Bath #2		+		3	+		4/2	+		+		see note Master Bath
Utility Room	+			4		+	2	+		+		Ceiling 8'-0" Finish 2
Hall			+	3	+		3	+			+	Ceiling 8'-0"
Garage	+			3			3	+		+		Ceiling 9'-0" Match wall finish

FINISH NOTES:

BASE:
1. 4" oak – match cabinets
2. 2" "Slimline", oak veneer
3. Coved tile – match floor and wall tiles
4. 4" rubber cove base – brown

WALLS:
1. Wallpaper
2. Semi-gloss latex paint
3. Flat latex paint
4. 4" ceramic tile
5. Wood panel, light oak, full height

CEILINGS:

As noted. match paint

NOTE:

All materials selected by owner

FIGURE 8–3
Finish Schedule—Lee Residence

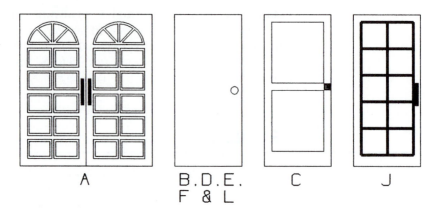

MARK	SIZE	DESCRIPTION	REMARKS
A	pr 3'-0"x6'-8"	1¾" panel stained	w/½ moon lites. custom
B	3'-0"x6'-8"	1¾" flush s/c paint	w/self closer
C	3'-0"x6'-8"	1⅜" pocket panel stained	
D	2'-6"x6'-8"	1⅜" flush h/c paint	stained @ powder room
E	2'-0"x6'-8"	1⅜" flush h/c stained	
F	3'-0"x6'-8"	1⅜" flush h/c paint	stained @ Mstr bedroom
G	4'-0"x6'-8"	Bi-pass closet w/mirror	
H	6'-0"x6'-8"	Wood frame sliding glass	custom design
J	3'-0"x6'-8"	Wood 10 lite patio	custom design
K	16'-0"x7'-0"	Wood garage door w/opener	custom design
L	2'-6"x6'-8"	1¾" panel stained	

FIGURE 8–4
Door Schedule

2. Architectural schedules may include:
   a. Door and window schedules
      (1) Identifying letters or numbers at the window locations
      (2) Identifying letters or numbers at the door openings
   b. Finish schedule
      (1) Specific materials (GWB, paint, wallpaper) to be used in certain areas
3. Structural schedules may include:
   a. Foundation footing schedule
   b. Reinforcement schedule
   c. Beam, column, girder, girt, and so on (commercial/industrial only)
   d. Framing schedules (types and sizes of materials required)
4. Plumbing schedules may include:
   a. Fixture schedule
5. Mechanical schedules may include:
   a. Equipment schedule (HVAC)
   b. Power supply schedule

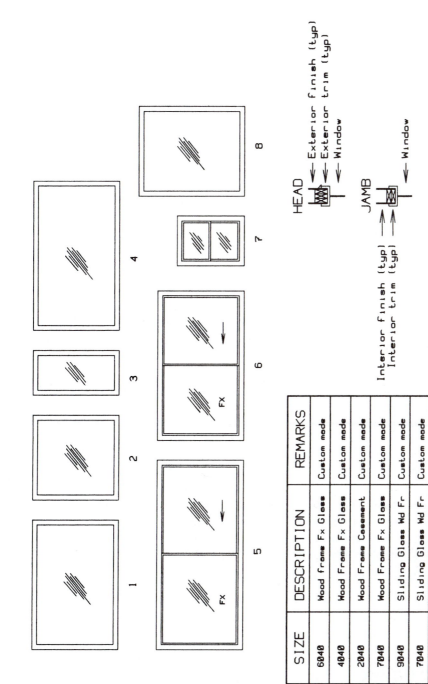

MARK	SIZE	DESCRIPTION	REMARKS
1	6040	Wood Frame Fx Glass	Custom made
2	4040	Wood Frame Fx Glass	Custom made
3	2040	Wood Frame Casement	Custom made
4	7040	Wood Frame Fx Glass	Custom made
5	9040	Sliding Glass Wd Fr	Custom made
6	7040	Sliding Glass Wd Fr	Custom made
7	2030	Wd Fr Double-hung	Custom made
8	4050	Wd Fr Fx Glass	Custom made

FIGURE 8–5
Window Schedule

137

6. Electrical schedules may include:
   a. Power and lighting schedule
      (1) Entrance panel circuit-breaker placement
   b. Fixture schedule

Refer to figures 8–3, 8–4, and 8–5. The schedules listed are more likely to be included in commercial plans. The door and window schedules, and the finish schedule, along with an electrical fixture schedule, are usually the only schedules included in residential plans.

Refer to Sheet C-1, Plot Plan, Lee Residence. The plot plan for the Lee residence indicates no curb or gutter at the street. Although not noted, the street has an asphalt surface. All utilities are available along the street, or the right-of-way parallel to the street, outside of the property lines. The distance maintained for the separation of site improvements and on-site construction at the Lee residence is 5'-0" (1.5 m) on all sides.

Refer to figure 8–2, the General Notes, Architectural Plans, and figure 8–3, the Finish Schedule, for the Lee Residence. The finish schedule supplies information regarding the materials required for each room in the house at all levels. The finish schedule is divided into three areas:

1. Floor and base sections, identifying the material(s) to be installed on the floor and at the base of the walls.
2. Walls section, identifying the drywall types, painting, and wall coverings.
3. Ceilings section, identifying ceiling heights and the finishes to be installed on them (if any).

For example, per the finish schedule, the kitchen finish requirements are as follows:

Floor: Quarry tile for floor, to be selected by owner

Base: 4" (10.16 cm) wood base to match color of cabinets

Walls: All exposed walls to be covered with wood paneling, to be selected by owner except the breakfast nook area; breakfast nook walls to be padded to match seat coverings (kitchen side only)

Ceiling: Off-white semi-gloss latex paint inside light fixture recess with matching color for exposed ceiling areas

Remarks: Ceiling height to be 7'-0" (2.13 m) A.F.F. except at recess for light fixture; recess to be 7'-6" (2.29 m) A.F.F.

In addition, the General Notes specify information that may not be indicated in the schedule.

SITEWORK

The Lee residence requires excavating and grading to change the location and height of some of the earth on the property. There is also some mass excavation required for the lower level foundation. A sufficient quantity of earth is removed for installation of the drain at the walls and maneuvering about the work area. The completed work includes the back-fill necessary upon completion of all other below-grade installations. No landscaping, other than a few trees, is specified. This indicates that there is a separate landscape plan or the owner is doing his or her own landscaping.

If the utilities terminate some distance away from the project, the utility extensions from the termination to a location near the property are installed at the owner's expense. Any additional repairs to the street resulting from the extensions are also at the owner's expense.

The edge of the street nearest the Lee Residence is 10'-0" (3.05 m) from the property line. This area is for future sidewalk, curb, and gutter that are not required at this time. The street is 26'-0" (7.92 m) wide. The plumber and electrician must make the taps at the street, trench and lay the necessary materials, install the metering, and so on, for installation into the residence. This work is all covered in the off-site work. Any repairs necessary to the street are included in the contract for the off-sites. All of the work at the street (metering, and so on) must be per local codes and utility requirements, or under the jurisdiction of the area or national building codes. Specifications, schedules, and/or plans must also note the type of materials to be used.

Plumbing

Refer to Sheet P-1, Lee Residence. The plumbing includes all pipe (black, galvanized iron, copper, or plastic ABS) with the respective connections, accessories, and fixtures necessary to dispose of all liquid waste, and the installation of fuel lines (gas). The sewer location, if too low for the sewer main, must have a sump pump added to force the waste disposal from the residence to the main. The sewer main is 8'-0" (2.44 m) below the street surface. The lowest point at the Lee residence is approximately 4'-0" (1.22 m) higher; therefore, no pump is required. The location of the water and sewer mains, the taps, trenching, installation of lines to the structure, backfilling, and any metering devices necessary are all a part of the off-site plumbing installation. The gas utility company is responsible for the installation to the gas meter, usually located immediately adjacent to a structure. The plumber may be required to install the service but does not make the taps or meter installation. The plot plan indicates supply from the street to the Lee residence for water, sewer, and gas connections to the west side of the residence, entering or exiting at the Utility Room.

Piping

Refer to Sheet P-2, Lee Residence. The piping includes galvanized iron, copper, or PVC pipe with the respective connections, accessories, and fixtures necessary to install the water supply lines. Galvanized iron pipe may still be in use in some areas, but copper and plastic pipes are most commonly used today because of their ability to withstand corrosion and reduce health hazards. Black pipe is installed for the gas lines.

Electrical

Refer to Plot Plan, Sheet C-2, Lee Residence. Electricity for the Lee residence must extend laterally from the transformer supply on the south side of the street, under the street and into the property, to a convenient location for the service entrance. The plot plan indicates that the electric service entrance is located on the southwest side of the garage. All site-improvement and off-site work must be included for the completion of the service. This includes street repair, trenching, conduit, and wire installation.

STRUCTURAL FOUNDATION PLANS

See Sheets S-1, Lower Level, and S-2, Main Level, Lee residence. Both the masonry foundation wall, with the concrete footing, and the monolithic slab construction are required for the lower-level foundation and patio slabs. A short masonry stem wall and footing is used along the north wall of the lower level and around the unexcavated areas (main level) on the south, east, and west sides with a slab-on-grade over these walls. The footing is expanded for the fireplace area at both the lower and main levels and for the stairwell at the lower level. An additional footing is noted along the depressed slab at the living room and for the garage separation wall. These footings are known as **thickened slab footings.** They are an additional 4″ (101.6 mm) deep and taper from 8″ (203.2 mm) wide to 1′-0″ (304.8 mm) wide at the slab. All slabs are 4″ (101.6 mm) thick except the garage. The garage has a 6″ (152.4 mm) high concrete curb on three sides. The slab starts at 6″ (152.4 mm) thick at the north end (adjacent to the residence) and slopes 2″ (50.8 mm) southward to a thickness of 4″ (101.6 mm) at the garage entrance. If necessary, the footing and foundation walls located at the garage entrance may be replaced by a **grade beam.** A grade beam is an enlarged footing separate from the slab with additional reinforcement. This is only necessary where soil and/or structural conditions warrant such a change.

The walls on three sides (south, east, and west) of the lower level are constructed of 8″ (203.2 mm) CMU a full 8′-0″ (2.44 m) above finish floor (A.F.F.). The walls are also constructed around three sides of the stairwell and the fireplace. Because the walls are below grade and are supporting the structure above, they are solid grouted. As previously mentioned, these walls may be solid concrete in lieu of the masonry.

MOISTURE PROTECTION

The foundation wall is protected from moisture penetration by a cementitious polymer with a protection board. This protection is to be applied to the structure masonry walls as well as the retaining walls extending to the east and west from the sides of the residence. The installation procedure is referred to as **parging** where the material is troweled onto the walls to a thickness of approximately 60 mils. A perforated, sloped tile drain is installed parallel to the dwelling walls through each retaining wall and beyond the patio slab to assist in drainage away from the dwelling.

See figure 8–6, Tyvek® Housewrap, Lee Residence. The frame wall structure uses a Tyvek® plastic wrapper, a product developed for use in the same manner as building paper, which is applied over the framing or sheathing (if used) prior to the installation of siding. This material is considered moisture protection because of its ability to resist moisture penetration. The material will allow moisture changes to escape to the outside but will not allow moisture to penetrate inward.

FIGURE 8–6
Tyvek® Housewrap.
Permission of Dupont, Tyvek
Housewrap.

The roofing material to be installed over rigid insulation (see the later section on insulation) is a one-piece, clay S tile over a 43 lb/sq (19.55 kg/sq) asphalt felt underlayment.

FRAMING

Refer to Sheets A-1 thru A-8, Architectural, and S-1 thru S-8, Structural Plans, Lee Residence. The structural framing includes the upper level floor structure, the north exterior wall on the lower level, all walls on the main and upper levels, two chimneystacks, and the roof structure.

The exterior walls for the lower level are framed with 2 × 6 (50.8 mm × 152.4 mm) PTMS sill plate on the north wall at slab level, and the south, east, and west walls of the main level and the garage. A 2 × 8 (50.8 mm × 203.2 mm) PTMS sill plate is installed on the masonry walls. The bottom of the upper level floor joist is a nominal 8'-2" (2.49 m) A.F.F. due to the height of the masonry walls (8'-0" [2.44 m] above the lower level slab). The exterior framing includes 2 × 6 (50.8 mm × 152.4 mm) studs with double top plate. The studs may be 92½" (2.35 m) with three (3) top plates instead of the normal double top plate. An alternate method of the wall is to use 10'-0" (3.05 m) studs cut to the proper height using the double top plate.

On the east and west walls, 2 × 6 (50.8 mm × 152.4 mm) balloon framing is installed to accommodate the vaulted/cathedral ceilings. The interior bearing walls are also 2 × 6 (50.8 mm × 152.4 mm) balloon-framed (see floor plan and sections). All partition walls on the lower level are the same height as the exterior walls (8'-2" [2.5 m]). All main level and upper level partitions are 8'-1" (2.49 m) U.N.O. The fireplaces and the flue stacks are framed with 2 × 4 (50.8 mm × 102.4 mm) and 2 × 6 (50.8 mm × 152.4 mm) lumber, as shown on the plans or as required by local codes and ordinances.

The main roof structure is constructed with three (3) variations of scissors trusses produced to give the exterior roof slope and to provide for the interior vaulted and cathedral ceilings. The trusses are manufactured with a 2 × 8 (50.8 mm × 203.2 mm) top chord and 2 × 6 (50.8 mm × 152.4 mm) bottom chord. The structural garage roof may be constructed using conventional framing or with gable trusses. The end trusses at the east and west walls and the extended wall between the kitchen and dining room along the upper patio (balcony) are *gable-end trusses*.

The finish schedule indicates the rooms that are to be trimmed with wood and the location of wood paneling to be installed. The keynotes on the floor plan and/or section(s) also indicate wood stairwells and railings, balusters, and newel posts. The door and window schedules identify the type and location of each item to be installed in the residence. The doors and windows may also be identified with a manufacturer's numbering system.

INSULATION

The exterior walls have R-19 kraft-backed fiberglass insulation installed between the studs from foundation to roof structure. The floor and ceiling joists are to have R-30 unfaced fiberglass batt (under floor) or roll insulation (ceilings at roof structure). Rigid foil-backed fiberglass insulation, 1½″ (38.1 mm) thick, is installed over the structural roof and sheathing.

PLUMBING

Refer to Sheet A-1, Architectural Plans, and P-1, Plumbing Plans. The plumber uses the floor plan fixture locations along with the isometric drawings to determine the types, sizes, and lengths of material necessary for the water and waste system installations. Reading the blueprint using both the floor plans and the isometrics allows for a better picture of items and locations. The isometric plumbing drawing, for example, shows the complete waste disposal system including all off-site, site improvement, and on-site parts from the farthest fixture location in the residence to the sewer main. The drawing further shows the three floor levels. Pipe sizes are indicated for the plumbing contractor. The fixtures are excluded from the diagram but the location is noted on the floor plans and the General Notes specify the fixtures and fixture manufacturer. The piping isometric offers the same comparisons with the floor plans. The location of each fixture is noted and can be identified on the floor plans. The hot and cold water lines, with sizes, are also given on the drawing.

To further assist in identifying materials and locations, interior elevations (details), such as the master bathroom elevations, are provided so that the plumbing contractor can again coordinate the work with a cabinet installer. Wherever plumbing, piping, and cabinetry are associated, an interior elevation is drawn. By identifying the type of cabinet and the location of the fixture, and making use of the isometric drawings, the piping and plumbing can be located in the proper area so that no conflict is incurred with the cabinet installation.

HVAC

See Sheets M-1 and M-2, HVAC plans for the Lee Residence. The plans indicate a heating unit (furnace) in the utility room. The specifications in the General Notes indicate that the unit is a combination heating/cooling system with a built-in humidifier and a separate compressor unit for cooling located on the outside of the wall next to the utility room. The ductwork for the upper level is located in the trusses or soffited ceilings. Duct and air-supply registers are located in a soffit in the master bath, in the master bedroom walls, in the master closet, kitchen ceiling, and the wall of the dining room on the upper level. The ducts and supply registers for the main level are located in the den and powder room ceilings. The living room is supplied through under-floor ducts embedded in, or beneath, the main floor slab with the registers exposed at the step-down from the foyer into the living room. The lower level air is supplied from ductwork in the floor joists or in soffits above (ceilings) with the registers located in the walls of bedrooms #2 and #3, bath #2 ceiling, the hall ceiling, and the family room. The cubic feet per minute (CFM) rating is noted at each supply air register. A mechanical engineer calculates the quantity of air required for each room. These calculations aid in determining the size of duct required for each location.

One return air duct with return air grille is located in the floor of the entry hall to the master bedroom and one return air grille is located in the base of the partition wall separating the hall from the utility room at the air plenum on the lower level. The stairwell into the lower level is a satisfactory return for the air from the dining room and the main level and none is required for the lower level for the same reason. The furnace has an air plenum at the floor level to handle the main supply and return air intake. The unit is self-contained with exception of the air-conditioning compressor. All of the controls are built into the main unit. The thermostat is both manually and automatically controlled.

ELECTRICAL

See Sheet E-1 and E-2, Electrical Plans for the Lee residence. As previously mentioned, electrical on-site blueprints include information on indoor lighting and power equipment from the entry switchgear (service entrance) to the light switches, receptacles, fixtures, and electrical appliances. All of the electrical layout may be identified on the architectural floor plan. Electrical schedules may or may not be found on residential plans. It is preferable to include them since they indicate any special equipment or lighting fixtures to be used in the installation.

The service entrance equipment for the Lee residence includes a panel enclosing the circuit breakers necessary for disconnecting the various branch circuits within the residence. The service entrance panel is a 120VAC/240VAC, 200A, service supplied by a 1/0 AWG USE (underground service, electrical—an NEC classification) lateral service feeder from the transformer. The circuits from the service entrance to the convenience outlets and switches are referred to as branch circuits. The power and lighting plan(s) identify(s) which circuit is to be connected to which circuit breaker (CB). This is determined from the load calculations supplied by the electrical engineer or calculated by the contractor. The branch circuits may be directly supplied from the service entrance panel or they may be operated through a sub-panel. A sub-panel is one connected to the load side of the service entrance panel. The load side of the service entrance panel is any part of the panel supplied from the interior electrical bus (the copper bars to which the circuit breakers are connected) *after* the main 200A breaker. The load side of the circuit breaker is the one to which the wires are connected for the individual branch circuits.

The sub-panel may be used for convenience of location for energizing or de-energizing a circuit or, in the more modern concept, a Smart House service may be installed. A Smart House service is a computerized or automatic electronic control used for controlling the circuits. A computerized system may operate complete areas of power and lighting by just touching the monitor screen identifying the area desired. An electronically controlled service can operate in the same manner by touching switches in the panel. The systems may be reduced voltages (24VAC) that control the 120VAC/240VAC circuits at the touch points or switches. The reduced voltage operates electronic devices, which, in turn, close the normal 120VAC power and lighting circuits.

CHAPTER EXERCISES

Completion

1. The Lee Residence exterior walls are constructed with _____" (_____ mm) studs.

2. The lower level framing may require _____ lf (3.05 m) studs cut to fit.

3. Interior partition (non-bearing) studs are _____"(_____ mm).

4. The roof structure is a _____ system.

5. The sub-flooring to be installed at the upper level may be installed with 1" (25.4 mm) OSB® or _____" (_____ mm) CDX plywood.

6. There are _____ risers on the stairs connecting the lower level and the main level.

7. The roof structure over the garage is identified as _____ framing.

8. Window type "Mark 4" is a _____.

9. The electric service entrance panel has a maximum capacity of _____ A.

10. A(n) _____ system is installed throughout the Lee residence for communications purposes.

11. The hot water heater is connected to the _____ service.

12. The plastic membrane used for protection on the exterior frame walls is called _____ manufactured by DuPont.

13. The garage requires 5/8" (15.88 mm) "X" GWB on the ceiling and the _____ wall.

14. The mechanical contractor installs the _____ for regulating heating and cooling.

Multiple Choice

_____   1. The electrical service entrance equipment has:
a. Place for 30 CB's
b. A rating of 120/240VAC and 150A
c. 45 branch circuits
d. A place for a light socket connection

_____ 2. The HVAC system includes:
   a. A self-contained heat pump
   b. A hot water heating system
   c. An all-electric baseboard heating system
   d. A combination air-conditioning, humidifier, and gas-fired heating unit

_____ 3. The electrician is responsible for all off-site work including:
   a. Inspection of the installation
   b. Installation of the power supply at the utility service
   c. Back-filling all trenching regardless of trade
   d. The power tap to and including the service entrance equipment

_____ 4. The power tap for the service is located:
   a. On the south side of Mary Street
   b. On a pole along the property line
   c. With a street-lighting circuit
   d. None of the above

_____ 5. The off-site electrical service:
   a. Is a lateral service
   b. Is parallel to the south side of Mary Street
   c. Both a and b
   d. Neither a nor b

_____ 6. The structure setbacks are:
   a. 20'-0" (6.1 m) from the south property line and 30'-0" (9.14 m) from the southeast property line
   b. 20'-0" (6.1 m) from the south property line and 20'-0" (6.1 m) from the southwest property line
   c. No setbacks indicated
   d. Plotted from the northwest and northeast property lines

_____ 7. The two retaining walls extending perpendicular to the east and west walls:
   a. Are 12'-0" (3.66 m) long
   b. Are to be moisture protected
   c. Are as high as the masonry walls of the lower level
   d. All of the above

_____ 8. Insulation for the exterior framed walls includes:
   a. A blown material such as rockwool
   b. 16" (406.4 mm) wide batts or rolls
   c. 24" (609.6 mm) wide batts or rolls
   d. Foam insulation

_____ 9. The insulation for the roof is:
   a. Foil-backed batt insulation on the underside of the roof structure
   b. 1½" (38.1 mm) composite board rigid insulation
   c. 1½" (38.1 mm) coated rigid fiberglass insulation
   d. The air space between the roofing material and the roof deck

_____ 10. The roofing is:
      a. A one-piece "S" tile application
      b. A wood shake roofing material
      c. Asphalt composition shingles
      d. None of the above

True or False

T F 1. Footings for all stem walls are a minimum 2'-0" × 1'-0" (609.6 mm × 304.8 mm).

T F 2. The underground USE cable is installed in a 2" (50.8 mm) conduit.

T F 3. The service entrance is rated at 120/240VAC and 200A.

T F 4. The nearest connection to the sewer line is located 175'-0" (53.34 m) from the residence.

T F 5. The roofing is a concrete tile over a 43 lb/sq (19.5 kg) underlayment.

T F 6. Normally, the electrician is responsible for maintaining all wiring to and including the HVAC unit.

T F 7. The piping to the hot water heater is type M, ¾" (17.78 mm) ID copper pipe.

T F 8. The water main is 4" (101.6 mm) DIA.

T F 9. The electrical work on premises includes a communications system.

T F 10. At least one convenience outlet in the dining room, living room, and den is partially energized by a switch.

PART III

Commercial Blueprint Reading

CHAPTER 9

Commercial Construction Documentation

Commercial plans are determined by the function of the structure. Commercial construction includes structures developed for institutional structures (for example, schools, hospitals, and nursing facilities) and any *non-habitable* structure such as offices, warehouses, and industrial manufacturing plants. Multi-family structures, such as apartments, condominiums, motels, and hotels, are also included in commercial construction.

COMMERCIAL PLAN GROUPS

See figure 9–1, Commercial Plan Groups. Commercial plans can be quite large, with as many as fifty sheets in a set of plans. The plans are organized into six specific plan groups. Each group is identified with the first letter of the group: Civil Plans, "C"; Architectural Plans, "A"; Structural Plans, "S"; Plumbing Plans, "P"; Mechanical Plans (air-handling and air-conditioning plans), "M"; and Electrical Plans, "E." The letter identifies the group; a number with the letter identifies the sheet number within the group.

THE CONTRACT DOCUMENTS

Residential construction and commercial construction are similar only in adherence to all codes and ordinances required for both. A commercial project follows the same basic construction sequence described in the residential chapters, that is, off-site construction, site improvements, and on-site construction. The difference between residential and commercial construction is the documentation requirements and the manner in which the project is supervised. The owner of a commercial development normally hires a consultant such as the following:

1. An architect or engineer—to design the project and oversee the work as the owner's representative.

149

1. Civil ("C") plans:
   a. Site plan*
   b. Plot plan
   c. Utilities plans (water, sewer, gas, and/or electrical)**
   d. Paving plan**
   e. Street improvements plans**
   f. Landscape plans***
   g. Sections and details of each plan as required

*The site plan may be under separate contract and not included here.
**Utilities, paving, and improvement plans may be included in the plot plan.
***Landscape plans may be a separate set of plans and placed under separate contract.

2. Architectural ("A") plans:
   a. Floor plan
   b. Exterior elevation plan(s)
   c. Interior elevations (details)
   d. Reflected ceiling plan
   e. Roof plan
   f. Sections:
          (1) Longitudinal, transverse, and partial wall sections
   g. Door, window, and hardware schedules
   h. Interior finish schedule
   i. Miscellaneous architectural details

*These may be found in the plans, the specifications, or both.

3. Structural ("S") plans:
   a. Structural General Notes*
   b. Foundation plan
   c. Structural floor plan (not at foundation level; above grade)
   d. Structural wall framing plan
   e. Masonry reinforcement plan (if masonry is used in lieu of framing)
   f. Roof framing plan
   g. Structural sections:
          (1) Longitudinal, transverse, and partial wall sections
   h. Structural schedules:*
          (1) Footing, reinforcement, column, pier, beam, lintel, joist, etc.*

*These schedules and the Structural General Notes may be combined on one or more sheets, on separate sheets as indicated, and/or in the specifications.

4. Pluming ("P") plans:
   a. Piping isometric plan (potable water)
   b. Piping pictorial (if used)
   c. Pluming isometric plan (waste disposal)
   d. Pluming pictorial (if used)
   e. Piping and pluming details
   f. Fixture schedule*
   g. Miscellaneous pluming details

*These may be found on the plans, in the specifications, or both.

5. Mechanical ("M") plans:
   a. Floor layout (underfloor or wall supply and return – if necessary)
   b. Reflected ceiling plan (if required)
   c. Roof layout (if required)
   d. Equipment schedule(s)
   e. Equipment layout (pictorial – risers, etc.)
   f. Control diagrams
   g. Miscellaneous mechanical details

6. Electrical ("E") plans:
   a. Plot plan (exterior power and lighting)
   b. Power plan (interior receptacle layout)
   c. Reflected ceiling plan (interior lighting layout)
   d. Power, lighting, fixture, and equipment schedules
   e. Equipment pictorials (one-line and riser details)
   f. Feeder and control diagrams
   g. Miscellaneous electrical details

FIGURE 9–1
Commercial Plan Groups

2. A construction management company—to supervise the construction and verify that the architectural and engineering procedures are followed.

3. General contractor—to supply the field personnel (subcontractors and their employees) to actually construct the project.

See appendix IV, Bid Documents. There must be a logical sequence of events and documentation stating requirements, dividing the responsibilities, and offering some legal protection for all parties involved in a project. Whether it is the contractor, the estimator, or some field member using the blueprint, they *must be able to read the pertinent information influencing the work of the trade(s) in which the contractor is involved, and must be informed of the procedural requirements of the project.* A knowledge of the contract documents assists in this endeavor. This does not mean that the field personnel must know everything described in them. Knowledge of the documents also aids the contractor, the estimator, or the field personnel, to better understand the set of plans.

Included in the documents are the **Invitation** or **Advertisement to Bid,** the **Instructions to Bidders,** and the **Contract Documents.** The information included in these documents contains the legal requirements to be adhered to by everyone from the owner to the subcontractors selected to perform the work on the project.

The Invitation to Bid

The Invitation to Bid is a letter to a selected group of general contractors known and qualified by an owner, developer, architect, or engineer requesting them to tender a bid on the proposed project. Only those parties who receive such a letter may bid the project. The invitation may include such information as the following:

1. Owner of the project
2. Location of the project
3. Bid time and date
4. Some minimal information regarding insurance

The Advertisement to Bid

The Advertisement to Bid is the same as the letter of invitation except that it is placed in a newspaper or periodical widely read in construction circles, requesting qualified general contractors to bid on a project. Such an advertisement is required for government bidding. This method may also be applied when there are insufficient qualified contractors on a known list, or if the project is in an area where the owner has no knowledge of qualified general contractors.

Instructions to Bidders

The Instructions to Bidders describe what is expected of those bidding on the project. The information in the Invitation to Bid, or the Advertisement to

Bid, is repeated and expanded into more detail along with other instructions, such as:

1. The cost for the plans and specifications (if required)
2. The requirements for a bid security (bond)
3. Material substitutions allowed (if any)
4. The manner in which the bid is handled (open or sealed bid)

THE AGREEMENT

The agreement is separated from the other documents mentioned above because they are issued only to the winning bidder(s). Sample documents may also be included with the Instructions to Bidders. There are a variety of such documents, including those provided by the military, public works, Army Corps of Engineers, and private projects. Many private construction projects and some of the public works projects use documentation provided by the American Institute of Architects (AIA), Form A401 (revised), or the Engineering Joint Contractor Document Committee (EJCDC) form. The agreement includes information on bid requirements, bid forms, bonding, and procedures for a project. The documents may be of the standard varieties, or customized to fit the needs of the owner, architect, engineer, and/or contractor. The following paragraphs explain the major portions of the agreement.

TECHNICAL SPECIFICATIONS (CSI MASTERFORMAT)

See figure 9–2, CSI, MasterFormat. The Construction Specifications Institute (CSI) established a widely recognized format of organization for the technical specifications. This nationwide organization—a group composed of architects, engineers, manufacturers' technical writers, contractors, and other interested parties—has established this uniform system of identification. This format includes specifications for sixteen (16) divisions. The specification writers have adopted instructions garnered from these groups. The results are the specification standards noted in the MasterFormat.

See table 9–1. The specifications are broken down into *divisions, sections,* and *subsections of a division.* The breakdown is referred to as the *scope format.* The scope of a specification determines how detailed the specification is. The division detail is the **broadscope** format with section titles. When only the broadscope is used, the specifications are written in paragraph form with the section numbers and titles only. Figure 9–1 shows the divisions as they are listed in the broadscope specification.

If the information needs more detail, the specification is broken down into subsections. This is referred to as the **mediumscope** format. The mediumscope breaks the sections down into major subsections with numbers and titles. The subsections expand the information noted in the sections.

When the specification is written in a very detailed form, paragraphs are written to explain the information even further. This is called breaking the division down into the **narrowscope** format. The narrowscope breaks the work down into paragraphs under the subsections. The specifications in this text are examples of these formats.

Division 1- General Requirements
  01010 Summary of Work
  01020 Allowances
  01025 Measurements & Payments
  01030 Alternates/Alternatives
  01040 Coordination
  01060 Workmen's Comp. & Ins.
  01200 Project Meetings
  01300 Submittals/Substitutions
  01400 Quality Control
  01500 Construction Facilities
  01600 Materials & Equipment
  01700 Contract close-out

Division 2 - Sitework
  02000 Scope of Work
  02010 Subsurface Investigation
  02100 Site Preparation
  02200 Earthwork
  02500 Paving & Surfacing
  02900 Landscaping

Division 3 - Concrete
  03000 Scope of Work
  03100 Cosite Formwork
  03200 Reinforcement
  03300 Cast-in-Place Concrete
  03400 Precast Concrete

Division 4 - Masonry
  04000 Scope of Work
  04100 Mortar and Grout
  04200 Brick
  04300 Concrete Masonry Units

Division 5 - Metals
  05000 Scope of Work
  05100 Structural Metal Framing
  05200 Structural Light Gauge Metal Framing

Division 6 - Wood and Plastics
  06000 Scope of Work
  06100 Rough Carpentry
  06200 Finish Carpentry

Division 7 - Thermal and Moisture Protection
  07000 Scope of Work
  07100 Waterproofing
  07200 Insulation
  07300 Roofing Tile
  07600 Sheet Metal
  07900 Sealants & Caulking

Division 8 - Doors and Windows
  08000 Scope of Work
  08100 Metal Doors & Frames
  08200 Wood & Plastic Doors
  08250 Door Opening Assemblies
  08500 Metal Windows

Division 9 - Finishes
  09000 Scope of Work
  09200 Lath & Plaster
  09250 Gypsum Board (GWB)
  09300 Tile
  09500 Acoustical Treatment
  09650 Resilient Flooring
  09630 Carpet
  09900 Painting
  09950 Wallcovering

Division 10 - Specialities
  10000 Scope of Work
  10500 Lockers
  10800 Toilet & Bath Accessories

Division 11 - Equipment
  11000 Scope of Work
  11700 Medical Equipment

Division 12 - Furnishings
  12000 Scope of Work
  12100 Office Furniture
  12200 Draperies
  12300 Rugs
  12400 Art Work

Division 13 - Special Construction
  13000 Scope of Work
  13100 Boiler
  13200 Incinerator

Division 14 - Conveying Systems
  14000 Scope of Work
  14100 Elevators
  14200 Hoisting Equipment
  14300 Conveyors

Division 15 - Mechanical
  15000 Scope of Work
  15050 Basic Mechanical Materials & Methods
  15100 Heating, Ventilation & Air Conditioning
  15400 Basic Plumbing Materials & Methods
  15450 Plumbing

Division 16 - Electrical
  16000 Scope of Work
  16050 Basic Electrical Materials & Methods
  16400 Service and Distribution
  16500 Lighting
  16600 Special Systems
  16700 Communications

FIGURE 9–2
CSI MasterFormat

   Division 1 in the CSI MasterFormat contains information about the responsibilities and limitations of the owner, contractor, subcontractor, and specific details for submitting product information sheets, alternate and alternative proposals, allowances for special equipment and materials, change

TABLE 9–1
Breakdown of the Scope of a Specification

Division:	DIVISION 4 - Masonry	}		}	}
		}Broadscope	}		}
Section:	04000 Scope of Work	}		}	}
			}Mediumscope	}	
Subsection:	04010 General Requirements		}		}
					}Narrowscope
Paragraph:	1.1 Division 1 shall be considered a part of this Division.				}

orders and work authorizations, specific insurance requirements, payment procedures, quality control, and temporary facilities.

Division 2 through 16 specify the material and equipment requirements, workmanship requirements, and code requirements. Instructions for a trade or combination of trades are included in each division. Each contractor or subcontractor bids the work according to the division and/or section of a division pertaining to the trade or trades in which the contractor or subcontractor is involved. For example, Division 7, Thermal and Moisture Protection, includes work pertaining to thermal insulation, underground moisture protection, roofing, sheet metal flashings, roof accessories and sealants. Specialty contractors (subcontractors) working in insulation will bid those portions of the division pertaining to the insulation materials and working requirements. Manufacturers or suppliers specializing in roof accessories, such as prefabricated roof hatches or skylights, may also bid their own products directly to the owner.

The CSI MasterFormat is used for the specifications of the Frontier Manufacturing Company.

THE PROJECT MANUAL

In addition, a separate book of information, called the **project manual,** is included with most commercial and industrial construction plans. The project manual states all of the legal requirements, conditions of the contract, a list of the organizations whose instructions are to be followed throughout all of the construction, and a format of specifications supplying material, labor, and equipment requirements necessary for the project. These will be explained in a later chapter.

General and Special Conditions

The General Conditions are the standard format governing a project. A standard format established for the General Conditions is provided in AIA form A201. The form includes administrative and procedural controls governing a project. Such information as the clause regarding release from injury or harm (the "hold harmless" clause), rights of rejection of bid, recision of contract, specific insurance requirements, litigation rights, payment procedures, and accounting are thoroughly explained. Instructions regarding addenda prior to acceptance of contract or work authorization and change orders after acceptance of contract are also provided.

Special conditions are established and incorporated into the contract documents by agreement between the owner, architect/engineer, and general contractor. The changes made in the Special Conditions may modify the General Conditions, delete one or more portions of the General Conditions, or supply additional instructions inherent to the specific project.

Additional Documents

There may also be a special bid form included with the agreement. The form may require such information as the type of company bidding (sole proprietor, partnership, corporation, minority) and the signature of the party legally appointed to sign such documents. The general contractor may be required to submit the list of subcontractors whose bids were chosen to perform the work on the project.

A requirement for certification of a contractor's qualification, known as the *bid bond*, and *payment and/or performance bonds*, can be made as well. Most institutional and government projects insist upon them. The *bid bond* is submitted with the bid proposal.

Payment and performance bonds may be required when the bid is accepted for the contract. The *payment bond* is a guarantee that all product costs and labor wages will be met in accordance with the contract. The *performance bond* is a guarantee that the work will progress in accordance with the schedule established for the project.

The Project Manual

The specifications and drawings are designed to coordinate with one another. The project manual includes the following:

1. General Project Information. All parties responsible for the development of the project are included on the cover page of the project manual as well as on the set of plans. The cover page identifies the names and addresses of the Owner(s), Architect(s), Civil Engineer(s), Mechanical Engineer(s), Electrical Engineer(s), and Structural Engineer(s).
2. Index of the Specifications. These are laid out in the CSI MasterFormat, Divisions 1 through 16, identifying the administrative and trade responsibilities.
3. Specifying Organizations. This is a list of several organizations that have their own specifications that are incorporated into the project specifications either in writing or by inference.
4. Specifications per the CSI MasterFormat. The General and Special Requirements (similar to the General and Special Conditions) and the specifications are detailed.

See appendix IV, Project Manual for Frontier Manufacturing, Inc. All information found in the project manual is part of the contract documents. Any discrepancies noted between the specifications and the set of plans must be rectified prior to bidding or construction. Such problems are directed through the proper channels from subcontractor to general contractor, and from the general contractor to the architect, engineer, or both, for clarification. In most cases the clarification request must be made in writing.

If the discrepancy is noted with sufficient time (four to ten days minimum) prior to a bid, an *addendum* may be prepared and all bidders notified. If the discrepancy is noted following the contract, the party making the discovery must again notify the proper individual(s). In any change made, the owner, architect, engineer, or other authorized assigned person (contractor, superintendent), issues a *work authorization* and/or *change order* in writing before any work is to be done.

CHAPTER EXERCISES

Matching

Match the contract documents with the descriptions.

_____ 1. General Conditions

_____ 2. Specifications

_____ 3. Project manual

_____ 4. Special Conditions

_____ 5. Payment bond

_____ 6. Contract documents

_____ 7. Bid bond

_____ 8. Invitation to Bid

_____ 9. Bid form

_____ 10. Section 10100

_____ 11. Construction Specifications Instate

_____ 12. American Institute of Architects

_____ 13. Performance bond

_____ 14. Instructions to Bidders

_____ 15. Addendum

a. Section of Division 10

b. Spec writing organization

c. Request for bid by letter or advertisement

d. Part of legal documents describing legal responsibilities

e. A correction to the bid request

f. The manual of Specifications

g. Legal document expanding information on the Invitation

h. Supplement to General Conditions

i. The agreement

j. Form used to present bid to owner

k. A guarantee of payment

l. An assurance of contractor's ability to produce a quality project

m. A guarantee to complete a project

n. The explicit instructions regarding responsibilities of all parties

o. The trade information and directions for materials, labor, and equipment

Multiple Choice

_____   1. The term *specification in construction* means:
  a. The legal documents
  b. The project manual
  c. Directions written for a trade
  d. None of the above

_____   2. The Contract Documents include:
  a. The General and Special Conditions
  b. The Specifications only
  c. The list of trade organizations
  d. All of the above

_____   3. The General and Supplemental Conditions include:
  a. Responsibilities of the owner
  b. Responsibilities of the Architect/Engineer
  c. Responsibilities of the Contractor
  d. All of the above

_____   4. A bid bond:
  a. Is supplied by the owner
  b. Is issued for all government project bids
  c. Is the same as the payment and performance bonds
  d. Costs the bidder 100% of the bid total

_____   5. The Specifications:
  a. Are unnecessary for commercial and government work
  b. Are part of the Project Manual
  c. Include twenty (20) division breakdowns
  d. Are written by the AIA

_____   6. There are three (3) types of CSI Specification formats. They are:
  a. Narrowscope, largescope, and largerscope
  b. Broadscope, Narrowscope, and Informal
  c. Informal small, informal medium, and informal broad
  d. Broadscope, mediumscope, and narrowscope

_____   7. The Invitation to Bid is:
  a. A request to contractors to bid on a project
  b. A request to partake in an invitation for a party
  c. A demand for a payment and performance bond
  d. None of the above

True or False

T F   1. The Instructions to Bidders are directions on the proper estimating procedures of a project.

T F   2. The American Institute of Architects has written the basic requirements for Division 1 of the Specifications.

T F   3. The contract documents include the project manual only.

T F   4. A Bid Bond is always necessary with a private commercial project.

T F   5. A Specification may include a broadscope, mediumscope, and narrowscope expansion of directions for material, labor, and equipment requirements.

T F   6. An addendum is a change in Specifications made prior to the bid date.

T F   7. The Specifications include a division defining requirements for steel construction.

T F   8. General Conditions and General Requirements are interchangeable.

T F   9. The invitation to bid is the same as the advertisement to bid.

T F 10. The legal documents include the contract.

T F 11. The Specifications include information for sixteen (16) divisions.

T F 12. A change in plans issued after contract is referred to as an addendum.

T F 13. Division 11, Equipment, supplies information regarding swimming pool construction.

T F 14. The work described in Division 9, Finishes, includes finish carpentry.

T F 15. The Project Manual includes information regarding the owner, architect, and engineering companies that took part in the development of the plans for a project.

Completion

1. A contract may be broken if the contractor cannot _____.

2. The Instructions to Bidders is provided along with the plans and _____.

3. The bid bond is included for the purpose of determining the _____ of a contractor.

4. Government requests for bids are normally found in _____.

5. The bid submission on government contracts and some private contracts demands a list of the _____.

6. A contract document includes the General Conditions and, possibly, a section referred to as the _____.

7. The _____ documents that are supplied to a contractor include the Instructions to Bidders, bid proposals, and contract back-up.

8. A contractor that is the successful bidder may _____ on the contract only if all notification, in writing, was not provided to the contractor.

9. There are _____ trade divisions in the CSI MasterFormat.

10. An addendum is a change in specifications or instructions supplied to the bidder _____ contract.

Refer to the Project Manual, appendix IV

Multiple Choice

_____ 1. The project manual indicates that the owner of Frontier Manufacturing is:
   a. Janus Corporation
   b. Brophy Electric Company
   c. Christle Associates
   d. None of the above

_____ 2. The initials ASHRAE found in the list of support organizations represent:
   a. The ASHRAE Corporation
   b. The American Society of Roofing Architects and Engineers
   c. The Association of Standard Housing Regulations, Administration, and Effort
   d. The American Society of Heating, Refrigeration, and Air-Conditioning Engineers

_____ 3. Division 6 includes:
   a. Beams and supports
   b. R/S beams, posts, sheathing, siding, joists, trusses, and roof decking
   c. All interior framing
   d. All of the above

_____ 4. The exterior finish specified for the Frontier Manufacturing building is:
   a. Slumpstone CMU and a one-coat stucco finish
   b. Slumpstone and precision CMU
   c. Precision CMU only
   d. EIFS and Slumpstone

_____ 5. The HVAC includes:
   a. Radiant heating and a heat pump for the office areas
   b. Swamp cooling for the whole building
   c. Air-conditioning throughout
   d. None of the above

_____ 6. Division 1:
   a. Is to be included as part of Division 12 only
   b. Is inferred as a part of all the divisions
   c. States the requirements for concrete work
   d. All of the above

_____ 7. Division 12:
   a. Covers information regarding equipment
   b. Is known as the Mechanical division
   c. Is not included in the contract
   d. All of the above

_____ 8. The format used for the project manual and specifications is called:
   a. The Legal Format
   b. The CSI MasterFormat
   c. The Contract Format
   d. The AIA Format

_____ 9. All of the divisions except Division 1 are referred to as:
a. The trade divisions
b. The Special Requirements
c. The Instruction to Bidders
d. None of the above

_____ 10. The AIA:
a. Has a form, A401, revised, used in the specifications
b. Is an organization made up of certified architects
c. Is formally known as the American Institute of Architects
d. All of the above

_____ 11. Division 2, Earthwork, includes:
a. Landscaping and paving
b. Excavating and grading
c. Shoring and mass excavations
d. All of the above

_____ 12. The division considered the most diversified is:
a. Division 9, Finishes
b. Division 6, Wood and Plastics
c. Division 7, Thermal and Moisture Protection
d. Division 16, Electrical

_____ 13. Included in Division 4 are:
a. Concrete slab construction
b. Mortar, grout, reinforcement, and masonry units
c. Caulking and sealants
d. Clay roofing tiles

_____ 14. The division that will normally be responsible for supplying steel reinforcement in commercial construction projects is:
a. Division 3, Concrete
b. Division 4, Masonry
c. Division 5, Metal
d. Division 6, Wood and Plastics

_____ 15. The divisions most commonly considered in carpentry construction include:
a. Divisions 1, 4 and 14
b. Divisions 6, 9 and 12
c. Divisions 6, 8 and 9
d. Divisions 6, 14 and 15

True or False

T F   1. The American Institute of Architects has written the basic requirements for Division 1 of the specifications.

T F   2. A specification may include a broadscope, mediumscope, and narrowscope expansion of directions for material, labor, and equipment requirements.

T F   3. The specifications include a division defining requirements for steel construction.

T F   4. General Conditions and General Requirements are interchangeable.

T F   5. There are six major areas covered in a blueprint.

T F   6. A blueprint is a set of plans or drawings.

T F   7. Most commercial blueprints include schedules describing information not found directly on a plan.

T F   8. The specifications include information on sixteen (16) divisions.

T F   9. A change in plans issued after contract is referred to as an addendum.

T F   10. The work described in Division 9, Finishes, includes finish carpentry.

T F   11. The project manual includes information regarding the owner, the architect, and engineering companies that took part in the development of the plans for a project.

T F   12. The project manual is not part of the legal documents.

T F   13. Thermal and Moisture Protection are included in Division 8.

T F   14. Power requirements for Frontier Manufacturing Company are found in the specifications only.

T F   15. The Project Manual includes the General and Special Requirements.

Completion

1. Commercial construction _____ are broken down into the six plan groups.

2. A(n) _____ is written to advise of changes in bidding procedures or plans.

The Specifications in the Project Manual, appendix IV, or the CSI MasterFormat, are to be followed for the remaining questions.

3. A section of Division 2, identified as _____, requires that all hazardous material must be removed from a job-site prior to any other work.

4. Information on dumbwaiters is found in Division _____.

5. No corrections should be made in the workplace after contract without a written _____ or _____.

6. Sheet metal work is included in Division _____.

7. _____ is the section in Division 16, Electrical, stating the requirements for intercom systems.

8. The site facilities are supplied by the _____.

9. There are two types of roofing on the Frontier Manufacturing building. They are _____ and _____.

10. The exposed portions of the perimeter walls are constructed of _____ CMU.

11. The steel columns used for support of the glu-lam beams are _____″ (_____ mm) DIA.

12. The wood and steel truss joists are manufactured by _____.

13. The size of the center glu-lam beam measures _____ × _____ × _____.

14. The plant office is to have _____ insulation on the interior side of the exterior walls.

15. The office windows are to be _____ insulated.

10

Commercial Construction

The complexity of commercial projects makes it necessary to be more explicit in the details of the construction. There are areas of construction that are not likely to be found in residential plans, such as structural steel; conveyance systems—hoists, elevators, or conveyor systems; and specialized concrete systems—caissons and pilings, till-up wall construction, multi-level concrete floors, or concrete roof decks.

Where such items are required for commercial structures, structural elevations, sections, and details must be added to enable understanding of the construction design. Therefore, the set of plans is more complex and more detailed than one finds in normal residential plans. As a result, specifications, for the materials and equipment necessary for the project are identified in more detail. This may be accomplished by use of more detailed drawings and instructions within the plans and/or in the project manual.

Other than the information and instructions found on each plan sheet within a set of plans, special instructions are found in the Structural General Notes. Schedules identifying the materials and their locations are also included. Structural requirements for commercial/industrial buildings are discussed in the following segments of this chapter.

CONCRETE

Structural Concrete

See figure 10–1, Structural Concrete Construction. Structural concrete for commercial construction is more complex than for residential construction. For example, figure 10–1 shows footings that are larger, deeper, and require more additional strength to support the structure.

As mentioned in the chapter introduction, there may be special footings and **pilings.** *Pilings* are column-like extensions from the foundation of a structure placed into the earth to a deeper solid natural base. Along with the pilings, **capitals** and **bell footings** may be necessary. A *capital* is a pre-formed tapered concrete unit (square or round) placed on the top of a piling

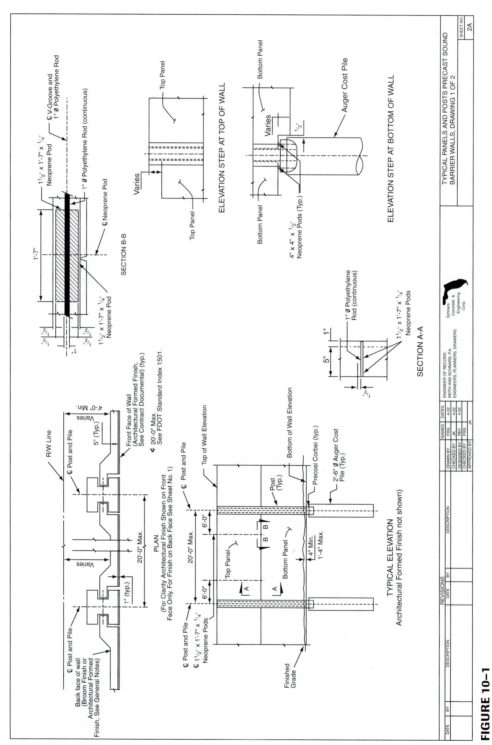

FIGURE 10–1
Structural Concrete Construction

with the larger face supporting the structure above. A *bell footing* is similar to a capital except it is placed in the earth with the larger face down and the piling set upon it.

Mat footings and **spread footings** may also be required. A *mat footing* is an extra-large concrete pad under the concrete slab that supports whole sections of a structure including the footings and foundation walls. A mat footing may actually cover the whole area under the foundation below the slab and footings or on the foundation capitals and pilings for additional support.

Spread footings are used as an additional concrete support placed directly under the floor slab at the base of steel and concrete columns (*refer to figure 1–10*).

Another foundation support similar to the mat footing is a **slurry** or **lean concrete** mixture that is used to fill extremely large areas of excavated earth. Where the earth is very soft (sandy) to a depth of 5'–0" (1.52 m) or more (this depth may vary with the area), it may be removed and a large formed slab, made of the slurry or lean concrete, is placed into the cavity.

Commercial above-grade concrete installations include **C.I.P (cast- or concrete-in-place)** or **tilt-up** construction. *C.I.P.* is the basic form of concrete placement on the job. Cast-in-place includes concrete hand-mixed and placed, placement from an on-site mixing plant, or ready-mix truck. *Tilt-up* construction is a pre-cast concrete system also in common use for commercial and industrial construction (see section on pre-cast concrete below).

Compressive Strength.   *Compressive strength* of concrete is determined by how much weight or stress concrete can withstand and the quality of the *mixture* and *additives* that may be included. The normal compressive strength of commercial concrete foundation construction ranges from 2000 psi (909.1 kg/cm^2) to 6000 psi (2727.3 kg/cm^2) or higher. An exception is the slurry/lean concrete mentioned above. The compressive strength of the slurry/lean concrete is usually 1000 psi (454.55 kg/cm^2) to 1500 psi (681.83 kg/cm^2). Foundation walls may be from 6" (152.4 mm) to 24" (609.6 mm) thick.

Pre-Cast Concrete

See figure 10–2, Pre-Cast Tilt-Up Walls. Concrete that is prepared (formed, placed, and cured) in advance of the structure's need is called **pre-cast** concrete. Pre-cast concrete includes special structural products such as beams, columns, and walls that are produced in the concrete plant or on the job.

In commercial construction, the most common pre-cast unit is the tilt-up wall. For example, the walls for the Frontier Manufacturing plant (see chapters 12 and 13) could be tilt-ups in lieu of the masonry that is called for. A tilt-up wall is normally prepared on the job site. The structural footings and slab are installed and cured. A non-stick surfacing is sprayed or brushed over the slab to prevent any additional concrete from adhering to it. Forms, reinforcement, and any other embeds, are laid out on the slab. Concrete is then placed in the forms and left to cure. Upon completion of the cure, the forms are removed and the concrete tilt-up wall is raised into place, and supported. Supports remain on the walls until all walls are placed and the structural roof

FIGURE 10–2
Pre-cast Tilt-up Walls.
Courtesy of Tectonics,
Inc.

FIGURE 10–3
Major Types of Pre-cast
Concrete Floor and Roof
Panels

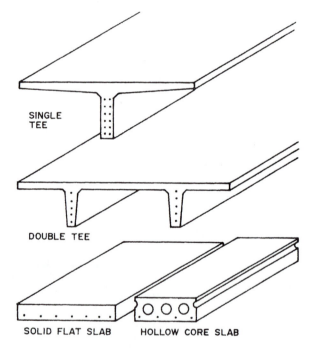

SINGLE
TEE

DOUBLE TEE

SOLID FLAT SLAB   HOLLOW CORE SLAB

components are installed connecting them together. The supports are then removed and the remaining structure is completed.

See figure 10–3, Pre-Cast Concrete Floor and Roof Panels. Another common form of pre-cast construction is the floor slab. This concrete form is used in lieu of the combination steel deck with lightweight concrete placed over it. The thickness of the slab is dependent upon its use. The single and double tees are used for structures where there *may be* heavy traffic such as in multi-level parking structures. The solid slab would be more likely used for roof construction. The hollow-core slab is commonly found in office structures.

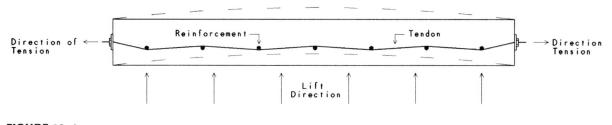

FIGURE 10–4
Pre- and Post-Tensioning

Pre- and Post-Tensioning

Pre-Tensioning.   *See figure 10–4, Pre- and Post-Tensioning.* One of two special reinforcing systems installed in pre-cast concrete beams used for commercial, industrial, and highway (bridge) construction is referred to as *pre-tensioning* construction. The reinforcement used is called a **tendon,** a flexible wire, cable, or steel rod, similar to rebar. The tendon (or tendons) is (are) installed within the full length of the pre-cast unit to be tensioned. It (or they) is (are) then drawn taut to give additional strength to the unit. The tensioning is done in the manufacturing plant *during the concrete cure process.* This system increases the concrete strength of the unit because of the compressive and tensile strengths supplied by the components.

Post-Tensioning.   The second reinforcing system is a similar construction procedure to pre-tensioning. The system is referred to as *post-tensioning.* The reinforcement tendon(s) is (are) placed in a slab or other concrete structure in the same manner as pre-tensioning. *When the slab is fully cured,* tension is then applied to the cables. This system also increases the concrete strength of the unit for the same reason as in pre-tensioning.

STEEL REINFORCEMENT

See figure 10–5, Steel Reinforcement and appendix III. Also refer to chapter 4, the section on Steel Reinforcement. In commercial construction, all concrete and/or masonry foundation footings and walls will include *steel reinforcement.* Rebar sizes of #4 and #5 are the most common for residential. Large commercial structures use #5 rebar to #11, grade 60, 75, or 80 kps. Tall commercial structures, bridges, tunnels, and the like, may use the larger sizes such as #14 and #18. Any other sizes in between or above are special ordered.

The smaller rebar sizes (#3 and #4) are used for *ties, loops saddles* and *hooks. Ties* are used to wrap the heavier rebar to assist in holding the rebar in place until the concrete is placed and cured. This is a common procedure found in support columns for bridges or concrete columns within a structure. *Loops, saddles,* and *hooks* are found in wall construction over openings, in pilasters, or areas requiring additional reinforcement. These, too, are used to hold the larger rebar in place until the concrete is placed and cured.

FIGURE 10–5
These workers are installing reinforcing bars in the forms for a foundation. The vertical bars were cast in the footing and extend up the height of the wall. Courtesy of the city of Austin, Texas. Photo by Anne S. Easterling.

MASONRY

Concrete is also heavily used with masonry. As mentioned in chapter 4, structural masonry walls require a combination of concrete block or brick installed with mortar, grout, and reinforcement.

Mortar and Grout

Chapter 4 also identifies mortar as a concrete mix that includes a fine aggregate (sand) as well as a fluidifier additive to aid in binding the masonry units together. The compressive strength of mortar for commercial use is 2000 psi (909.1 kg/cm^2). Grout is also identified as a concrete mix, similar to regular concrete, with a 3/8″ (0.95 cm) aggregate, and can increase wall strength. Grout can improve the compressive strength of a wall to 3125 psi (1420.45 kg/cm^2) or more.

Masonry Reinforcement

See figure 10–6, Masonry Reinforcement. The drawing is an example of typical masonry construction and reinforcement design. Steel reinforcement used in masonry construction includes the rebar, previously discussed in concrete, along with horizontal joint reinforcement. Commercial construction often includes larger sizes than found in residential construction. Depending upon the structure and its use, rebar may be required at much closer intervals than would be required for residential. It is not unusual to have vertical and/or horizontal rebar spaced at 16″ O/C in commercial construction. A 9-gauge, horizontal steel reinforcement may also be used.

FIGURE 10–6
Masonry Reinforcement

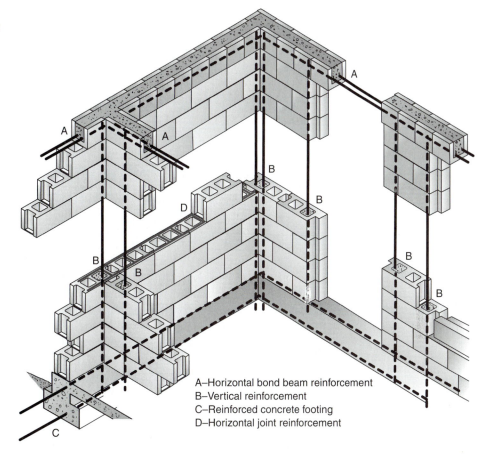

A–Horizontal bond beam reinforcement
B–Vertical reinforcement
C–Reinforced concrete footing
D–Horizontal joint reinforcement

Masonry Accessories.   The two masonry accessory classifications, masonry and non-masonry, as referred to in chapter 4, are considered the same for both commercial and residential construction. As in concrete installations, many of the non-masonry embeds are supplied by others to be installed by the brick/block mason.

STRUCTURAL STEEL

Structural Steel is rarely considered in residential construction, but is found in many areas of commercial/industrial construction. The term, *structural steel,* refers to metal support systems required for a structure. The support systems include columns, beams, girders, joists, and the reinforcement necessary as a part of the system. Structural steel is the strongest and most versatile material available to the construction industry. Several important details and symbols are necessary to understand structural steel construction drawings. The following sections define these details and symbols.

See figure 10–7, Common Rolled-Steel Shapes Used in Construction. The sizes and shapes of steel are very diverse—from angle iron to wide-flange beams. Each shape has a specific purpose. Wide-flange beams are the primary support columns or beams in a structure. The American standard S-shape (I-beam) is used as a secondary support column or beam. Channel iron and angle iron are called miscellaneous shapes. They may be used as connectors with the larger

FIGURE 10–7
Common Rolled-Steel Shapes
Used in Construction

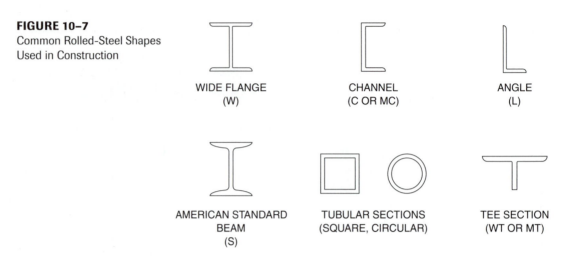

WIDE FLANGE
(W)

CHANNEL
(C OR MC)

ANGLE
(L)

AMERICAN STANDARD
BEAM
(S)

TUBULAR SECTIONS
(SQUARE, CIRCULAR)

TEE SECTION
(WT OR MT)

structural columns and beams. Miscellaneous structural steel is used as additional support for the heavier steel components.

See figure 10–8, Structural Steel Shop Drawing. This drawing is an example of work required in the planning of a steel structure. A structural steel set of plans will include such detail designs to assist the plan reader in determining how to give the steel structure rigidity and strength. The detail notes the size and type of steel units required, the connections necessary, and how the connections are to be made (bolted, riveted, welded, or combinations thereof).

See figure 10–9, Welding Symbols. Structural steel construction requires welding of connections to ensure strength and stability to the steel structure. Included in the details in figure 10–9 is the identification of welding systems. There are several different symbols—the *structural symbol* and the *types of weld* symbols. The structural symbol identifies the location of the weld, the type of weld, whether welded one side or both sides, and other information. The weld symbols are identified as fillet, V-groove, Y-groove, and surface welds of various types.

See figure 10–10, Various Configurations of Open Web Joists. Floor and roof support systems for multi-level structures are constructed with both beams and joists. The structural beams, concrete walls, or masonry walls support the various types of joists noted in figure 10–10. The joists may support the floor above in a multi-story structure, or may be required to support the roof structure above.

See figure 10–11, Steel Deck Shapes and Sizes. The floor structure may be one of the concrete panel types shown in figure 10–3 or may be a steel deck. Steel decking is also manufactured in several designs. The basic design is called a *fluted* deck. Where a steel deck is installed, a lightweight or standard-weight concrete or wood decking is applied over it.

COMMERCIAL FRAMING

When concrete, masonry, or structural steel is not required for wall construction, either wood or metal-stud framing may be used. The construction is identical to that described in chapter 5 and figures 5–8 and 5–16. There are two distinct differences between residential and commercial framing.

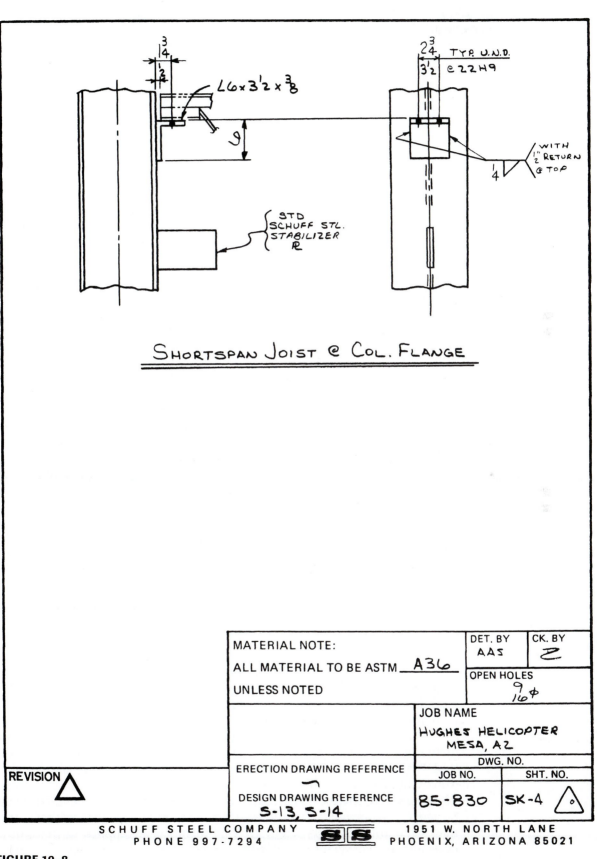

FIGURE 10–8
Shop Drawing

FIGURE 10–9
Welding Symbols

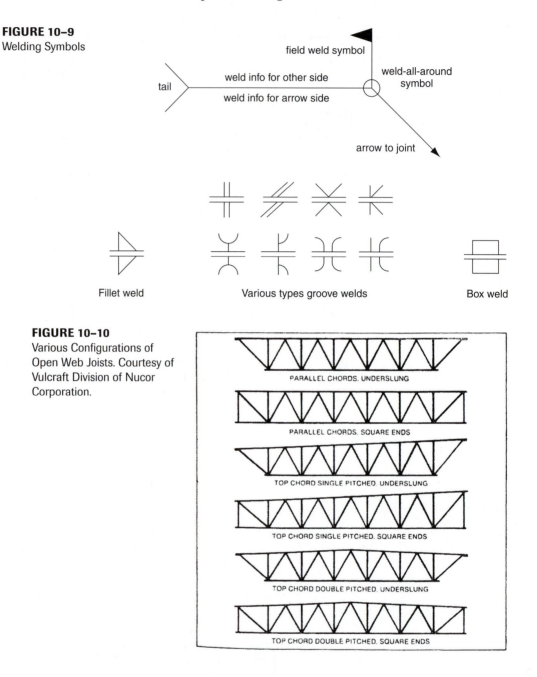

field weld symbol

weld-all-around symbol

tail

weld info for other side

weld info for arrow side

arrow to joint

Fillet weld   Various types groove welds   Box weld

FIGURE 10–10
Various Configurations of Open Web Joists. Courtesy of Vulcraft Division of Nucor Corporation.

PARALLEL CHORDS. UNDERSLUNG

PARALLEL CHORDS. SQUARE ENDS

TOP CHORD SINGLE PITCHED. UNDERSLUNG

TOP CHORD SINGLE PITCHED. SQUARE ENDS

TOP CHORD DOUBLE PITCHED. UNDERSLUNG

TOP CHORD DOUBLE PITCHED. SQUARE ENDS

One difference may be that the wood frame materials require a fire-retardant treatment for exterior bearing wall framing and the roof structure. This requirement is not at all unusual. The fire-retardant treatment is done in a similar manner as the termite treatment given lumber components (see chapter 5).

The second difference is that interior and exterior metal-stud framing both use heavier gauge steel studs. The type of structure determines the gauge of the stud. For example, where a residential structure may use 25-gauge and 20-gauge studs, commercial construction uses 20-gauge studs (minimum) if the walls are non-bearing. Where the metal-stud framing is bearing-frame, either 18-gauge or 16-gauge studs are used. The studs and track may also be welded together, rather than screwed together. Where horizontal members are applied in walls, or in rafter and joist installations, *stiffeners* are welded at all connections.

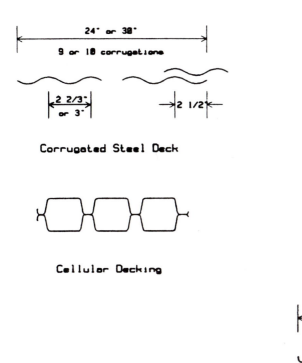

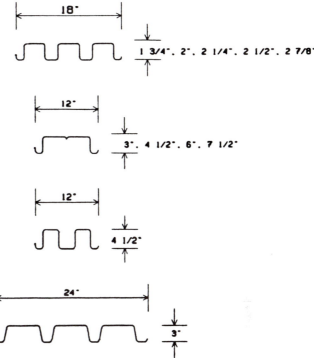

Fluted Cold-rolled Steel Decking

FIGURE 10–11
Steel Deck Shapes and Sizes

ROOFING

Where necessary, commercial roofing makes use of special built-up roof (BUR) materials for flat roofs. Sloped roofs are treated in the same way as in residential construction. The exception may be in the materials used in the structural support of the roofing (see framing) and/or the type of underlayment.

The procedures for BUR vary from a single-ply (one layer) application such as an EPDM (*E*thylene, *P*ropylene and *D*iene *M*onomer), or SBS, a modified, layered bitumen sheet, to a multi-ply system with from three to five plies of standard roofing felts. EPDM is a rubberized single-ply bituminous roof sheeting applied to concrete, wood, or insulated roof decks. SBS is a three-ply-in-one combination single-ply system consisting of two layers of bituminous sheet material with a polyester sheet inserted and the sheets compressed together. The material is applied as a single-ply system. Both the EPDM and SBS materials are available in 1 sq (square) (9.29 m^2) and 3 sq (27.87 m^2) rolls. The standard 3-ply or 5-ply systems may also be used.

There are several types of roofing materials for sloped roofs common to commercial roof construction. Some of the materials used for residential, such as composition shingles, plastic panelized roofing, or metal paneling may be used where allowed. Codes may require that commercial sloped roof be either tile (clay or concrete) or one of the metal roofing systems such as standing seam (galvanized or copper) roofing.

CHAPTER 11

Off-Site Construction and Site Improvements

Each project has the possibility of off-site construction work. In the case of the Frontier Manufacturing Company, there is work involving the entry approach onto the property, retaining walls, and a storm sewer connection. These items are further discussed in the succeeding sections of this chapter.

See Sheets C-1, Site Plan, and C-2, Plot Plan, Frontier Manufacturing, Inc. The site plan and legal description on the plan indicate the benchmark is located at Broadway and Main Street and is at elevation 500.0' (152.4 m). The datum point is identified at the intersection of Broad Street and First Avenue next to the project at elevation 504.0' (153.62 m). The point of beginning (POB) for the project is the northwest corner, nearest the datum point, starting at elevation 507.0' (154.53 m). The length of the property is 260.0' (79.25 m) along the north property line, 125.0' (38.1 m) along the east property line, 240.0' (74.37 m) along the south property line, and 126.59' (38.58 m) along the west property line.

The specifications for the off-site construction and site improvements include excavating and grading, surfacing (asphalt and concrete), landscaping, and, if necessary, concrete and masonry construction. Following the CSI MasterFormat, instructions for these trades is located in Division 2, Earthwork, Division 3, Concrete, Division 4, Masonry, and Division 5, Metals.

OFF-SITE/SITE IMPROVEMENT

Entry Approach (Apron)

See figure 11–1, Entry Approach, and refer to Sheet C-2, Plot Plan. There is grading required for the apron. The plan and the detail in figure 11–1 show that the apron slopes from the finish property elevation to street level. Measurements and elevations are noted on Sheet C-2, plot plan. They are as follows:

The approach is 36'-0" (10.97 m) long and 15'-0" (4.57 m) wide from the street curb to the interior (top) end of the approach at the parking lot. The finish-grade elevations are indicated with a point (+) and the elevation.

175

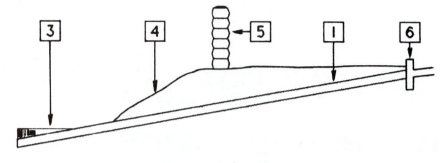

Detail A

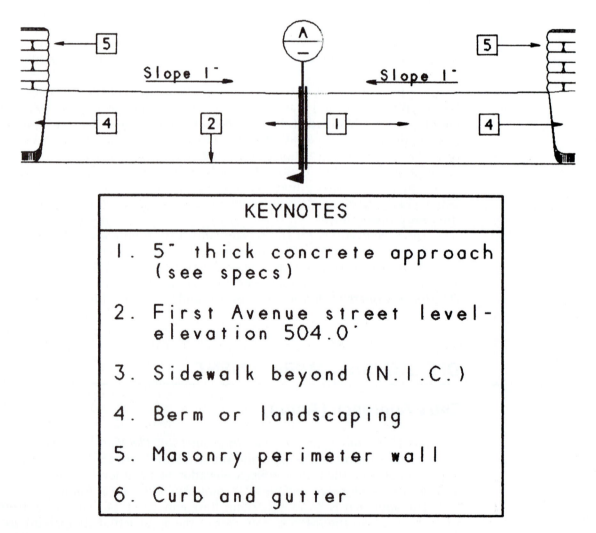

KEYNOTES

1. 5" thick concrete approach (see specs)

2. First Avenue street level- elevation 504.0'

3. Sidewalk beyond (N.I.C.)

4. Berm or landscaping

5. Masonry perimeter wall

6. Curb and gutter

FIGURE 11–1
Entry Approach

The plan indicates that the finish grade at the property entrance is at elevation 507.5' (154.69 m) and the street elevation is 504.0' (153.62 m). Therefore, the apron must slope 3'-6" (1.07 m) from the parking area to the street (approximately 4¼" per foot [108 mm per 304.8 mm]). It is constructed using 3500 psi (1587.6 kg/cm^2) concrete, and ties into the asphalt parking area and the gutter at street level.

Curb and Gutter

See figure 11–2, Curb and Gutter Detail. The curb and gutter detail and the specifications for Division 2 indicate that the curb is 4" (101.6 mm) wide by 18" (457.2 mm) deep with 6" (152.4 mm) exposed above the finish asphalt surface. The elevation of the curb and gutter will vary with the elevation of the finish surface throughout the project parking and driveway areas (U.N.O.). The exposed height will always remain the same. This detail is similar to the Department of Transportation (DOT) detail for curbs and gutters found in most areas of the country.

Asphalt Surfacing

Refer to Sheet C-2, Plot Plan. The finish surface elevations of the parking area and driveways are noted on the plot plan with the higher elevations nearest the curb and gutter and the lower elevations along the center line of these areas. At the rear of the building, the loading dock is sloped toward the loading area. The asphalt at the extreme east end of the property is the same as the rest of the parking lot and driveways. The asphalt surfacing is specified indicating a 10" (254 mm) sand or gravel base with a 4" (101.6 mm) cementitious base and a 6" (152.4 mm) asphalt surface and seal coating overall. The specifications also note that the finish surface shall be striped for parking and for traffic direction.

Swales and Drains

Refer to Sheet C-2, Plot Plan. The roof drains are extended into the interior curbs at the office portion, or onto splash blocks around the plant/warehouse to direct the water away from the structure into the *swales* constructed in the parking area. A *swale* is, by definition, *a natural or man-made depression in the earth that allows water to flow from one point to another. A swale may also be constructed in any finished surfacing (asphalt or concrete) on a plan.*

Another construction note regarding the surfacing is the requirement for swales directed to a basin installed in the asphalt. The swales are constructed to direct water away from the structure and into the drainage basin (see Figure 11-4) or the street where drainage already exists. The swale on the west parking area directs the flow to the entry approach, as does the one on the north side of the structure from the fence and gate. The swale on the southeast corner of the asphalt drive area directs water away from the loading ramp.

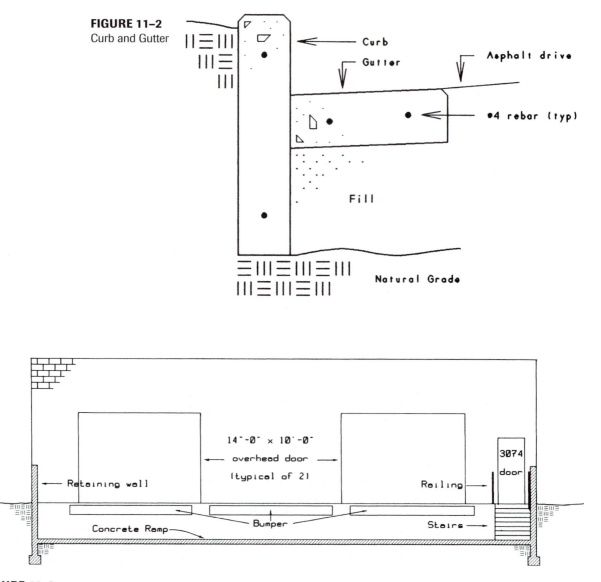

FIGURE 11–2
Curb and Gutter

FIGURE 11–3
Loading Dock, Full View

See figure 11–3, Loading Dock, Full View, and figure 11–4, Drainage System. Also refer to Sheet C-2, Plot Plan. Water is drained from the loading ramp area through the installation of a 6″ (152.4 mm) wide by 8″ (203.2 mm) deep trench drain, with a steel grate, at the base of the loading dock. The specifications indicate that the drain is constructed with 4″ (101.6 mm) thick concrete on the sides and bottom. A bulkhead (diverter wall) shall be installed at the north end of the drain to accommodate a 4″ (101.6 mm) DIA (ID) cast iron steel pipe. The pipe is installed from the trench drain to an open storm basin, 3′-0″ (0.91 m) long by 2′-0″ (0.61 m) wide by 18″ (457.2 mm) deep. The drain is located in the northeast area of the property. The connection point of the pipe at the trench drain and the basin is called an *invert*. An invert is the point at which a change in depth of a drain, basin, or sewer connection occurs. Another pipe is connected between the basin and the storm sewer along First Avenue. The purpose

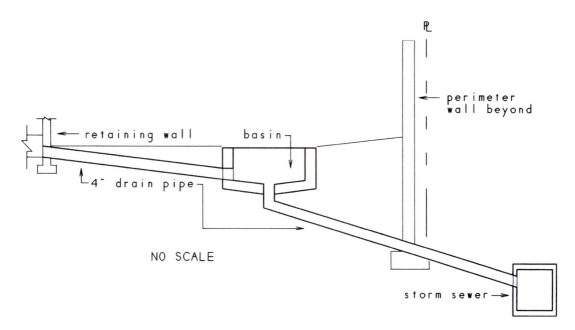

FIGURE 11–4
Drainage System

of the basin is to provide additional drainage to reduce the possibility of an overflow of the trench at the loading dock.

CONCRETE

Concrete Loading Dock and Service Area

Refer to figure 11–3; also see Sheet A-2, Architectural Plans, East Elevation. The loading dock deck and the sloped dock entry area, extending the full length of the east end of the warehouse, are both 6″ (152.4 mm) thick, 3500 psi (1587.59 kg/cm^2) concrete with 6 × 6/W2/9-W2.9 (152.4 mm × 152.4 m/W2.9-W2.9) WWF 1½″ (38.1 mm) below the concrete surface. A concrete pedestrian stair is built into the dock on the north end. The concrete dock driveway is 4′-0″ (1.22 m) below the finish floor and dock elevation. The concrete is installed over a 10″ (245 mm) compacted base extending 20′-0″ (6.1 m) to the east from the loading dock. The area is sloped from the finish elevation of the asphalt surfacing to the base of the loading dock, or 2′-8″ (8.14 m) in 20′-0″ (6.1 m) (approximately 1½″ per foot [38.1 mm per 304.8 mm]).

Concrete Sidewalks

Refer to Sheet C-2, Plot Plan. There are also concrete sidewalks surrounding three sides of the office area and along the south side of the structure to the manufacturing area exterior door. The sidewalks are 3′-0″ (9.1 m) wide and 5″ (127 mm) thick over 4″ (101.6 mm) compacted fill. The entry sidewalk is 6′-0″ (1.83 m) wide with the same specifications.

MASONRY

Masonry Retaining Walls

Refer to figure 11–3 and Sheet A-2, Architectural Plans. The masonry retaining walls on the north and south sides of the loading dock extend 20'-0" (6.1 m) from the east end of the structure to the end of the loading ramp. The walls are 8 × 8 × 16 (203.2 mm × 203.2 m × 406.4 mm) precision (smooth face) CMU. The retaining walls are installed over a 1'-6" × 1'-0" (457.2 mm × 304.8 mm) concrete footing. A solid 8 × 2 × 16 (203.2 mm × 50.8 mm × 406.4 mm) concrete cap block is installed over the top of each wall, therefore, the walls are 8'-2" (2.49 m) at the structure, 4'-2" (1.27 m) of which is exposed above the finish floor elevation of the dock. A maximum depth of 5'-6" (1.68 m) is exposed from the dock to the east end of each wall.

An additional depth of 2'-0" (0.61 m) is added to the depth of the retaining wall below the finish ramp elevation to the top of the footings. When concrete or masonry walls are constructed along a slope, or a change in depth of a structure occurs, the footings are usually installed in steps. Steps occur as often as required to maintain a minimum depth below grade, usually 1'-4" (0.41 m) to 2'-0" (0.61 m) in length. The steps in the retaining wall for the loading dock are installed to accommodate the masonry units along the slope; that is, the equivalent of one or two lengths of block (16" [406.4 mm] to 32" [812.8 mm]) and one or two courses of block (8" [203.2 mm] to 16" [406.4 mm] high).

Masonry Perimeter Walls

Note: *The slumpstone walls identified in this section are common to the southwestern portion of the country. Since this structure is to be in the southwest, the slumpstone has been used. See figure 11–5 and refer to Sheet C-2, Plot Plan. Also refer to figure 1–9.* There are slumpstone fence walls surrounding the property. The slumpstone block is a CMU manufactured to look like adobe brick, an old Spanish/Indian material made from the natural adobe earth and straw. The slumpstone is 8 × 6 × 16 (203.2 mm × 152.4 mm × 406.4 mm).

The plot plan indicates that the east and south walls are 8'-0" (2.44 m) above finish grade. The north wall extending westward from the east property line to the chain-link fence is also 8'-0" (2.44 m) above finish grade. The remaining north wall extending westward to the west property line from the chain-link fence, and the west wall, are 3'-0" (0.91 m) above finish grade.

A retaining wall is also required for a portion of the perimeter walls. The elevation at the corner of Broad Street and First Avenue is identified as elevation 504.0' (153.62 m). The elevation of the landscaping and berm between the walls and the parking lot is 508.68' (55.04 m). The depth for the retaining walls on this project is, therefore, 5'-4" (1.62 m). The 3'-0" (0.91 m) high perimeter wall along Broad Street requires a tapered masonry retaining wall similar to the walls at the loading dock. The retaining wall tapers from 5'-4" (1.62 m) at the northwest corner of the property (the corner at Broad Street and First Avenue) to a minimum 8" (203.2 mm) at the southwest corner (on the Broad Street side).

The south and east walls require no retaining wall since the adjoining properties are at approximately the same elevation as the finish grade of

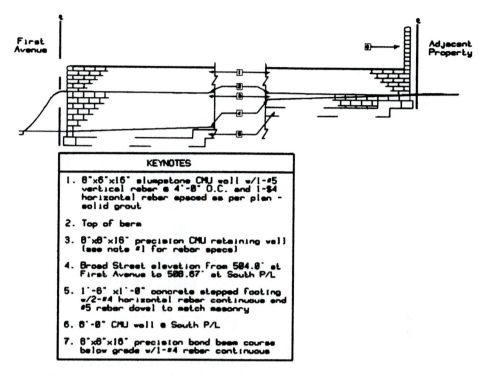

FIGURE 11–5
Slumpstone Fence Walls

the property. All masonry below finish grade is 8 × 8 × 16 (203.2 mm × 203.2 mm × 406.4 mm) smooth-faced precision units.

The specifications note that all the perimeter masonry walls are solid grouted with a grout cap. A grout cap is made from an additional amount of grout, approximately 1″ (25.4 mm) to 2″ (50.8 mm) high, installed on top of the wall and rounded to a smooth finish. The grout cap is often used in lieu of a masonry slab cap, especially when used with slumpstone or natural stone.

See figure 11–6, Slumpstone Retaining Walls. A retaining wall is required for the north and west perimeter walls from sidewalk level to the finish grade level to aid in the prevention of erosion of the soil between the property and the sidewalks. An additional 6′-0″ (1.83 m) slumpstone wall is noted that parallels the perimeter walls adjacent to the sidewalk (figure 11–6). This information, too, is provided by the civil engineer and included in the specifications.

A 6 × 8 × 16 (152.4 mm × 203.2 mm × 406.4 mm) precision, split face, fluted, or scored fence block (CMU) could be used in lieu of the slumpstone. The fence walls may be installed with pilaster block columns at 24′-0″ O/C. Reinforcement is at 4′-0″ intervals between the pilasters and in the pilasters themselves. Rather than using the pilasters, the block may be solid grouted with reinforcement at 4′-0″ intervals.

STEEL REINFORCEMENT

Refer to figures 11–2 through 11–6; also see Sheets S-1 and S-2, Structural plans. The plans and specifications indicate that the concrete loading dock and driveway area, extending the full length of the east wall, include 6 × 6/W2.9 × W2.9 WWF

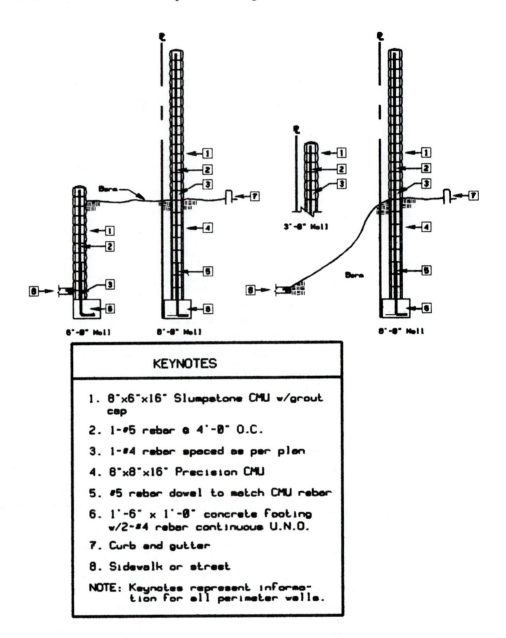

FIGURE 11–6
Slumpstone Retaining Walls

(102.4 mm × 102.4 mm/W2.9 × W2.9) embedded in the concrete driveway. The specifications further note that the wall footings require 2-#4 horizontal rebar and the walls and slabs have #5 horizontal and vertical rebar as specified in the details noted in figures 11–2 and 11–3. The perimeter walls are installed with 2-#4 rebar (U.N.O.) and 1-#5 vertical dowel rebar in the footings. 1-#5 rebar is inserted vertically in the walls at 4'-0" (1.22 m) O/C, horizontally, to match the footing dowels. The fence wall also includes 1-#4 horizontal rebar spaced 4'-0" (1.22 m), vertically, in the 8'-0" (2.44 m) walls and in the top course of the 3'-0" (0.91 m) walls.

BELOW-GRADE MOISTURE PROTECTION

See Sheet C-2, Plot Plan. Also refer to figures 11–2 through 11–6. All retaining walls are to be protected with moisture protection according to the specifications. The protection system is a self-adhering bituminous membrane "installed as per manufacturer's specifications." This statement is not an unusual one because most systems—moisture protection, insulation, surfacing, and so on—must be installed per manufacturer's specifications in order to gain approval and certification of their products and procedures to install the system.

FENCES AND GATES

Refer to Sheet C-2, Plot Plan. Additional site improvements include two 8'-0" (2.44 m) high chain-link fences and gates on the north and south sides of the structure. The fence on the north side is divided into two equal fixed sections with a 14'-0" (4.27 m) long rolling gate, electrically operated, centered in the fence. The fence along the sidewalk on the south side of the building is 28'-0" (8.53 m) long including a 4'-0" (1.22 m) wide swing gate for personnel use only.

UTILITIES

Refer to Sheet C-2, Plot Plan. The water, gas, and electrical service utilities are located in a 15'-0" (4.57 m) wide easement along the south portion of the property. The electric power enters from the adjoining property to the east. The water and gas utilities enter from Broad Street on the west. These utilities enter the structure at the west end of the manufacturing/warehouse structure. All metering is established on the exterior of the building within the fence. The architect and engineer have been granted permission to construct the masonry and chain-link fences across the easement as per the utility companies and local codes and ordinances. The utilities extend approximately 130'-0" (39.62 m) from the street to the point of entry into the structure.

The sanitary and storm sewer lines are located on the north side of the property. The storm drainage system has been previously discussed. The sanitary sewer is located at the northwest corner of the manufacturing/warehouse structure and extends to the First Avenue sewer and storm mains.

LANDSCAPING

There are no specifics for the landscaping other than that noted on the plot plan and in the specifications. All landscaping is to be under separate contract between the owner and the landscape architect. The information included in the specifications is to be a part of the landscape contract.

ELECTRICAL

There are two lamps built into the 3'-0" (0.91 m) perimeter wall at the entry approach and floodlights mounted on the top of the parapet as indicated on the plot plan.

CHAPTER EXERCISES

True or False

T F   1. The benchmark is located at Broad Street and First Avenue.

T F   2. The property is on the corner of Main Street and Broadway.

T F   3. The legal description states that the property is separate from any other industrial or commercial properties.

T F   4. The North and South boundaries are the same length.

T F   5. The construction included in this chapter is referred to as the on-site construction.

T F   6. The POB is farthest from the datum point located at Broad Street and First Avenue.

T F   7. Most of the work included in this chapter is covered in Divisions 6 through 16.

T F   8. There are no utility easements within the boundaries of the Frontier Manufacturing Company property.

T F   9. The entrance to the property is made from Broad Street.

T F 10. The property is enclosed with a chain-link fence.

Matching

_____   1. Approach

_____   2. Swale

_____   3. Cementitious

_____   4. DOT

_____   5. Plot plan

_____   6. Elevation

_____   7. Legal Description

_____   8. Datum Point

_____   9. Point of Beginning

_____ 10. Site plan

a. Point above sea level

b. Department of Transportation

c. Plan with natural contours

d. Location of property

e. Starting point of survey

f. Sloped earth or surface to direct water flow

g. Starting point of property layout

h. Finish grades noted in this plan

i. Entry to the property

j. Cement-like materials

Completion

1. All work except the structure is included under site _____ or off-site construction.

2. The _____ ramp and approach apron (ramp) are both installed with 3500 psi (1587.6 kg/cm^2) concrete.

3. The north property line of the Frontier Manufacturing Company is _____ feet.

4. The depth of the curb surrounding the parking/driveway is _____ cm.

5. The 0.91 m and 2.44 m high perimeter walls have exposed masonry units called _____.

6. The size of all below-grade masonry units at the retaining walls is _____.

7. All asphalt surfacing shall be laid over a _____" (_____ mm) compacted base material.

8. The lowest area of the parking/driveways leading away from the structure is a(n) _____.

9. The lowest area of the loading dock ramp includes a 6" (152.4 mm) wide _____ drain.

10. All water runoff is directed to the _____ drain on First Avenue.

11. A _____ pipe connects the trench drain to a storm drain on the northeast corner of the property.

12. All curb and gutter installations are to meet the requirements of the federal _____.

13. The asphalt surfacing is _____ mm thick.

14. The sidewalks are _____" deep over 4" (101.6 mm) compacted base.

15. The loading dock ramp is 6" (152.4 mm) deep, 3500 psi (1587.59 kg/cm^2) concrete with _____ WWF 1^1/$_2$" (38.1 mm) below the concrete surface.

16. The retaining walls on both sides of the loading dock have a 203.2 mm × _____ mm × 406.4 mm concrete cap on top.

17. The perimeter retaining walls are _____' (1.62 m) deep.

18. All masonry walls are placed on _____ (457.2 mm × 304.8 mm) footings.

19. The exposed walls on the west property line are _____' (_____ m) high.

20. To prevent the berm from eroding away from the perimeter walls, exposing the retaining walls, another _____, 6'-0" (1.83 m) wall may be installed.

21. There are _____ fences installed between the perimeter walls and the structure.

22. A(n) _____ operated rolling gate is installed on the north side of the structure.

23. The _____ plans are under separate contract to the owner, therefore, the plans are not included with the Frontier Manufacturing Company blueprint.

24. There is a(n) _____ on the south side of the property for use by the utility company(ies).

25. The plot plan indicates the installation of a $1^{1}/_{2}''$ (38.1 mm) DIA copper pipe by _____' (39.62 m) water service from the street to the structure.

Multiple Choice

_____ 1. The datum point used for the survey of the Frontier Manufacturing Company property is located:
   a. At Broad and Main Streets
   b. At elevation 504.0' above sea level
   c. On the Plot Plan only
   d. Is not shown

_____ 2. The legal description of the property indicates:
   a. The range location
   b. The township location
   c. Where the records are located
   d. All of the above

_____ 3. Site improvements and off-sites are:
   a. Both included as one area
   b. All construction on a property excluding the structure
   c. Both a and b
   d. Neither a nor b

_____ 4. The property point of entry (apron or approach) on the Plot Plan:
   a. Is located on First Avenue just off Broad Street
   b. Is 30' (9.14 m) wide
   c. Is asphalt surfaced
   d. None of the above

_____ 5. The curb and gutter to be installed along the perimeter of the paved areas is:
   a. Installed per DOT Specifications
   b. Machine-formed
   c. Asphalt formed
   d. 4" (101.6 mm) by 18" (457.2 mm) with a 12" (304.8 mm) wide gutter

_____ 6. The property measures:
   a. 260.0' × 125.0' × 244.0' × 126.02'
   b. 38.41 m × 74.37 m × 79.25 m × 36.1 m
   c. Neither a nor b
   d. Both a and b

_____   7. The asphalt surfacing for the driveway/parking areas is specified as follows:
   a. 6″ (152.4 mm) asphalt surface over 4″ (101.6 mm) cementitious base over 12″ (304.6 mm) compacted base
   b. 6″ (152.4 mm) asphalt surface over 4″ (101.6 mm) cementitious base over 10″ (254 mm) compacted base
   c. 4″ (101.6 mm) asphalt surface over 6″ (152.4 mm) cementitious base over 10″ (254 mm) compacted base
   d. 10″ (254 mm) asphalt surface over 12″ (304.8 mm) cementitious base over 6″ (152.4 mm) compacted base

_____   8. Swales are sloped in the asphalt:
   a. For esthetic design purposes
   b. To keep vehicles from crashing into the structure
   c. To direct the water flow away from the property
   d. To direct the water flow onto the landscaping

_____   9. The trench drain and the open storm drain on the property:
   a. Are installed to remove water from the loading dock area and the western portion of the property
   b. Are installed with a connecting CI pipe
   c. Are for esthetic design only
   d. None of the above

_____   10. The approach apron and loading ramp both:
   a. Include 6 × 6/W2.9-W2.9 WWF
   b. Are 3500 psi (1,587.59 kg/cm^2)
   c. Are 6″ (152.4 cm) thick
   d. All of the above

_____   11. All retaining walls are:
   a. 8′-0″ (2.44 m) high
   b. Constructed using smooth-faced precision 8″ × 8″ × 16″ (203.2 mm × 203.2 mm × 406.4 mm) CMU
   c. Constructed from 8″ × 6″ × 16″ (203.2 mm × 152.4 mm × 406.4 mm) slumpstone CMU
   d. Exposed to view

_____   12. The change in elevation of the site walls occurs:
   a. At the junction of the chain-link fence on the North side of the structure and at the Southwest corner of the property
   b. At the junction of the chain-link fence on both sides of the structure
   c. At the junction of the Southwest corner and the East end of the entry approach
   d. At the Northwest and Northeast corners of the property

_____   13. The entry approach is 26′ (7.92 m) long by 15′ (4.57 m) wide by:
   a. 245 mm deep
   b. 101.6 mm deep
   c. 152.4 mm deep
   d. 50.8 mm deep

_____ 14. The trench drain and open storm drain:
  a. Remove water from the whole East section of the property
  b. Connect with the storm sewer on First Avenue
  c. Are both pre-cast concrete units
  d. All of the above

_____ 15. The landscape areas:
  a. Are included in the contract
  b. Are to have no trees or shrubbery
  c. Are to be automatically sprinkled
  d. None of the above

_____ 16. If used, the additional perimeter retaining wall shall be:
  a. Constructed from slumpstone CMU of the same size as the perimeter walls
  b. 6'-0" (1.83 m) high overall (O/A)
  c. Installed parallel and adjacent to the public sidewalk or street
  d. All of the above

_____ 17. All perimeter walls shall be installed with:
  a. A 2" (50.8 mm) high concrete cap
  b. A grout cap
  c. No reinforcement
  d. None of the above

_____ 18. Steel reinforcement is:
  a. Supplied by the steel fabricator
  b. Deformed #4 and #5 rebar
  c. Installed as per plans and specifications
  d. All of the above

_____ 19. The chain-link fence:
  a. Is 12'-0" (3.66 m) high
  b. Is to include one electrically operated rolling gate
  c. Extends East and West from the structure
  d. None of the above

_____ 20. All site improvements/off-sites include:
  a. All construction inside and outside the property excluding the structure
  b. All construction including the structure
  c. All construction within the property boundaries only
  d. All construction having to do with grading and excavating only

CHAPTER 12

On-Site Construction—
The Office

There are two different construction types in the Frontier Manufacturing Company structure. The office construction includes a concrete slab, with exterior masonry walls, wood (or alternate metal) interior framing, insulation, and a wood hip roof structure with tile roofing. Construction for the manufacturing/warehouse facility includes special slab construction, loading dock construction, special equipment requirements, and a flat structural roof and roofing system. The personal care facilities (wash/restroom and break room) are also much different than the office facility. To better understand the differences, this chapter discusses the office construction only. The manufacturing/warehouse is discussed in chapter 13.

MAIN OFFICE AREAS

See figure 12–1, Foundation Details, and Sheet S-1, Foundation Plan, Frontier Manufacturing Company. Also refer to appendix IV, the Project Manual. The foundation plan indicates an $8 \times 8 \times 16$ (203.2 mm × 203.2 mm × 406.4 mm) masonry foundation (stem) wall over a 2'-0" × 1'-0" (0.61 m × 0.30 m) concrete footing. The stem walls are to be a minimum 2'-0" (0.61 m) deep along the north, south, and west sides of the office area. This footing depth will vary in accordance with geographic location, the soils report, and weather conditions as noted in chapters 3 and 4, as well as with local codes and ordinances. The detail also indicates that the footing contains 2-#4 continuous horizontal rebar and 1-#5 rebar dowel to match the masonry wall reinforcement. The specifications state that there shall be a minimum rebar lap, both horizontally and vertically, of 48 bar diameters (2'-0" [0.61 m]) for #4 rebar and 40 bar diameters (2'-1" or 2'-0" [0.61 m], nominal) for #5 rebar. For this reason the dowel in the footing extends a maximum 2'-0" (0.61 m) above the finish floor (A.F.F.), so that the dowel and vertical wall rebar can be tied together for rigidity and continuity.

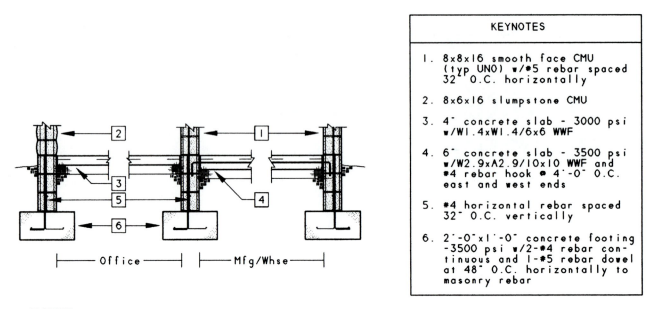

KEYNOTES

1. 8x8x16 smooth face CMU
   (typ UNO) w/#5 rebar spaced
   32" O.C. horizontally

2. 8x6x16 slumpstone CMU

3. 4" concrete slab - 3000 psi
   w/WI.4xWI.4/6x6 WWF

4. 6" concrete slab - 3500 psi
   w/W2.9xA2.9/10x10 WWF and
   #4 rebar hook @ 4'-0" O.C.
   east and west ends

5. #4 horizontal rebar spaced
   32" O.C. vertically

6. 2'-0"x1'-0" concrete footing
   -3500 psi w/2-#4 rebar continuous and 1-#5 rebar dowel
   at 48" O.C. horizontally to
   masonry rebar

FIGURE 12–1
Foundation Details

Concrete

Refer to appendix IV, the Project Manual. The floor slab for the office is 48'-0"
(14.6 m) by 34'-4" (10.46 m) by 4" (101.6 mm) deep and rated at 3000 psi
(1360.8 kg/cm^2) at 28 days. The concrete slab is placed abutting the masonry
wall on all sides, requiring the installation of an expansion or isolation
(moisture) control joint along the perimeter of the slab. The east wall, adjoining the manufacturing/warehouse area, is included in the manufacturing/
warehouse construction.

Exterior Wall Construction

*See Sheets A-2, Architectural Plans, and S-1 and S-2, Structural Plans. Also refer
to appendix IV, the Project Manual.* The office walls above grade are 8 × 6 × 16
(203.2 mm × 152.4 mm × 406.4 mm) solid grouted slumpstone masonry to a
height of 12'-0" (3.66 m) A.F.F. Reinforcement for the masonry walls is indicated
in the keynotes of the foundation plan and in the structural wall sections.

Structural Roof

*See Sheets C-2, Plot Plan, A-3, Architectural Roof Plan, and S-3, Structural Roof Plan.
Also refer to appendix IV, the Project Manual.* The roof over the office area is a
3:12 (⅛ [3.18 mm] roof pitch) combination truss and jack truss hip roof. The
trusses have a 2 × 6 (50.8 mm × 152.4 mm) top chord and a 2 × 4 (50.8 mm
× 101.6 mm) bottom chord spaced at 24" (0.61 m) O/C in all directions. The
ridge of the roof structure is level with the height of the wall between the office
and the manufacturing/warehouse structure, (20'-0" [6.10 m] A.F.F.) The
trusses are fastened to a 2 × 10 (50.8 mm × 254 mm) ledger at the masonry
wall, and a 2 × 8 (50.8 mm × 203.2 mm) at the bottom chord, 12'-0" (3.66 m)

A.F.F. A rafter tail extending 2'-0" (0.61 m) horizontally beyond the plate line is also included. The roof is sheathed with 4' × 8' × ½" (1.22 m × 2.44 m × 12.7 mm) CDX plywood or exterior grade OSB®.

Interior Construction

See Sheets A-1 and A-2, Architectural Plans, and S-2, Structural Plan. Also refer to the Project Manual. The interior office walls are non-bearing partition walls to a height of 9'-0" (2.74 m) A.F.F., at 24" (0.61 m) O/C, using 4" (101.6 mm), 20 gauge, galvanized cold-rolled steel studs. The hall partitions and the plumbing wall between the office bathroom and kitchen are 6" (152.4 mm), 20 gauge, galvanized cold-rolled steel studs, also at a height of 9'-0" (2.74 m) A.F.F. The demising (separation) wall between the showroom and the offices is 12'-0" (3.66 m), at 16" (152.4 mm) O/C, to the underside of the roof trusses. An exposed 6 × 12 (152.4 mm × 304.8 mm) DF #1, R/S wood beam, located over the reception area, is installed as part of the separation wall. The beam is supported by two exposed wood posts (one on each end), 6 × 6 (152.4 mm × 152.4 mm) DF #2, R/S.

The interior perimeter slumpstone masonry has a 2" (50.8 mm) thermal insulating wall system (Styrostud®, or equal). There are 2 × 4 (50.8 mm × 101.6 mm) furring strips installed at each corner and at the top and bottom of the wall system to aid in the installation of drywall. The strips are screwed or nailed to the masonry. All interior walls are to have a combination of R-11 thermal and sound batt insulation in the stud walls.

Roofing

Refer to appendix IV, the Project Manual, and Sheet A-3, Architectural Plans. The specifications indicate that the 3:12 sloped roof over the office area is to have a clay S-tile system over a 43 lb/sq (19.55 kg/9.29 m^2) felt underlayment. Each tile is exposed as per manufacturer's directions and fastened to the roof sheathing with a tile-tie system, or on batten boards. The tile-ties are commonly used with the Spanish clay barrel tile or S-tile. Batten boards are 1 × 4 (25.4 mm × 101.6 mm) strips installed horizontally (parallel to the eave) and spaced according to the allowable exposure of the tiles. The specifications also call for a pre-manufactured galvanized metal or structural plastic ridge vent. A ridge trim is to extend along the ridge and hips over the vents for additional weather protection. The tile used does not require a rake trim since the roof has no *rakes* (barges). A *rake* trim is a specially formed tile that fits over the rake end of a gable roof.

THE FINISH SCHEDULE

Drywall

Refer to figure 12–2, Finish Schedule, Frontier Manufacturing, Inc., and appendix IV, the Project Manual. Per the finish schedule, all interior partition walls are specified with one layer of ⅝" (15.9 mm), type "X," GWB extending the full height of the walls (9'-0" [2.74 m] A.F.F.). The interior partitions have drywall on

Finish Schedule

LOCATION	FLOOR	BASE	WALLS N	WALLS S	WALLS E	WALLS W	CEILING	REMARKS
Office #1	2	1	1	1	1	1	1	
Office #2	2	1	1	1	1	1	1	
Office #3	2	1	1	1	1	1	1	
Office #4	2	1	1	1	1	1	1	
Office #5	2	1	1	1	1	1	1	
Office #6	2	1	1	1	1	1	1	
Reception	3	1	1	1	1	1	1	
Showroom	3	1	1	1	1	1	1	
Plant Office	1	3	1	1	1	1	2	
Kitchen	3	2	1 2 3	1 2 3	1 2 3	1 2 3	1	
Restroom	3	2	1 2 3	1 2 3	1 2 3	1 2 3	1	
Wash Room/ Restroom	1	3	1 2 3	1 2 3	1 2 3	1 2 3	2	
Break Room	3	3	1 2 3	1 2 3	1 2 3	1 2 3	2	

FLOORS:

1. Exposed concrete
2. Carpet
3. Vinyl composition tile

BASE:

1. Wood trim - 3"
2. Coving
3. 4" vinyl base - self-adhering

WALLS:

1. 5/8" X GWB
2. Paint
3. Ceramic tile

CEILINGS:

1. Acoustical tile
2. 5/8" X GWB

NOTES:

1. All finish materials to be selected by owner from standard styles and colors.
2. See specifications for other information.
3. Exterior walls of plant office, break room and restroom areas are to be covered with T-1-11 siding

FIGURE 12–2
Finish Schedule, Frontier Manufacturing, Inc.

both sides. The demising wall has two layers of ⅝" (15.9 mm), type "X," GWB both sides full height to the underside of the trusses (12'-0" [3.66 m] A.F.F.). One side of the wall shall have drywall installed to the underside of the roof structure. The underside of the trusses shall also have ⅝" (15.9 mm), type "X", GWB installed. All unexposed drywall above ceiling height is to be fire-taped.

Ceramic Tile

See Sheet A-1, Architectural Plan, and refer to figure 12–2 and appendix IV, the Project Manual. The finish schedule shows that 4" (101.6 mm) square wall tiles are installed on the kitchen walls between the backsplash over the counters and the wall cabinets, and to 6'-0" (1.83 m) A.F.F. on all walls in the balance of the kitchen and the office restroom. The tiles are embedded in a thinset mortar and grouted. The colors are to be selected by the owner.

Acoustical Ceiling

Refer to figure 6–8, Acoustical Ceiling Tile System, 12-2, Finish Schedule, and appendix IV, the Project Manual. Also see Sheet A-4, Architectural Plan. A suspended ceiling system, known as an *acoustical ceiling tile (ACT) system,* is installed using a metal T-bar support system and compressed fiberboard cut into sizes of 2′ × 2′ (0.61 m × 0.61 m) or 2′ × 4′ (0.61 m × 1.22 m). The tiles range in thickness from ½″ (12.7 mm) to 1½″ (38.1 mm), with smooth or fissured surfaces. The smooth surfaces are usually under ¾″ (1.91 cm), offering less acoustical control and normally have no fire rating. The thicker tiles with fissured surfaces are rated from ¾-hour to one-hour fire resistance.

The T-bar support system is composed of horizontal wall angles, T-bar runners, and tie wires. The tie wires are installed first, fastened to the roof structure above. They are sufficiently long enough to fasten the acoustical system at the proper height. The wall angle is attached horizontally to the walls of the area using the system. The T-bar runners are fastened to the wall

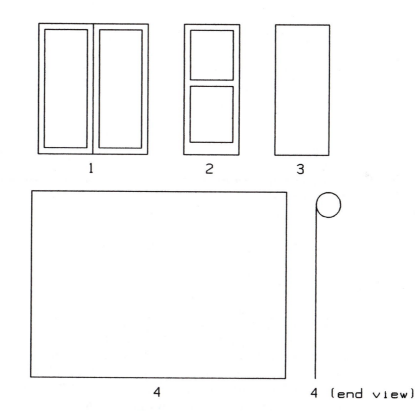

	1		2		3	

4   4 (end view)

MARK	SIZE	DESCRIPTION	QTY	REMARKS
		DOOR SCHEDULE		
1	pr 3′-0″x7′-0″	aluminum storefront	1	anodized finish
2	3′-0″x7′-0″	hollow metal w/HM frame	3	pre-painted by mfr.
3	3′-0″x7′-0″	birch. s/c. 13/8″. flush	9	stain grade
4	14′-0″x10′-0″	steel overhead roll-up	2	motorized

FIGURE 12–3
Door Schedule

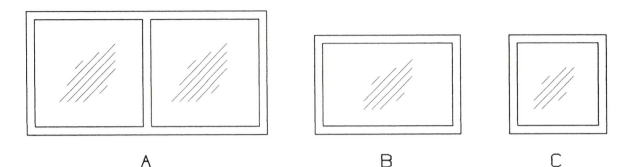

A   B   C

WINDOW SCHEDULE				
MARK	SIZE	DESCRIPTION	QTY	REMARKS
A	10'-0" x 5'-0"	Fixed	2	Fit masonry opening
B	6'-0" x 4'-0"	DO	3	DO'
C	4'-0" x 4'-0"	DO	5	DO
'NOTE: Plant office window made for frame construction.				

FIGURE 12–4
Window Schedule

angles spaced to match the size of the ceiling tiles to be placed in them. The main T-bars runners are one piece extending the full length of the shortest length of the ceiling and fastened to the wall angle and the tie wires. The secondary runners are then placed at the proper spacing and fastened to the wall angles and the main runners. In seismic areas, a metal tubing or rod is required at 9 sq ft (7.5 m^2) for stability and resistance to lateral forces.

Interior Wood Finishes, Doors, and Windows

See figures 12–3, Door Schedule, 12–4 Window Schedule. Also refer to figure 12–2 and appendix IV, the Project Manual. The specifications and the door and window schedules state all the information necessary for the door and window types, sizes, and finishes, including the trim.

All exterior doors are hollow metal (HM) doors and frames. All interior doors are solid core (s/c), birch, and flush, with stain finish. The frames are all knockdown hollow metal (KDHM). All windows are aluminum framed with fixed, fire-retardant, vandal-proof, tinted, and double-insulated plastic glass. The interior sides of the windows are to be trimmed with a material matching the base trim.

Carpeting and Flooring

Refer to figure 12–2 and appendix IV, the Project Manual. The floors of the restrooms, kitchen, break room, reception area, and showroom are to have vinyl composition tiles (VCT) on the floors. The tiles may range from 8" (203.2 mm) to 12" (304.8 mm) squares. The specifications and finish schedule note that the owner is to select the size, style, and color. The carpeting is specified as commercial grade with pad and edge tacking. Again, the owner selects the color and style. The carpeting is installed in office areas as noted.

Painting and Wall Coverings

Refer to figure 12–2 and appendix IV, the Project Manual. The specifications state that all exposed interior walls that are not covered with tile are to be painted. The R/S exposed beam and support posts are to be stained with a dark walnut stain. Unless otherwise directed by the owner, there are no other wall coverings (wallpaper or paneling).

CHAPTER EXERCISES

Completion

1. The size of the office area is 48'-0" (14.63 m) by _____ (_____ m).

2. The exterior office walls are constructed with _____ CMU.

3. There are 2 × 4 (50.8 mm × 101.6 mm) _____ on the interior side of the exterior walls.

4. The concrete slab is _____ psi (_____ kg/cm²).

5. A _____' (_____ m) demising wall is built between the offices and showroom.

6. All interior _____ are constructed to 9'-0" (2.74 m) A.F.F.

7. The batt insulation in the ceiling is rated at _____.

8. The windows and doors are both _____ and vandal-proof.

9. The drywall required for the interior walls is _____" (_____ mm).

10. The structural roof system is a(n) _____ truss roof system.

11. The roofing is applied over a(n) _____ deck.

12. The interior doors are all 3'-0" × 7'-0" (0.91 m × 2.13 m) flush _____.

13. All offices and halls are to have a _____ finish.

14. The perimeter of the concrete slab abutting the masonry walls on three sides has a(n) _____ joint installed.

15. The top of the footings at the office area are _____' (_____ m) deep below grade.

True or False

T F   1. There is rigid insulation used in the office area.

T F   2. The framing is all wood using construction grade 92½" × 2 × 6 (2.35 m × 50.8 mm × 152.4 mm) studs.

T F   3. The restroom is not equipped for use by persons with disabilities.

T F   4. The kitchen includes a sink and refrigerator.

T F   5. All the offices are the same size.

T F   6. The entry doors to the offices are called hollow metal doors.

T F   7. There are three entrances into the office area.

T F   8. All office doors shown on the floor plan are marked with a circled #2.

T F   9. The measurements from the exterior outside corner to the windows are to the center of the windows.

T F   10. There is a pony wall and a countertop shown at the reception area.

T F   11. All floors are to be covered with VCT except the showroom.

T F   12. All frame walls contain an insulation that controls both heat and sound transmission.

T F   13. The door exiting to the plant area is a hollow metal door and frame.

T F   14. All windows on each side of the office area are the same size.

T F   15. The foundation wall is constructed with 203.2 mm × 203.2 mm × 406.4 mm precision CMU.

T F   16. The roof trusses have a top chord of 2 × 6 (50.8 mm × 152.4 mm) and a bottom chord of 2 × 4 (50.8 mm × 101.6 mm).

T F   17. The underside of the trusses is to have ½″ (12.7 mm), type "X," GWB installed.

T F   18. A rough-sawn (R/S) 6 × 12 (152.4 mm × 304.8 mm) beam and 6 × 6 (152.4 mm × 152.4 mm) posts are installed in the demising wall at the reception area.

T F   19. The roofing called out is a Spanish S-tile over a 43 lb/sq (19.55 kg/9.29 m^2) underlayment.

T F   20. The roof is sloped 3″ per lineal foot (76.2 mm per 304.8 mm).

Multiple Choice

_____   1. The concrete for the footings is rated at:
     a. 2500 psi (1136.36 kg/cm^2)
     b. 4000 psi (1818.18 kg/cm^2)
     c. 3500 psi (1590.91 kg/cm^2)
     d. 3000 psi (1363.64 kg/cm^2)

_____   2. The perimeter of the concrete slab has a(n):
     a. Construction joint installed
     b. Expansion joint installed
     c. Isolation joint installed
     d. All of the above

_____   3. The exposed exterior office walls are:
   a. Steel-framed walls at 24″ (609.6 mm) O/C
   b. 8 × 8 × 16 (203.2 mm × 203.2 mm × 606.4 mm) slumpstone masonry
   c. 2 × 6 (50.8 mm × 152.4 mm) wood-framed walls @ 16″ (406.4 mm) O/C
   d. 8 × 6 × 16 (203.2 mm × 152.4 mm × 406.4 mm) slumpstone masonry

_____   4. The roof system consists of:
   a. Sloped trusses 2 × 6 (50.8 mm × 152.4 mm) top chord and ½″ (12.7 mm) plywood
   b. A tile roofing material and 43 lb/sq (19.55 kg/9.29 m^2) underlayment
   c. Both a and b
   d. Neither a nor b

_____   5. The structural interior wall framing consists of:
   a. 2 × 6 × 92½″ (50.8 mm × 152.4 mm × 2.35 m) studs with sill plate and double top plate
   b. 4″ × 9′-0″ (50.8 mm × 2.74 m) 20 gauge galvanized steel studs and track
   c. 6″ × 9′-0″ (101.6 mm × 2.74 m) 20 gauge galvanized steel studs and track
   d. 2 × 4 × 10′-0″ (50.8 mm × 101.6 mm × 25.4 m) wood framing with sill plate and double top plate

_____   6. The concrete slab is:
   a. 3000 psi (1363.64 kg/cm^2)
   b. 2500 psi (1136.36 kg/cm^2)
   c. 4000 psi (1818.18 kg/cm^2)
   d. None of the above

_____   7. The stem wall is:
   a. 1′-6″ (0.46 m) deep
   b. 2′-0″ (0.61 m) deep
   c. 1′-8″ (0.51 m) deep
   d. Slumpstone masonry

_____   8. The truss system requires that the trusses:
   a. Have a sill plate under the trusses
   b. Have ½″ (12.7 mm) GWB fastened to the top chord
   c. Are exposed
   d. Have ⅝″ (15.9 mm), type "X," GWB fastened to the underside

_____   9. The interior office partitions comprise:
   a. ⅝″ (15.9 mm), type "X," GWB on both sides of a 6″ × 9′-0″ (152.4 mm × 2.74 m) 20 ga stud and track
   b. ⅝″ (15.9 mm), type "X," GWB on both sides of a 4″ × 9′-0″ (101.6 mm × 2.74 m) 20 ga stud and track
   c. ½″ (12.7 mm), type "X," GWB on both sides of a 6″ × 9′-0″ (152.4 mm × 2.74 m) 20 ga stud and track
   d. ½″ (12.7 mm), type "X," GWB on both sides of a 4″ × 9′-0″ (101.6 mm × 2.74 m) 20 ga stud and track

_____ 10. The interior walls contain:
   a. R-19 thermal batt insulation
   b. R-11 combination thermal and sound insulation
   c. R-11 thermal batt insulation
   d. R-19 combination thermal and sound insulation

_____ 11. The wall dividing the showroom from the office areas:
   a. Is insulated the same as the other walls
   b. Is 12'-0" (3.66 m) tall to the underside of the roof trusses
   c. Has a wood beam and posts installed within the wall
   d. Includes all of the above

_____ 12. The windows are manufactured with:
   a. Steel frames and plate glass
   b. Aluminum frames with fire-protection and vandal-proofing glazing
   c. Single-hung windows
   d. Sliding glass windows

_____ 13. The entry doors are:
   a. A storefront entry
   b. Composed of a pair of 3'-0" × 7'-0" (0.91 m × 2.13 m) doors
   c. Fully glazed
   d. All of the above

_____ 14. The kitchen is finished with:
   a. Base and wall cabinets along the north and east walls
   b. 9'-0" × 6'-0" (2.74 m × 1.83 m)
   c. A drywall ceiling
   d. Painting full height all walls

_____ 15. The restroom is finished with:
   a. Standard fixtures and all ceramic tile walls
   b. Handicap facilities with ceramic tile to 6'-0"
      (1.83) m A.F.F.
   c. A 7'-0" (2.13 m) ceiling
   d. None of the above

CHAPTER 13

On-Site Construction—
Manufacturing/Warehouse

See *Architectural and Structural Plans, Frontier Manufacturing. Also refer to appendix IV, the Project Manual.* As previously mentioned, the construction for the manufacturing/warehouse area, referred to hereafter as *the plant area,* includes special materials and procedures. These requirements are found in the specifications in the project manual and the various schedules included with them. The work necessary is under more careful scrutiny, including more stringent government and owner inspections of material, installation, and care in material storage. Most of the details are explained in the plans through the use of keynotes.

CONCRETE

Concrete Footings

In accordance with the specifications, the concrete footings are 2'-0" × 1'-0" (0.61 m × 0.30 m) at 3500 psi (1590.91 kg/cm^2). The concrete requirement for the slab, as per specifications, is also 3500 psi (1590.91 kg/cm^2) at 6" (152.4 mm) thick. The footings continue completely around the structure and along the face of the loading dock with step footings from the main slab level to the bottom of the loading dock wall. The retaining walls on each side of the loading dock also have step footings from the loading dock to their ends.

Refer to figure 1–9, Keynotes, and Sheet S-1, Structural Plans. The drawing in figure 1–9 is the same detail describing the column supports for the plant as the detail in the plans. The roof support system requires additional concrete where interior column supports are located. A special footing, referred to as a mat footing, is placed where the columns are installed. This is done at the same time as the perimeter footings are placed. This area at the mats is left undone until the columns are installed and the roof structure is completed. Concrete is then placed over the mats with control (isolation) joints and finished to the level of the main slab areas.

Concrete Slab

See figure 13–1, Flat Formwork. Per the specifications, as mentioned, the concrete requirement for the slab is 3500 psi (1590.91 kg/cm²), and 6″ (152.4 mm) thick. The slab is placed in sections with a cutback at the column footings. The slab is placed in staggered placements. Flat 6″ (152.4 mm) high GI steel forms, similar to the form shown in figure 12–1, are installed to form the six sections on the foundation plan. The forms are used to separate the slab sections as well as to form a *cold-key expansion joint.* Three sections may be placed at one time. For example, the northwest end, the southwest end, and the middle section on the east side may be placed at the same time. This leaves the three other areas open and the areas being placed accessible. When the concrete in the first three areas cures, the forms are removed for the next placement. A moisture barrier is placed in the keyed joints, using thin strips of material such as polystyrene foam, neoprene, or bituthene, and the remaining areas are placed.

　　See figure 13–2, Slab/Wall Connection. Per the detail in figure 13–2, a 6 × 6/W2.9-W2.9 (152.4 mm × 152.4 mm/W2.9-W2.9) welded wire fabric is embedded in the slab prior to the placement. There may or may not be rebar in the concrete, depending upon the locale and structural requirements. If

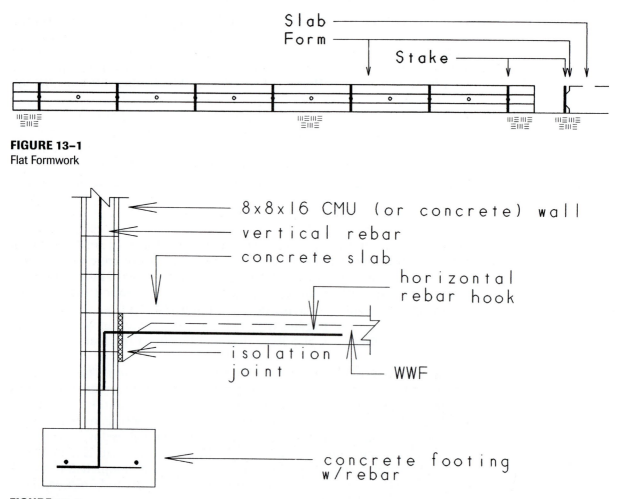

FIGURE 13–1
Flat Formwork

FIGURE 13–2
Slab/Wall Connection

rebar were required, it would be placed horizontally in the perimeter of the slab with a hook (bent portion of the bar) placed vertically downward in the masonry and the longer portion extending into the slab. Such reinforcement is usually 4'-0" (1.22 m) O/C. When a slab abuts a wall, instead of extending over the wall, an isolation control joint completely surrounding the finished slab is required. There may also be requirements for additives in the concrete for additional strengthening, or reducing slippery surfaces, or keeping dust from adhering to the concrete. These are required only if demanded by the owner, architect, or engineer and are included in the specifications.

Loading Dock

Refer to figure 11–3. The loading dock is installed with the same compressive strength concrete (3500 psi [1590.91 kg/cm^2]) and reinforcing requirements as required for the footings.

MASONRY

The plant walls are $8 \times 8 \times 16$ (203.2 mm $\times$ 203.2 mm $\times$ 406.4 mm) precision (smooth-faced) CMU. The plans show that the walls are 16'-0" (4.88 m) high on the north, east, and south sides, and 20'-0" (6.1 m) high on the west side adjacent to the office area. The specifications also supply information for the mortar, grout, and reinforcement. The walls are solid grouted for both strength and fire resistance. A solid-grouted masonry wall is rated as a two-hour (minimum) fire-retardant wall if standing alone, as are these walls.

See Sheet S-1, Structural Floor Plan and Details. There is additional strengthening and thickening of the walls where the roof structures require special wall support. These walls may be steel beam columns, or a combination of steel and concrete, or they may be reinforced masonry pilasters. Concrete, steel, or concrete and steel are used with concrete or steel wall construction. Where the main walls are constructed of masonry, the supports are reinforced masonry pilasters.

A sheet metal coping is installed over a 2×8 (50.8 mm $\times$ 203.2 mm) DF common, or utility HF, continuous wood cap on the top of the masonry walls. Where weather concerns are prevalent, PTMS (mudsill) may be required. Fasteners, sufficiently long enough to penetrate into the masonry, without damaging the coping, are used for the installation. The fasteners are installed at all sheet laps and at 2'-0" (0.61 m) O/C between the laps.

ROUGH CARPENTRY

Wall Framing

The office and personnel areas within the plant, like the main office area, are also constructed with metal stud framing to 9'-0" (2.74 m) A.F.F., using 6" (152.4 mm) -20 gauge studs, at 24" (0.61 m) O/C, in all walls, and 6" (152.4 mm) -20 gauge joists (unpunched) at 16" (0.41 m) O/C, for the ceilings. The exterior walls are covered with ½" (12.7 mm) exterior grade CDX plywood or OSB® sheathing outside and ⅝″ (15.9 mm), type "X," GWB on the interiors. The walls and ceiling also have R-11 thermal and sound batt insulation identical to the office areas. The exterior (top) of the ceiling joists are covered with a double layer of ½″ (12.7 mm) CDX plywood.

ROOF STRUCTURE

Beams and Beam Supports

Refer to Sheet S-3, Structural plans, and figure 1–8. The plant roof is supported by a combination of steel pipe columns, glue-laminated beams, and open web trusses. The two steel support columns, as previously mentioned, are 6″ (101.6 mm) DIA with a bottom plate attachment for installation in the mat footing. The columns are bolted and welded into place. The top of each column has a specially fabricated hinge connector. The connector is constructed to allow the center glu-lam beam and one end of the smaller glu-lam beams to rest in it. The opposite end of the smaller glu-lam beams rest on a steel plate inserted in the top of the masonry pilasters at the east and west ends of the plant. Straps may also be fastened to the beams and embedded in the masonry walls and pilasters. The total support beam is made up of the three separate beams. The center beam is 6¾″ × 27″ × 24′-0″ (146.1 mm × 685.8 mm × 7.32 m). The two smaller beams are 6¾″ × 18″ × 31′-0″ (146.1 mm × 457.2 mm × 9.45 m). The hinge connectors may be pre-manufactured or may require customizing. Whenever a metal support accessory is custom-made it must meet standards that may be even more stringent than the manufactured accessory.

Roof Joists and Ledgers

Refer to Sheet S-3, Structural Plans. As per the specifications, the roof joists are manufactured by Trus-Joist. The type of joist is a TJL, 14″ × 27′-6⅛″ (355.6 mm × 8.36 m) at 24″ (0.61 m) O/C. The joists span each way from the glu-lam beams to a 3 × 10 (76.2 mm × 254 mm) ledger fastened along the north and south walls. The joists are connected to the glu-lams and the ledgers with joist hangers recommended by the manufacturer. The manufacturer also supplies all necessary accessories for a complete system.

Roof Deck

The roof deck is made up of 4′-0″ (1.22 m) wide × ⅝″ (15.9 mm) thick, 5-ply CDX plywood (or OSB®, if permitted). The plywood (or OSB®) may be in either 8′-0″ (2.44 m) or 12′-0″ (3.66 m) lengths to be used to cover the joist system.

Built-Up Roofing (BUR)

See Sheet A-3, Architectural Plans, and appendix IV, the Project Manual. A roof is considered flat where no slope exists or is no more than a 3:12 slope. As noted in chapter 6, many varieties of roofing felts and procedures are found in BUR. The roofing system used for the plant roof is one of the asphalt multi-ply systems. The roof deck is plywood over which an insulating system is applied. The built-up roofing (BUR) system is applied over the insulation. The specifications note several roofing material manufacturers, but the system specified is a GAF (manufacturer's name) IO4G. The number and letter code is the manufacturer's way of identifying the system and materials as well as what base is used with the system. The symbols are identified as follows:

1. I = insulated deck
2. 0 = no base sheet
3. 4 = 4 plies of "Gafglas Ply 4" asphalt impregnated felts
4. G = gravel surfacing over the final layer and flood coat

The materials are applied in the following manner:

1. There are 4 applications (one over the insulated deck and three between roof plies) of Type II asphalt ply coat each at 25 lb/sq (11.34 kg/9.29 m^2)
2. There are 4 plies of asphalt-impregnated roll material
3. A flood-coat of 60 lb/sq (27.22 kg/9.29 m^2) is applied over all
4. 450 lb/sq (304.12 kg/9.29 m^2) of white gravel is embedded in the flood coat

DOORS AND WINDOWS

Refer to Door and Window Schedules, figures 12–3 and 12–4. There are three personnel doors and two overhead garage doors in the exterior masonry walls. The personnel doors are located on the north near the plant office and on the south next to the electrical switchgear. The third door is in the plant west wall where it enters the hall in the main office area. The overhead doors are located at the east end of the building at the loading dock. The personnel doors are hollow metal (HM) doors and frames. The garage doors are motorized 16 gauge metal roll-up doors with hollow metal (HM) steel frames.

FINISHES

Exterior Wall Finish

See figure 13–3, Exterior Insulation and Finish System. The precision CMU plant walls are to be covered with an exterior cement plaster system. The system is both aesthetic and insulating, thus the name given the system, *Exterior Insulation and Finish System (EIFS).* As discussed in chapter 6, the plastering is similar to the one-coat or two-coat stucco system without metal lath. The material is applied over a polyisocyanurate or polystyrene foam base with a fiber reinforcing mesh and a base coat used as an adhesive and sealer. The finish coat is then applied by either spray or brush.

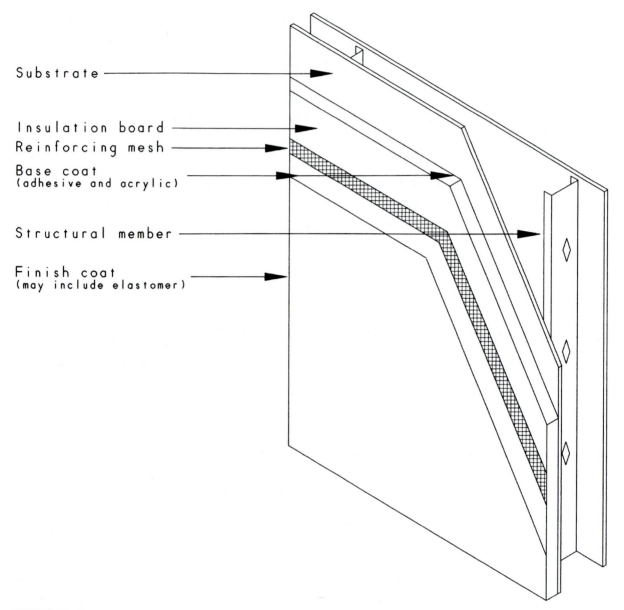

Substrate

Insulation board
Reinforcing mesh

Base coat
(adhesive and acrylic)

Structural member

Finish coat
(may include elastomer)

FIGURE 13–3
Exterior Insulation and Finish System

Drywall

Refer to the Finish schedule, figure 12–2. All interior walls and ceilings of the plant office, wash/restroom, and break room, are specified with one layer of ⅝″ (15.9 mm), type "X," GWB, extending the full height (9′-0″ [2.74 m]) of the walls and the full area of the ceilings.

Ceramic Tile

Refer to the Finish schedule, figure 12–2. 4″ (101.6 mm) square wall tiles are installed to a 6′-0″ (1.83 m) height on all walls in both the employee wash/restroom and the break room. The tiles are embedded in a thinset mortar and grouted. The colors are to be selected by the owner.

Wall Coverings

Refer to the Finish schedule, figure 12–2. The plant office and personnel area exterior wall face has a 7/16″ (1.11 cm) T-1-11 panelized siding, available in sizes of 4′ × 8′ (1.22 m × 2.44 m) to 4′ × 12′ (1.22 m × 3.66 m) sheets, installed over the plywood sheathing. T-1-11 has the appearance of a board-and-batten siding. Board-and-batten is an original aesthetic wood siding utilizing 2 × 12 (50.8 mm × 304.8 m), DF select, or Pine boards, installed vertically on the walls, with a 1 × 4 (25.4 mm × 101.6 mm) or 2 × 4 (50.8 mm × 101.6 mm) select grade member over the board seams (joints).

Painting

All exposed interior drywall at the plant office and personnel area walls and ceilings is to be painted. The interior masonry plant walls are painted with a sealer, primer, and oil-based latex finish coat. The underside of the roof structure is also painted to match. The exterior T-1-11 plant office finish is also to be painted to match the plant walls.

SPECIALTIES

See Sheet A-1, Architectural Floor Plan. There are lockers installed in the wash/restroom area along two walls, the east wall and the south wall next to the shower area.

HVAC

See Sheet M-1, Mechanical Plan and the Project Manual. There are five gas-fired air-handling heating units mounted on the roof. There are also two self-contained air-conditioning units (heat pumps). One, a 10-ton unit, is mounted on the plant roof. The second, a 5-ton unit, is mounted in the joists of the main office area. The ductwork for the plant area is fastened to the roof joists equally spaced on both sides of the plant. The ductwork for the office is laid in the joists or ceiling of the main office area. The plant office is to have a room air-conditioning unit at the discretion of the owner.

PLUMBING

See figure 13–4, Washbasin. There is one water closet, a shower, and one large washbasin in the restroom. This is also the locker room. The basin is a commercial/industrial type with a foot pedal operation so that several persons can wash simultaneously. There are also three floor drains installed, two in the wash/restroom (one in the shower area) and one in the break room.

FIGURE 13–4
Washbasin. Courtesy of International Sanitary Ware Manufacturing Co.

ELECTRICAL

Plant Power Supply

See Sheet E-1, Electrical Plan. The transformer outside the southwest corner of the plant supplies power to the 800A, 480VAC to 240/208VAC, switchgear located on the inside of the wall at the same location. The switchgear supplies power to all of the machinery—mixers, kilns, spray booth, and conveyors—that are located throughout the plant. One A-frame floor crane is included in the plant construction. The electrical contractor supplies the power to the crane when the manufacturer's erector representative completes the installation of the crane.

The switchgear controls each piece of equipment, or series of equipment, with a separate breaker on the main panel. The output power supplied to the plant is 3-phase 480/240VAC for the machinery. The plant receptacles are 1-phase 240VAC, 25A (minimum), three-wire, twist-lock receptacles. All convenience outlets are the standard 120VAC, 15A or 20A, duplex receptacles.

The electrical contractor is responsible for supplying and installing 240VAC, 20A (minimum) disconnects or outlets for connections to the motors for the overhead doors. The electrical or the door installers make the necessary connections to the motors.

Interior Plant Lighting

See Sheet E-1, Electrical Plan, Lighting Plan. Plant lighting is installed between the roof joists. The light fixtures are 400W, 208VAC, with high-intensity halogen vapor lamps, with self-contained transformers. There are thirty-seven (37) lamps as per the lighting plan. Lighting for the plant office, break room, and wash/restroom is supplied separately from the plant lighting. A sub-panel is installed for the circuitry for the office.

EQUIPMENT INSTALLATIONS

Manufacturing equipment and the location(s) are determined by the owner and are not included in the contract (N.I.C.). All equipment is to be installed by the equipment erector (a representative of the manufacturer) or by the owner after completion of the contract.

CHAPTER EXERCISES

Completion

1. The plant area has a concrete slab that is _____ psi (_____ kg/6.45 cm^2).

2. The _____ wall at the plant is a maximum 2'-0" (0.61 m) deep.

3. The loading dock is _____ (_____ m) deep from top to bottom.

4. The retaining walls on each side of the loading dock are _____ CMU.

5. The plant office has double layer roof installed with _____.

6. There are two _____ (_____ m) wide overhead doors.

7. The electrical switchgear is located at the _____ corner of the plant.

8. The masonry wall is 16'-0" (4.88 m) on the _____ side(s) of the plant.

9. There are _____ gas-fired heating units.

10. The steel columns used for the glu-lam beams are _____ (_____ mm) DIA.

11. _____ wood and steel joists are by Trus-Joist/MacMillan.

12. The size of the center glu-lam beam is _____ × _____ × _____ (_____ mm × _____ m × _____ m).

13. The plant office is finished with _____ siding.

14. There are a total of _____ windows in the plant office area.

15. The smaller glu-lams are _____ × _____ × _____
    (_____ mm × _____ m × _____ m).

True or False

T F   1. The crane is installed by the electrical contractor.

T F   2. The slab is divided into two separate placements, three areas
          in each.

T F   3. The concrete formwork system is a flying gang form system.

T F   4. The plant masonry walls are grout-capped.

T F   5. The plant is 86'-8" × 57'-4" (26.42 m × 17.47 m), excluding
          the loading dock.

T F   6. There are four personnel doors entering into the plant area.

T F   7. The owner supplies all equipment for the manufacturing area.

T F   8. The light fixtures for the plant area are incandescent 200W.

T F   9. The exterior walls of the plant are coated with an Exterior
          Insulating Finish System.

T F   10. The plant restroom has a standard vanity basin for washing.

T F   11. The exterior doors are all hollow metal and hollow-metal frame.

T F   12. The masonry walls are struck flush on the interior side for painting.

T F   13. The overhead doors are motor-driven.

T F   14. The length of the building including the loading dock is 97'-4"
          (29.67 m).

T F   15. The large square in the floor plan of the manufacturing area is
          the location of the paint booth.

Multiple Choice

_____   1. The electrical switchgear is located:
                a. Outside with the transformer
                b. Nearest to the loading dock
                c. Inside on the northwest corner of the plant area
                d. Inside on the southwest corner of the plant area

_____   2. The plumbing installation includes:
                a. Connections for a vanity basin and shower
                b. Connections for four floor drains
                c. Connections for two water closets
                d. None of the above

_____   3. The interior masonry plant walls are to be:
    a. Painted from floor to roof structure
    b. Left exposed with the natural masonry gray color
    c. Covered with drywall
    d. Covered with T-1-11 siding

_____   4. The roofing material for the plant roof is:
    a. GAF BUR I04G
    b. Insulated with pre-formed tapered insulation
    c. Both a and b
    d. Neither a nor b

_____   5. The plant office/personnel area is:
    a. Located on the northeast corner of the plant building
    b. Constructed of wood frame and siding
    c. Constructed with metal stud frame and exterior siding
    d. None of the above

_____   6. The break room is used for:
    a. The locker room
    b. The lunch room
    c. The dressing area
    d. None of the above

_____   7. The plant office:
    a. Is connected to the air-conditioning system
    b. Is to be supplied with a room air-conditioner
    c. Is located next to the main office entry door
    d. Is windowless

_____   8. The manufacturing area has:
    a. An overhead crane operated from the floor
    b. An overhead crane with overhead crane run and operator
    c. A floor crane operated from the floor
    d. No crane at all

_____   9. The mechanical contractor:
    a. Is responsible for both the gas and the electrical heating and cooling systems
    b. Is responsible for the installation of the plant air-conditioning equipment
    c. Must supply the electrical power to the air-conditioning equipment
    d. All of the above

_____   10. The slab for the plant:
    a. Is 6″ (152.4 mm) thick
    b. Has 6 × 6/W2.9-W2.9 (152.4 mm × 152.4 mm/W2.9-W2.9) WWF
    c. May have horizontal rebar along the slab perimeter
    d. All of the above

_____ 11. The exterior surface of the plant walls:
   a. Is painted to match the slumpstone color
   b. Is finished with a two-coat stucco system and painted
   c. Has an EIFS system installed over the masonry
   d. Is finished with a one-coat stucco system

_____ 12. The roof structure includes:
   a. Glue-laminated beams and TJI truss joists
   b. ½" (12.7 mm) CDX plywood deck with insulation and BUR over
   c. Both a and b
   d. Neither a nor b

_____ 13. The original name for T-1-11 siding is:
   a. Board and batten siding
   b. Shiplap siding
   c. V-groove siding
   d. Wood shingle siding

_____ 14. The loading dock area is:
   a. 6'-0" (1.83 m) above finish grade
   b. All concrete construction
   c. Concrete and masonry construction
   d. At grade level

_____ 15. The wall height at the west end of the plant is:
   a. 20'-0" (6.10 m)
   b. 20'-4" (6.20 m)
   c. 16'-0" (4.88 m)
   d. None of the above

Fundamental Everyday Mathematics

The purpose of this appendix is to offer the instructor and student an alternate chapter in the event that a simple mathematics review is required.

ADDITION AND SUBTRACTION

See figure 1. All forms of work require some mathematics, in the field or in the office. Each day the field crews are measuring for excavation and trenching layouts, for concrete, masonry, and lumber layouts, and for calculations of the number of courses for roof materials. This is true even for blueprint reading. When looking at a drawing, there are multiple measurements indicated.

Many of these measurements must be added or subtracted from one another to attain the correct measurement being sought for a layout or installation. For example, in figure 1, the measurement from the outside corner of the wall to the center of the window and the center of the door are shown in a frame wall. There is no measurement given for the wall on either the side of the window or the side of the door to the corners or between the door and window. The wall measurements are as follows:

> Window size: 4040 (4′-0″ × 4′-0″)
> Door size: 3068 (3′-0″ × 6′-8″)
> Wall measurement: 3′-6″ + 5′-6″ + 3′-0″ = 12′-0″

Therefore:

> 3′-6″ − ½ of window width − 2′-0″ = 1′-6″ to end of wall at window
> 3′-0″ − ½ of door width − 1′-6″ = 1′-6″ to end of wall at door
> 12′-0″ − (1′-6″ + 1′-6″ + 4′-0″ + 3′-0″) = 2′-0″ between door and window

The layout carpenter daily determines this sort of calculation either mentally, by hand, or with a calculator.

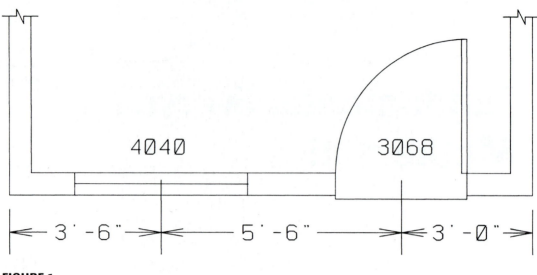

FIGURE 1
Partial Wall Plan

FRACTIONS AND DECIMALS

See appendix III, Inch to Fraction or Decimal Part of a Foot. The chart in appendix III shows both the fractional and decimal equivalent of inches per foot. Like the chart, the numbers as used above can be written in the same two ways. The average calculator uses the decimal system. When calculating by hand (written), the fraction is often used. For example, the numbers could be written as follows:

3'-6" = 3$^{1}/_{2}$ ft (fraction) or 3.5 ft (decimal)

10'-4" = 10$^{1}/_{3}$ ft (fraction) or 10.33 ft (decimal)

5'-7" = 5$^{7}/_{12}$ ft (fraction) or 5.58 ft (decimal)

RATIO AND PROPORTION (MULTIPLICATION AND DIVISION)

One use of fractions in construction in the field is the almost daily application of the ratio and proportion formulas (equations). The dictionary defines a ratio as "a fixed relation in degree, number, and so on, between two similar things; proportion; in mathematics, the quotient of one quantity divided by another of the same kind, and usually expressed as a fraction." When two such ratios, or fractions, are placed in a format forming an equation, they become one of the common simple algebraic expressions in any of the following ways:

a:b = c:d   a/b = c/d   a÷b = c÷d

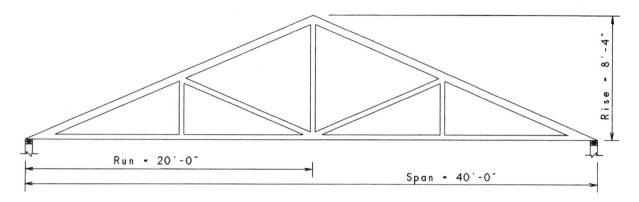

FIGURE 2
RISE and RUN

See figure 2. The proportion formula can be readily used when three of the four parts of the equation are known. One of the most common uses for proportion equations is found in framing for roof structure calculations for **rise and run.** For example, the **span** in a transverse section of a $^5/_{12}$ gable is 40 lf (lineal feet). The run of a true gable is one half ($^1/_2$) the distance of the span. With the proportion formula (equation), the *rise* of the gable at the ridge can be determined. The rise is determined as 8′-4″ as follows:

Span (exterior bearing wall to opposite exterior bearing wall) = 40′-0″

Run ($^1/_2$ of the span) = 20′-0″

The roof slope is $^5/_{12}$ (5 unit rise for each equal 12 units horizontally) = $^5/_{12}$

The denominator (bottom number of the slope fraction)—$^5/_{12}$—is the run (horizontal measurement) and the numerator (top number) is the rise (vertical measurement). Since the other measurements (span and run) are in feet, the unit measure for the $^5/_{12}$ is also converted to feet as follows:

5 lf/12 lf

As noted above, the run is the horizontal measurement from exterior bearing wall to the center (ridge) of the gable. The calculation is as follows:

$$\frac{a}{b} = \frac{c}{d}$$

Where:

a = 5 lf

b = 12 lf

c = the unknown (x lf)

d = 20 lf

Therefore:

$$\frac{5 \text{ lf}}{12 \text{ lf}} = \frac{x \text{ lf}}{20 \text{ lf}}$$

The numerator on one side of the equation is multiplied by the denominator (called cross-multiplication) on the opposite side as follows:

5 lf · 20 lf = x lf · 12 lf

The unknown part of the equation (x) is to be left on one side by itself. This is done by dividing both sides of the equation by the 12 as follows:

100 lf ÷ 12 lf = (x lf · 12 lf) ÷ 12 lf

Since 12 lf ÷ 12 lf = 1 lf, the equation becomes:

100 lf ÷ 12 lf = x lf · 1 lf

or

100 lf ÷ 12 lf = x lf

Thus:

x lf = 8.33 lf or $8^{1}/_{3}$ feet or 8′-4″ rise

It should be noted here that the angle formed at the junction of a rise and run is a right angle (90°). This is important for calculations of rafter lengths. The use of the right angle is discussed in the section making use of the Pythagorean theorem.

Proportional calculations can be used in other situations as well. For example, a plot plan in a blueprint is the only place that indicates a retaining wall along one of the property lines. The information on the plan indicates that the height of the wall is 6.0′ (civil engineering style measurement) above grade. No length is indicated. How can the length be determined? There are two solutions to the problem. *The best possible solution is to get an answer from the engineer or architect.* Verify that the wall exists and, if so, ascertain if there is any other information needed.

Where time may be of the essence and the information is not available, the alternative is to use the proportion formula. This is one of the rare times when "scaling" (measuring with a rule or scale of some kind) is allowed. The architectural, engineering, and estimating professions frown on this procedure except in this type of situation. **The measurements indicated on a plan will otherwise take precedence over scaling in all instances.**

The plan is scaled at 1″ = 20.0′. The wall measures $3^{1}/_{2}$″ on the plan as determined by use of a tape measure. The inches are broken down into any desired increments (for example, $^{1}/_{8}$″, $^{1}/_{4}$″, $^{1}/_{2}$″) to produce a fraction. This fraction is used in the proportion calculation. In the example, the inches are converted into $^{1}/_{8}$″ increments. The following are part of the proportion formula: that fractional value calculated in the conversion and the scale of the plan (in this case 1″ = 20.0′). The 20 lf is the horizontal measurement of the scale and is, therefore, the denominator of the fraction with an unknown value for the numerator. The 8 from the $^{1}/_{8}$″ breakdown is the denominator of the other fraction in the proportion. The length of the wall is determined to be 70 lf:

$3^{1}/_{2}$″ = ([3 · 2] + 1) = $^{7}/_{2}$

There are eight $^{1}/_{8}$″ increments in each 1″, therefore:

$$^7/_2'' \cdot {}^4/_8'' = {}^{(7 \times 4)}/_8'' = {}^{28}/_8''$$

The formula is:

$$\frac{a}{b} = \frac{c}{d}$$

Where:

a = 28 (convert to lf)

b = 8 (convert to lf)

c = the unknown (x lf)

d = 20 lf

Therefore:

$$\frac{28 \text{ lf}}{8 \text{ lf}} = \frac{x \text{ lf}}{20 \text{ lf}}$$

28 lf · 20 lf = x lf · 8 lf

560 lf ÷ 8 lf = (x lf · 8 lf) ÷ 8 lf

x lf = 70 lf

The answer for this proportion calculation will be identical for any of the above fractions suggested. For example, the $3^1/_2''$ in $^1/_4''$ increments = $^{14}/_4''$, and in $^1/_2''$ increments = $^7/_2''$, and so on.

PYTHAGOREAN THEOREM (3-4-5 SYSTEM)

See figure 3. Another commonly used formula in construction is the Pythagorean theorem. Most field personnel use this formula frequently and probably never know it. The system is called the *3-4-5 system*. This system is used to determine whether a true right angle exists at a foundation or slab, or whether the framing corner is square, horizontally and/or vertically. The layout is stated as follows: If one side measures 3 units (inches, feet, and so on) and the perpendicular side

FIGURE 3
Pythagorean Theorem
(3-4-5 SYSTEM)

5 (c)

4 (a)

3 (b)

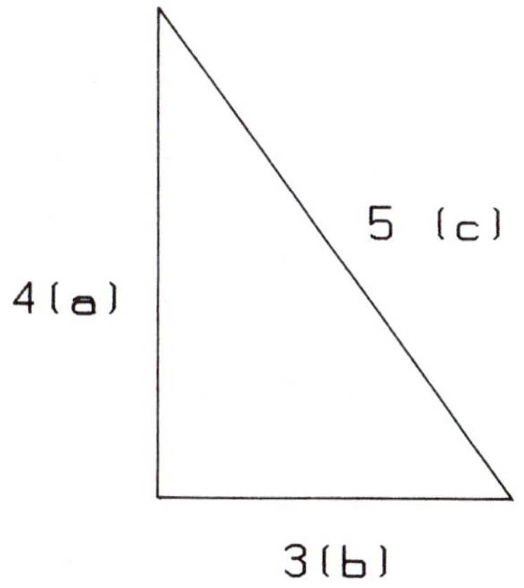

measures 4 units of the same measure, then the diagonal between the ends of them must equal 5 units of the same measure. In other words, the theorem states that "the sum of the squares of two sides of a right triangle is equal to the square of the hypotenuse (diagonal length opposite the right angle) of the triangle." The *square* of a number is the number multiplied by itself, such as $1 \cdot 1$ or $2 \cdot 2$. It is written mathematically as follows:

$$c^2 = a^2 + b^2$$

Where:

c^2 = the hypotenuse (diagonal)

a^2 = the one side

b^2 = the perpendicular side

In the 3-4-5 system, the theorem is determined as follows:

c^2 = 5 (diagonal)

a^2 = 4 (perpendicular or vertical [altitude])

b^2 = 3 (base or horizontal)

Therefore, if:

$$c^2 = a^2 + b^2$$

Then:

$$(5 \cdot 5) = (4 \cdot 4) + (3 \cdot 3)$$
$$25 = 16 + 9$$
$$25 = 25$$

Thus a true right triangle (or a true right angle) is formed. As previously mentioned, this formula is also used for determining the lengths of rafters. The truss manufacturer uses this formula along with the rise and run for this purpose. Carpentry contractors also use the formula for determining the lengths of conventional rafters. As an example, with the run and rise determined in the previous calculation, the rafter length can be calculated as follows:

Rise = 8.33 lf

Run = 20 lf

Rafter length = ?

Using the Pythagorean theorem, the rafter length is calculated as follows:

Where:

$$c^2 = a^2 + b^2$$
$$c^2 = (8.33 \text{ lf})^2 + (20 \text{ lf})^2$$
$$c^2 = 69.39 \text{ ft}^2 + 400 \text{ ft}^2$$
$$c^2 = 469.39 \text{ ft}^2$$

The square root (c) = 21.67 lf

Lumber is purchased in even lineal-foot increments, therefore, the length purchased is 22 lf.

LINEAL (LINEAR) MEASURE

See figure 4. Lineal measurements for determining perimeters (length around), heights, and depths of properties, buildings, rooms, and so on, are basic to construction calculations. To obtain square measure, two lineal measurements are required; for volume, three lineal measurements are required.

For example, an architect is preparing a conceptual estimate for an owner. Part of the information to be determined includes the size of the slab and the exterior wall framing for "shell" construction (exterior walls only). The rectangular building footprint measures 100 lf by 73 lf. The slab area and volume, the quantity of plate stock, sill plate, and studs can be determined quickly. All of the measurements start with the lineal feet of perimeter or the lengths of two sides as follows:

100 lf + 100 lf + 73 lf + 73 lf = }
or   }346 *lf*
(100 lf · 2) ÷ (73 lf · 2)   = }

The concrete slab for the structure is 6″ thick.

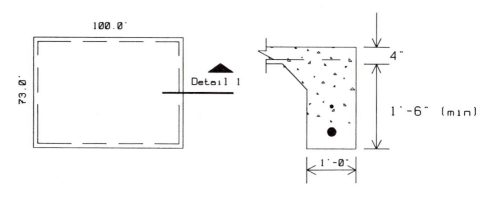

FIGURE 4
Lineal Measure

METRIC CONVERSIONS

See figure 5 and appendix III. All federal government work since 1994 requires plans to be dimensioned in metrics. It is hoped that all projects will be in metrics eventually, since most of the world uses them. To assist in calculations with the most common metric measures converted from metrics to equivalent English (American) measures, use the following conversions:

Lineal Measure	Square Measure	Volume Measure
1 in = 2.54 cm	$1 \text{ in}^2 = 6.45 \text{ cm}^2$	$1 \text{ in}^3 = 16.38 \text{ cm}^3$
or 25.4 mm		
1 ft = 0.3048 m	$1 \text{ ft}^2 = 0.0929 \text{ m}^2$	$1 \text{ ft}^3 = 0.0283 \text{ m}^3$

The metric equivalents of mass and liquid volume are calculated as follows:

1 lb = 0.454 kg; 2.2 lb = 1 kg   3.79 gal = 1 L (liter); 1 gal = 0.264 L (liter)

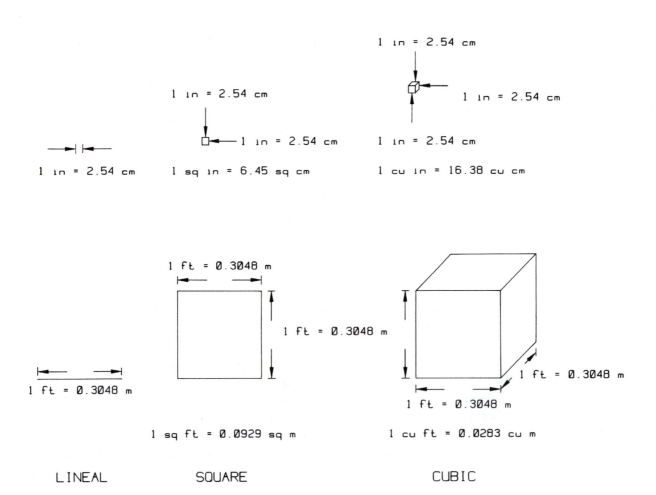

FIGURE 5

English/Metric Conversions

Note: in^2 = square inches (sq in); in^3 = cubic inches (cu in); ft^2 = square feet (sq ft); ft^3 = cu ft (cu ft).

See appendix III, Rebar (Standard Sizes). One other frequently noted measure is in reference to reinforcement steel bar (rebar). Rebar is sized in $\frac{1}{8}''$ diameter (DIA) increments. For example, a #4 bar = $\frac{4}{8}''$ or $\frac{1}{2}''$ DIA.

Many specifications refer to the laps in rebar in terms to the number of diameters of the rebar. The specification for standard footing installations may state "2–#4 rebar shall be installed continuously in the footing. There shall be 48 diameter laps at all ends of the rebar and at the corners." The length of the laps are calculated as follows:

$$\#4 = \frac{4}{8}'' \ (\frac{1}{2}'')$$

$$\frac{4}{8}'' \cdot 48 \text{ laps} = 4'' \cdot 6 = 24'' \text{ or } 2'\text{-}0'' \text{ laps}$$

ADDITIONAL EXERCISES

Hint: When calculating combinations of addition and subtraction, *add* all of the positives (+) together, then *add* all of the negatives together (−), then *subtract* the negative (−) total from the positive (+) total.

Addition and Subtraction

The property measures as follows:

North property line	= 766.0′
East property line	= 361.5′
South property line	= 738.67′
West property line	= 370.0′

1. Determine the total lineal feet of the perimeter of the property.
2. Determine the combined east and west property line length.
3. The slab in figure 4 measures a total of _____ lf.
4. The depth of the slab and footing in figure 4 is _____ deep.
5. Subtract the combined east/west footage in question 2 from the total lineal feet of the plat referred to in question 1.
6. The structure that is to be built on the slab in figure 4 requires 346 lf of sill plate fastened to the slab. Deduct the quantity of sill plate required for two sides of the slab, one long side and one short side.
7. There are 692 lf of double top plate required for the perimeter walls. Determine the quantity required for the same two sides as for the sill plate in question 6.
8. A delivery of lumber is made that includes 31,368 lf of 2 × 4, DF #2. The load also includes some 2 × 6, DF #2. The total lineal feet of lumber delivered is 104,572 lf. Determine the quantity of 2 × 6 delivered.

Fractions and Decimals

9. Add the following fractions:

$1/2'' + 4^1/4'' + 21^1/4'' + 5/16'' + 1/8'' =$

10. Subtract the following fractions:

$52^7/8'' - 12^1/2'' - 10^1/4'' - 19^1/8'' =$

11. Determine the total of the following:

$175^1/3 \text{ lf} + 300 \text{ lf} - 275^3/4 \text{ lf} =$

12. Calculate the answer for the following problem:

$12.66 \text{ lf} + 175.5 \text{ lf} - 90.99 \text{ lf} + 67.66 \text{ lf} - 200.17 \text{ lf} =$

Hint: When calculating combinations of addition and subtraction, *add* all of the positives (+) together; *add* all of the negatives (−) together; then *subtract* the negative (−) total from the positive (+) total.

Multiplication and Division

Hint: When calculating combinations of multiplication and division, *multiply* first, then *divide*.

13. $1^1/4'' \cdot 1/2'' =$
14. $75.35 \text{ lf} \cdot 131.8 \text{ lf} \div 52.1 \text{ lf} =$
15. $21^3/4'' \div 2'' \cdot 44^1/4'' =$
16. $357.08 \text{ lf} \cdot 260.01 \text{ lf} =$
17. $357.08 \text{ km} \div 260.01 \text{ km} =$
18. $5,286 \text{ ft} \cdot 2 = \underline{\hspace{1cm}} \text{ mi}$
19. $350 \text{ cu ft (ft}^3) \div 27 \text{ cu ft (ft}^3) = \underline{\hspace{1cm}} \text{ cu yd (yd}^3)$

Metrics

1. The dimension shown on a plan is 101′-10″. What is the metric equivalent?
2. A plot plan measures 245′-0″ × 133′-0″. Calculate the area.
3. Calculate the same area in metrics.
4. A mass excavation is 60′-0″ × 40′-0″ × 10′-0″. Calculate the volume in cubic feet and cubic yards. (1 cu yd = 27 cu ft).
5. Calculate the same volume in cubic meters.

General

1. A specification for rebar notes that the vertical wall rebar is a #8 that must be lapped 72 bar diameters. Determine the size of the lap.
2. The rise of a sloped roof is 14′-0″ and the run is 24′-0″. Calculate the length of a rafter excluding any overhang.
3. The lengths of a rectangular structure are 161 lf by 65 lf. Calculate the lineal feet of the perimeter.

4. Calculate the area of the flat plane of the structure in question 3.

5. Calculate the volume of concrete (in cubic yards) necessary for this area if the slab is 6″ thick. Note: $27 \text{ ft}^3 = 1 \text{ yd}^3$.

Construction Abbreviations

A	area	CJ	ceiling joist, control joint
AB	anchor bolt	CKT	circuit (electrical)
AC	alternate current	CLG	ceiling
A/C	air conditioning	CMU	concrete masonry unit
ACT	acoustical ceiling tile	CO	cleanout (plumbing)
A.F.F.	above finish floor	COL	column
AGGR	aggregate	CONC	concrete
AIA	American Institute of Architects	CONST	construction
		CONTR	contractor
AL, ALUM	aluminum	CU FT (ft³)	cubic foot (feet)
AMP	ampere	CU IN (in³)	cubic inch(es)
APPROX	approximate	CU YD (yd³)	cubic yard(s)
ASPH	asphalt		
ASTM	American Society for Testing Materials	d	pennyweight (nail)
		DC	direct current (elec.)
AWG	American wire gauge	DET	detail
		DIA	diameter
BD	board	DIAG	diagonal
BD FT (BF)	board foot (feet)	DIM	dimension
BLDG	building	DN	down
BLK	black, block	DO	ditto (same as)
BLKG	blocking	DS	downspout
BM	board measure	DWG	drawing
CC	center to center, cubic centimeter	E	East
		EA	each
CEM	cement	ELEC	electric, electrical
CER	ceramic	ELEV	elevation, elevator
CFM	cubic feet per minute	ENCL	enclosure
CIP	cast-in-place, concrete-in-place	EXCAV	excavate, excavation

EXT	exterior	KG	kilogram
FDN	foundation	KL	kiloliter
FIN	finish	KM	kilometer
FIN FLR	finish floor	KW	kilowatt
FIN GRD	finish grade	KWH	kilowatt-hour
FL, FLR	floor	L	left, line
FLG	flooring	LAU	laundry
FLUOR	fluorescent	LAV	lavatory
FOB	free-on-board, factory-on-board	LBR	labor
		LDG	landing, leading
FOM	face of masonry	LDR	leader
FOS	face of stud, flush on slab	LEV/LVL	level
FT	foot, feet	LIN FT (LF)	lineal foot (feet)
FTG	footing	LGTH	length
FURN	furnishing, furnace	LH	left hand
FX GL (FX)	fixed glass	LITE/LT	light (window pane)
GA	gauge	MAT'L	material
GAL	gallon	MAX	maximum
GALV	galvanize(d)	MBF/MBM	thousand board feet, thousand board measure
GD	ground (earth/electric)		
GI	galvanized iron	MECH	mechanical
GL	glass	MISC	miscellaneous
GL BLK	glass block	MK	mark (identifier)
GLB, GLU-LAM	glue-laminated beam	MO	momentary (electrical contact), masonry opening
GRD	grade, ground		
GWB	gypsum wall board		
GYP	gypsum	N	North
HB	hose bibb	NEC	National Electric Code
HDR	header	NIC	not in contract
HDW	hardware	NOM	nominal
HGT/HT	height	O/A	overall (measure)
HM	hollow metal	O.C. (O/C)	on center
HORIZ	horizontal	OD	outside diameter
HP	horsepower	OH	overhead
HWH	hot water heater	O/H	overhang (eave line)
ID	inside diameter	OPG	opening
IN	inch(es)	OPP	opposite
INSUL	insulation	PC	piece
INT	interior	PLAS	plastic
		PLAST	plaster
J, JST	joist	PLT	plate (framing)
JT	joint		

PR	pair	STL	steel
PREFAB	prefabricate(d)(tion)	STR/ST	street
PTN	partition	STRUCT	structural
PVC	polyvinylchloride pipe	SUSP CLG	suspended ceiling
		SYM	symbol, symmetric
QT	quart	SYS	system
QTY	quantity		
		T&G	tongue and groove
R	right	THK	thick
RD	road, round, roof drain	TOB	top of beam
REBAR	reinforced steel bar	TOC	top of curb
RECEPT	receptacle	TOF	top of footing
REINF	reinforce(ment)	TOL	top of ledger
REQ'D	required	TOP	top of parapet
RET	retain(ing), return	TOS	top of steel
RF	roof	TR	tread, transition
RFG	roofing (materials)	TRK	track, truck
RH	right hand	TYP	typical
S	South	UF	underground feeder (electrical)
SCH/SCHED	schedule		
SECT	section	USE	underground service entrance cable (electrical)
SERV	service (utility)		
SEW	sewer		
SHTHG	sheathing	W	West
SIM	similar	w/	with
SP	soil pipe (plumbing)	w/o	without
SPEC	specification	WC	water closet (toilet)
SQ FT (ft^2)	square foot (feet)	WDW	window
SQ IN (in^2)	inch(es)	WI	wrought iron
SQ YD (yd^2)	square yard(s)	WP	waterproof, weatherproof
STA	station	WT/WGT	weight
STD	standard		
STIR	stirrup (rebar)	YD	yard
		Z	zinc

SYMBOLS

&	and	″	ditto, inch, -es
∠	angle	′	foot, feet
@	at	%	percent
#	number, pound	ø	diameter

Reference Tables

TABLE 1–1
Inch to Fraction or Decimal Part of a Foot

Inch	Fraction	Decimal
1″	$\frac{1}{12}$ ft	0.083 or 0.08 ft
2″	$\frac{1}{6}$ ft	0.166 or 0.17 ft
3″	$\frac{1}{4}$ ft	0.25 ft
4″	$\frac{1}{3}$ ft	0.33 ft (0.34 ft)
5″	$\frac{5}{12}$ ft	0.417 or 0.42 ft
6″	$\frac{1}{2}$ ft	0.5 ft
7″	$\frac{7}{12}$ ft	0.583 or 0.58 ft
8″	$\frac{2}{3}$ ft	0.66 ft (0.67 ft)
9″	$\frac{3}{4}$ ft	0.75 ft
10″	$\frac{5}{6}$ ft	0.833 or 0.83 ft
11″	$\frac{11}{12}$ ft	0.916 or 0.92 ft

TABLE 1–2
English to Metric Equivalents

English			Metric
Lineal			
	1 in	=	25.4 mm
	1 ft	=	0.3048 m
	1 yd	=	0.9144 m
	1 mi	=	1.60934 km
Volume			
	1 qt (liquid)	=	0.946353 L
	1 gal	=	0.00378541 m^3
Weight			
	1 oz (avdp)	=	28.3495 gm
	1 lb (avdp)	=	0.453592 kg
Power			
	1 HP	=	0.7457 kw

TABLE 1–3
Metric to English Equivalents

Metric		English
Lineal Measure		
1 mm	=	0.03937 in
1 cm	=	0.3937 in
1 m	=	39.37 in
1 m	=	3.28084 ft
1 m	=	1.09361 yd
1 km	=	0.621371 mi
Area		
1 cm^2	=	0.15499 in^2
1 m^2	=	1,549.9 in^2
1 m^2	=	10.7632 ft^2
1 km^2	=	0.386 mi^2
Volume		
1 cc (cm^3)	=	0.6102 in^3
1 L	=	1.05669 qt (liquid)
1 m^3	=	35.314 ft^3
1 m^3	=	1.308 yd^3
1 m^3	=	264.172 gal
Weight		
1 kg	=	2.2046 lb
1 metric ton	=	2,204.6 lb
Power		
1 kw	=	1.34102 HP

TABLE 1–4
Drawing Scales

Plan Use	Ratio	Metric Length	English Equivalent (approx)
Details:			
	1:1	1000 mm = 1 m	12″ = 1′-0″ (Full scale)
	1:5	200 mm = 1 m	3″ = 1′-0″
	1:10	100 mm = 1 m	1½″ = 1′-0″
	1:20	50 mm = 1 m	½″ = 1′-0″
Floor Plans:			
	1:40	25 mm = 1 m	⅜″ = 1′-0″
	1:50	20 mm = 1 m	¼″ = 1′-0″
Plot Plans:			
	1:80	13.3 mm = 1 m	³⁄₁₆″ = 1′-0″
	1:100	12.5 mm = 1 m	⅛″ = 1′-0″
	1:200	5 mm = 1 m	1″ = 20′-0″
Plat Plans:			
	1:500	2 mm = 1 m	1″ = 50′-0″
City Maps (and larger):			
	1:1250	0.8 mm = 1 m	1″ = 125′-0″
	1:2500	0.4 mm = 1 m	1″ = 250′-0″

TABLE 1–5

Masonry Dimensions

English to Metric						
BRICK						
Nominal English Sizes				Nominal Metric Sizes		
W	H	L		W	H	L
Modular	4″	8″	8″	100mm	200mm	200mm
Roman	4″	6″	12″	100mm	150mm	300mm
Norman	4″	8″	12″	100mm	200mm	300mm
SCR	6″	8″	12″	150mm	200mm	300mm
CMU						
Stretcher	8″	8″	16″	200mm	200mm	400mm

TABLE 1–6

Rebar (Standard Sizes)

Bar	Diameter (Size)
#2	$\frac{1}{4}$″
#3	$\frac{3}{8}$″
#4	$\frac{1}{2}$″
#5	$\frac{5}{8}$″
#6	$\frac{3}{4}$″
#7	$\frac{7}{8}$″
#8	1″
#9	$1\frac{1}{8}$″
#10	$1\frac{1}{4}$″
#11	$1\frac{3}{8}$″
#14	$1\frac{3}{4}$″
#18	$2\frac{1}{4}$″

TABLE 1–6A

Welded Wire Fabric

Roll	Sheet
6×6 - W1.4 $\times$ W1.4	6×6 - W2.0 $\times$ W2.0
6×6 - W2.9 $\times$ W2.9	6×6 - W2.9 $\times$ W2.9
6×6 - W4.0 $\times$ W4.0	6×6 - W4.0 $\times$ W4.0
6×6 - W5.5 $\times$ W5.5	4×4 - W1.4 $\times$ W1.4
4×4 - W1.4 $\times$ W1.4	4×4 - W2.9 $\times$ W2.9
4×4 - W2.9 $\times$ W2.9	
4×4 - W4.0 $\times$ W4.0	

If the letter designation D is added, the fabric is deformed similar to rebar.

WWF is made into sheets or rolls depending upon the size and quantity required.

TABLE 1–7
Framing Ratios Per Stud Spacing

Spacing	Constant	Decimal Equivalent
12″ (304.8 mm) O/C	1	1.000
16″ (406.4 mm) O/C	¾	0.750
18″ (457.2 mm) O/C	⅔	0.667
20″ (508 mm) O/C	⅗	0.600
24″ (609.6 mm) O/C	½	0.500
32″ (812.8 mm) O/C	⅜	0.375
36″ (914.4 mm) O/C	⅓	0.333

TABLE 1–8
Nail Sizes

2d: 2 pennyweight × 1″ long
4d: 4 pennyweight × 1¼″ long
6d: 6 pennyweight × 1½″ long
8d: 8 pennyweight × 1¾″ long
10d: 10 pennyweight × 2″ long
16d: 16 pennyweight × 3″ long
20d: 20 pennyweight × 3½″ long
straw nail = 10d × 6″ long
spike = any nail 20d or larger × 6″ long

TABLE 1–8A
Surface Finishing Abbreviations, Yard
and Structural Lumber

Abbreviation	Definition
S1S	Smooth surface, one side
S1S1E	Smooth surface, one side, one end
S1S2E	Smooth surface, one side, two ends
S2S	Smooth surface, two sides
S2S1E	Smooth surface, two sides, one end
S2S2E	Smooth surface, two sides, two ends
S3S	Smooth surface, three sides
S3S1E	Smooth surface, three sides, one end
S3S2E	Smooth surface, three sides, two ends
S4S	Smooth surface, four sides
S4S1E	Smooth surface, four sides, one end
S4S2E	Smooth surface, four sides, two ends
R/E	Resawn (same as S1S or S1S2E)
R/O or R/S	Rough sawn (no smooth surfaces)

TABLE 1–9

Glue-Laminated Timber Sizing

Width		Depth	
Nominal	**Actual**	**Nominal**	**Actual**
3″	2¼″	6″	5⅛″
4″	3⅛″	8″	7½″
6″	5⅛″	10″	8¾″
8″	6¾″		
10″	8¾″		
12″	10¾″		
14″	12¼″		
16″	14¼″		

TABLE 1–10

Light Gauge Framing, Size and Weight per Lineal Foot

Size (Inches)	Metal Gauge	Net Weight (lb/lf)
Studs		
1½″	25	0.443
1½″	20	0.700
2½″	25	0.509
2½″	20	0.810
3″	25	0.555
3″	20	0.875
3¼″	25	0.575
3¼″	20	0.910
3½″	25	0.597
3½″	20	0.944
3⅝″	25	0.608
3⅝″	20	0.964
4″	25	0.641
4″	20	1.014
5½″	20	1.240
6″	20	1.290
Joists		
6″	20	1.486
6″	18	1.889
6″	16	2.339
6″	14	2.914
8″	18	2.215
8″	16	2.411
10″	16	3.142
10″	14	3.908

Courtesy of American Studco Corp.

TABLE 1–11
Roof Slope Table

Slope Ratio	Pitch Ratio	Conversion Factor	Waste Factor	
3:12	$\frac{1}{8}$	1.03	.05	1.08
3.5:12	$\frac{7}{24}$	1.04	.05	1.09
4:12	$\frac{1}{6}$	1.05	.05	1.10
4.5:12	$\frac{9}{48}$	1.06	.05	1.11
5:12	$\frac{5}{24}$	1.08	.05	1.13
5.5:12	$\frac{11}{48}$	1.10	.05	1.15
6:12	$\frac{1}{4}$	1.12	.05	1.17
6.5:12	$\frac{13}{48}$	1.14	.05	1.19
7:12	$\frac{7}{24}$	1.16	.05	1.21
7.5:12	$\frac{15}{48}$	1.18	.05	1.23
8:12	$\frac{1}{3}$	1.20	.05	1.25
10:12	$\frac{5}{12}$	1.30	.05	1.35
12:12	$\frac{1}{2}$	1.45	.05	1.50
18:12	$\frac{3}{4}$	2.0	.05	2.05
24:12	1	2.0	.05	2.05

TABLE 1–12
Numbers and Their Squares and Approximate Square Roots

Number	Square	Sq. Root	Number	Square	Sq. Root
1	1	1.000	51	2601	7.141
2	4	1.414	52	2704	7.211
3	9	1.732	53	2809	7.280
4	16	2.000	54	2916	7.348
5	25	2.236	55	3025	7.416
6	36	2.449	56	3136	7.483
7	49	2.646	57	3249	7.550
8	64	2.828	58	3364	7.616
9	81	3.000	59	3481	7.681
10	100	3.162	60	3600	7.746
11	121	3.317	61	3721	7.810
12	144	3.464	62	3844	7.874
13	169	3.606	63	3969	7.937
14	196	3.742	64	4096	8.000
15	225	3.873	65	4225	8.062
16	256	4.000	66	4356	8.124
17	289	4.123	67	4489	8.185
18	324	4.243	68	4624	8.246
19	361	4.359	69	4761	8.307
20	400	4.472	70	4900	8.367
21	441	4.583	71	5041	8.426
22	484	4.690	72	5184	8.485
23	529	4.796	73	5329	8.544
24	576	4.899	74	5476	8.602

TABLE 1–12 (Contd.)

Number	Square	Sq. Root	Number	Square	Sq. Root
25	625	5.000	75	5625	8.660
26	676	5.099	76	5776	8.718
27	729	5.196	77	5929	8.775
28	784	5.292	78	6084	8.832
29	841	5.385	79	6241	8.888
30	900	5.477	80	6400	8.944
31	961	5.568	81	6561	9.000
32	1024	5.657	82	6724	9.055
33	1089	5.745	83	6889	9.110
34	1156	5.831	84	7056	9.165
35	1225	5.916	85	7225	9.220
36	1296	6.000	86	7396	9.274
37	1369	6.083	87	7569	9.327
38	1444	6.164	88	7744	9.381
39	1521	6.245	89	7921	9.434
40	1600	6.325	90	8100	9.487
41	1681	6.403	91	8381	9.539
42	1764	6.481	92	8464	9.592
43	1849	6.557	93	8649	9.644
44	1936	6.633	94	8836	9.695
45	2025	6.708	95	9025	9.747
46	2116	6.782	96	9216	9.798
47	2209	6.852	97	9409	9.849
48	2304	6.928	98	9604	9.899
49	2401	7.000	99	9801	9.950
50	2500	7.071	100	10000	10.000

MASONRY MORTAR AND GROUT TABLES

Mortar, Quantity per Unit Masonry

1 cubic yard (cuyd) covers:	
Unit Size	Quantity
8 × 16 (203.3 mm × 406.4 mm) CMU	112.5 units
12 × 16 (304.8 mm × 406.4 mm) CMU	96 units
3c-8 (2⅔″ × 2⅔″ × 8″) SRC Brick	1,877 units
(67.56 mm × 67.56 mm × 203.2 mm)	

Grout, Quantity per Vertical Rebar Spacing

Vertical Wall Spacing	% of Wall Area Covered
16″ (406.4 mm) O.C.	50%
24″ (609.6 mm) O.C.	33.33%
32″ (812.8 mm) O.C.	25%
40″ (1016 mm) O.C.	20%
48″ (1219.2 mm) O.C.	16.67%

Masonry Unit Factors

Type of Unit	Size	Factor
Brick (3c-8)	2⅔″ × 2⅔″ × 8″	0.1294
	(67.56 mm × 67.56 mm × 203.2 mm)	
Brick	4″ × 4″ × 8″	0.2222
	(101.6 mm × 101.6 mm × 203.2 mm)	
Brick	4″ × 4″ × 12″	0.3333
	(101.6 mm × 101.6 mm × 304.8 mm)	
Concrete Masonry Unit	4″ × 4″ × 8″	0.2222
	(101.6 mm × 101.6 mm × 203.2 mm)	
Concrete Masonry Unit	6″ × 6″ × 8″	0.3333
	(152.4 mm × 152.4 mm × 203.2 mm)	
Concrete Masonry Unit	6″ × 6″ × 12″	0.5000
	(152.4 mm × 152.4 mm × 304.8 mm)	
Concrete Masonry Unit	6″ × 6″ × 16″	0.6666
	(152.4 mm × 152.4 mm × 406.4 mm)	
Concrete Masonry Unit	8″ × 4″ × 9″	0.2500
	(203.2 mm × 101.6 mm × 228.6 mm)	
Concrete Masonry Unit	8″ × 8″ × 8″	0.4444
	(203.2 mm × 203.2 mm × 203.2 mm)	
Concrete Masonry Unit	8″ × 8″ × 10″	0.5555
	(203.2 mm × 203.2 mm × 245 mm)	
Concrete Masonry Unit	8″ × 8″ × 12″	0.6666
	(203.2 mm × 203.2 mm × 304.8 mm)	
Concrete Masonry Unit	8″ × 8″ × 16″	0.8888
	(203.2 mm × 203.2 mm × 406.4 mm)	
Concrete Masonry Unit	12″ × 12″ × 12″	1.0000
	(302.8 mm × 304.8 mm × 304.8 mm)	

Grade Designation For Dimension Lumber

Category	Grades	Sizes
Light Framing	Construction, Standard	2″ to 4″ thick
	Utility, Economy	2″ to 4″ wide
Studs	Stud, Economy	2″ to 4″ thick
		2″ to 4″ wide
Structural Light Framing	Select Structural	2″ to 4″ thick
	Nos. 1, 2, 3 Economy	2″ to 4″ wide
Framing Appearance	Appearance	2″ to 4″ thick
		2″ and wider
Structural Joists and Planks	Select Structural Nos.	2″ to 4″ thick
	1, 2, 3 Economy	6″ and wider
Decking	Select Decking	2″ to 4″ thick
	Commercial Decking	4″ and wider
Beams, Stringers, Posts and Timbers	Select Structural	5″ and thicker
	Nos. 1, 2, 3	5″ and wider

Grade Designation For Douglas Fir (DF) and Pine Appearance Grade

Category	Douglas Fir (Finish Grades)	Pine (Select Grades)
Clears	C and better (Superior Finish)	C and better Selects
	D Prime Finish	
Factory		
Douglas Fir	Molding	Molding
Shop Grade	No. 3 Clear	No. 3 Clear
(Material to be	Nos. 1, 2, 3 Shop	Nos. 1, 2, 3 Shop
remanufactured		
into moldings,		
casings, base,		
jambs, etc.)		
Boards	Select, Construction, Standard, Utility, Economy	Nos. 1, 2, 3, 4, 5

Grade Designation for Plywood (per UBC Standards, Chapter 25–9)

Interior Type	Exterior Type	Premium
Shop and Mill	*Marine and Form*	*Structural*
N-N	Marine	C-D Structural I
N-A	Special Exterior	C-D Structural II
N-B	A-A	A-C Structural I
N-D	A-B	
A-A	A-C	
A-B	B-B (Concrete Forms)	
A-D	B-B	
B-B	C-C	
B-D	C-C (Plugged)	
Underlayment	A-A (High Density Overlay)	
C-D (Plugged)	B-B (High Density Overlay)	
Structural Standard	B-B (High Density Concrete Form Overlay)	
Standard w/Exterior Glue	B-B (Medium Density Overlay - Special Overlays)	

Note: For the meaning of the letters and their values see the local book of code standards or the American Plywood Association (APA) standards. The valuations are based upon density of the wood, glue applications, usage, splits and knots, fillers, etc.

The common usage of the letter "X," as in "CDX" plywood, refers to exterior grade glue. The "CD" refers to the structural grade (I or II).

Truss Joist TJI Series (Courtesy of Truss Joist)

Series Size	Flange Size (inches) (w × 1)[1]	Web Size and Type[2]	Web Depth (inches)
TJI/25	1.75″ × 1.5″	⅜″ STR I PLYWD	9½″, 11⅞″, 14″, 16″
TJI/35	2.3″ × 1.5″	⅜″ STR I PLYWD	11⅞″, 14″, 16″
TJI/35C	2.3″ × 1.5″	⁷⁄₁₆″ OSB	11⅞″, (14″-30″)
TJI/40C	2.3″ × 1.75″	⁷⁄₁₆″ OSB	11⅞″, (14″-30″)
TJI/55C	3.5″ × 1.5″	⁷⁄₁₆″ OSB	11⅞″, (14″-30″)
TJI/60C	3.5″ × 1.75″	⁷⁄₁₆″ OSB	11⅞″, (14″-30″)
TJI/15DF	1.5″ × 1.5″	⅜″ PP[3] OSB	9½″, 11⅞″
TJI/25DF	1.75″ × 1.5″	⅜″ PP[3] OSB	9½″, 11⅞″, 14″, 16″
TJI/35DF	2.3″ × 1.5″	⅜″ PP[3] OSB	11⅞″, 14″, 16″
TJI/55DF	3.5″ × 1.5″	⁷⁄₁₆″ PP[3] OSB	11⅞″, 14″, 16″
TJI/35P	2.3″ × 1.5″	¹⁵⁄₃₂″ STR I PLYWD	11⅞″, (14″-30″)
TJI/40P	2.3″ × 1.75″	¹⁵⁄₃₂″ STR I PLYWD	11⅞″, (14″-30″)[4]
TJI/55P	3.5″ × 1.5″	¹⁵⁄₃₂″ STR I PLYWD	11⅞″, (14″-30″)[4]
TJI/60P	3.5″ × 1.75″	¹⁵⁄₃₂″ STR I PLYWD	11⅞″, (14″-30″)[4]
196H	2.5″ × 3.85″	⅝″ & ¾″ STR I PLYWD	26.85″, 34.85″, 37.1″
196H	2.5″ × 4.65″	⅝″ & ¾″ STR I PLYWD	34.85″ or 37.1″
196L	2.25″ × 3.85″	⅝″ & ¾″ STR I PLYWD	26.35″ or 34.35″

[1] Width of flange lumber × thickness of flange lumber

[2] Oriented Strand Board (OSB) or Plywood (PLYWD)

[3] "Performance Plus" OSB

[4] In 2″ increments

Contract Documents

INVITATION TO BID
CHRISTLE & Associates
550 Broad Street
Las Vegas, Nevada 89000
(300)555-5555

October 30, 1998

Sir(s)/Madame(s):

You are invited to bid on a General Contract, including mechanical and electrical work, for a combination office/warehouse, wood frame and masonry construction, approximately 6,569 square feet. All bids must be on a lump-sum basis; *aggregate* bids will not be accepted.

Drawings and specifications may be obtained from the Architect along with the Instructions to Bidders at a cost of two-hundred dollars ($200.00), non-refundable. A maximum of four (4) sets may be purchased by any one company.

Plans may also be examined at the following plan room locations:

The Plan Room   The Bid Depository
35 Atlantic Avenue   156 Pacific Avenue
Las Vegas, Nevada   Las Vegas, Nevada

A bid (security) bond valued at fifteen percent (15%) of the bid must accompany each bid submitted in accordance with the Instructions to Bidders. The Architect and Owner reserve the right to reject any and all bids or waive any irregularities due to discrepancies in the bids.

(Signed) Steven Christle
Architect and Agent for
J.M. Land Co./Frontier Manufacturing
Caliente, Nevada

Advertisement to Bid

BID: November 15, 1998, office/warehouse, owned by J.M. Land Co., Caliente, NV, Project 12726, is open for bid. Christle Associates, Las Vegas, NV, (300) 555-5555, is representing the owner. Sealed bids are requested on a general contract, including mechanical and electrical work, for a wood frame and masonry structure approx. 6,569 square feet. All bids to be lump sum: no *aggregate* bids accepted. Bids to be received until 3PM PST, Thurs, November 15, 1998, at 550 Broad Street, Las Vegas, NV. No bids accepted after said time. Bids will be opened and read publicly. Plans and specifications may be examined at:

The Plan Room	The Bid Depository
35 Atlantic Ave.	156 Pacific Ave.
Las Vegas, NV	Las Vegas, NV

Copies may be obtained from the architect at a cost of $200/set, nonrefundable, maximum 4 sets. Bid bond of 15% of total bid proposal to be submitted with the bid in accordance with the Instructions to Bidders. Owner reserves right of refusal of any bid.

By order of:
Christle & Associates, Las Vegas, Nevada.

INSTRUCTIONS TO BIDDERS
CHRISTLE Associates
550 Broad Street
Las Vegas, Nevada
89000
(300)555-5555

October 30, 1992
Re: Office/Warehouse
Caliente, Nevada
Project 12726

TO: All Bidders.
All bids must be in accordance with these Instructions to Bidders in order to be considered.

Documents

Bonafide prime bidders may obtain a maximum of four (4) sets of Drawings and Specifications from the architect upon deposit of two-hundred and 00/100 dollars ($200) per set, non-refundable. No partial sets will be issued; no sets will be issued to sub-bidders (subcontractors) by the architect.

Examination

Bidders shall carefully examine the Documents and the project site to obtain first-hand knowledge of existing conditions. Contractors will not be given extra payment for any conditions determinable prior to bid by such examination of the Documents and the project site.

Questions

Submit all questions about the Plans and Specifications to the architect, in writing, at least ten (10) working days prior to the bid date. Replies shall be issued to all prime bidders of record as Addenda to the Plans and/or Specifications and will become a part of the Contract. The architect and owner will not be responsible for oral clarifications. Any questions after the ten (10) working-day period will not be accepted.

Substitutions

Unspecified products will not be accepted unless notification has been made ten (10) working days prior to bid date. Requests shall be accompanied by a description of the product, test approvals, and specifications of the product for verification by the architect. The architect, upon approval of said product, shall issue an Addendum to all bidders of record prior to bid date.

Basis of Bid

The bidder must include all unit cost items and all alternatives shown on the Bid Forms. Failure to comply may be cause for rejection. No aggregate bids or assignments will be considered.

Preparation of Bid

Bids shall be prepared on the Bid Forms supplied with the Plans and Specifications. Any alteration to the Forms shall be sufficient cause for bid rejection. Fill in all blanks and submit two (2) copies. Bids shall be signed with the name typed below the signature. Where bidder is a corporation, Bid Forms must be signed with the legal name of the corporation, the name of the state of incorporation, and legal signature of an officer authorized to bind the corporation to a contract.

Bid Security

Bid security shall be made payable to the architect, as representative and agent for the owner, in the amount of fifteen percent (15%) of the bid sum. Security shall be either by certified check or bid bond issued by a surety licensed to conduct business in the State of Nevada. The successful bidder's security will be retained until the contract is signed and the required Payment and Performance bonds submitted. The owner reserves the right to retain the security of the two (2) lowest bidders until the lowest bidder enters into contract or until sixty (60) days after bid opening, whichever is shorter. All other security will be returned as soon as practicable. Any bidders refusing to enter into contract with the owner shall have the security held for liquidated damages, not as a penalty. Security is to be submitted with the bid on bid day.

For the Owner:
(Signed) Steven Christle
Architect and Agent
Copies:
     Owner
     All bidders
     File

PROJECT MANUAL

for FRONTIER MANUFACTURING, INC.
CALIENTE, NEVADA

Owner: Frontier Manufacturing, Inc.
100 First Avenue
Caliente, Nevada 89–

Architect: Christle Associates
550 Broad Street
Las Vegas, Nevada 89109

Civil & Structural Engineers: Janus Corporation
1 Main Street
Caliente, Nevada 89–

Mechanical Engineer: Aquarius Mechanical & Plumbing, Inc.
375 Water Street
Las Vegas, Nevada 89–

Electrical Engineer: Brophy Electric, Inc.
935 Ampere Avenue
Las Vegas, Nevada 89–

FIGURE IV–1
Project Manual for Frontier Manufacturing, Inc.

GENERAL CONDITIONS

Definitions

For purposes of this contract, Frontier Manufacturing, Inc., of 100 First Avenue, Caliente, Nevada, 89–, is referred to as "the Owner."

The term "project" described in this Specification is an office/warehouse for the Owner located at Broad Street and First Avenue, Caliente, Nevada, 89–.

The term "contractor" means the person, firm, or corporation, identified as such in the agreement, responsible for the execution of the work contracted with the owner.

The term "subcontractor" means, without limitation, any person, firm, or corporation working directly or indirectly for the contractor, whether or not pursuant to a formal contract, that furnishes or performs a portion of the work, labor, or material, according to the drawings and/or specifications.

The term "agreement" means the construction agreement between the owner and the contractor.

The term "contract" means the agreement signed by the owner and the contractor, these Specifications, and all other documents listed as contract documents of this agreement.

The term "contract amount" means the dollar-value of the agreement as revised by approved contract change orders.

The term "work" includes all labor, material, and equipment necessary to produce the construction required by contract.

The term "change order" is a written order to the contractor, signed by the owner, issued AFTER the execution of the contract, authorizing a change in work or an adjustment in the original contract amount as agreed upon by the owner and the contractor.

The term "contract time" is the period of time allotted in the agreement for the completion of the work as revised by approved contract change orders.

Intent of the Documents

The agreement and each of the contract documents are complementary and they shall be interpreted so that what is called for by one shall be binding upon all. Should there be any conflicts in the documents, the contractor is to bring the discrepancies to the attention of the owner at once. It shall be the owner who shall make the responsible decision as to which document is correct and all other documents shall be immediately amended by addendum.

Duplication is not intended through any of the documents and no duplication for additional cost may be claimed.

Delays and Extensions of Time

Should there be excessive delays due to the owner, an employee of the owner, or a contractor of the owner, or by changes ordered in the work, or by acts of God, or by any other cause deemed by the owner as justifying the delay, the contract shall be extended by change order. The length of the extension shall be determined by the owner.

All requests for extension of contract shall be made to the owner no more than ten (10) working days after such delay occurs or they shall be otherwise waived. A continuing delay need not be put into writing unless it exceeds another ten (10) working-day period. Any delays caused by other than the above shall be at the expense of the contractor at a cost of one-thousand and 00/100 dollars ($1, 000) per day.

Assignments

This contract, or any rights hereunder, shall not be assigned by the contractor without the express consent of the owner.

FIGURE IV–1
Continued

Payment and Performance Bonds

Prior to any work, the contractor, at the discretion of the owner, shall supply the owner with a payment and performance bond in the amount of one-hundred percent (100%) of the contract. The cost of such bond shall be at the expense of the contractor.

Compliance with the Law

Contractor shall be responsible for complete compliance with all laws, including OSHA, ordinances, codes, or other regulations as may exist in the jurisdiction of authority in the locale of this contract.

Indemnification

The contractor shall indemnify and hold harmless the owner and all of the owner's heirs and assigns against any and all claims, damages, losses, and expenses, including attorney's fees, due to the performance of the work, provided that such claims, damages, losses or expenses, causing bodily harm, illness, or death due to negligence or omission of the contractor, subcontractor, or anyone directly or indirectly employed by the contractor or subcontractor, or anyone for whose acts any of them may be liable, regardless of whether or not it is caused in part by a party indemnified hereunder, and shall further indemnify and hold harmless the owner, all of the owner's heirs and assigns from the expense of such defense against all claims for damages, losses, and expenses claimed by any person, firm, or corporation.

FIGURE IV–1
Continued

INDEX TO SPECIFICATIONS

Division 1-General Requirements
01010   Summary of Work
01020   Allowances
01025   Measurement and Payment
01030   Alternates/Alternatives
01040   Coordination
01060   Workmen's Compensation and Insurance
01200   Project Meetings
01300   Submittals/Substitutions
01400   Quality Control
01500   Construction Facilities and Temporary Controls
01600   Materials and Equipment
01700   Contract Close-out

Division 2-Sitework
02000   Scope of Work
02010   Subsurface Investigation
02020   Demolition
02100   Site Preparation
02220   Earthwork
02270   Slope Paving
02510   Asphalt Concrete Paving
02525   Prefabricated Curbs
02580   Pavement Marking
02720   Storm Sewerage
02800   Site Improvements
02900   Landscaping

Division 3-Concrete
03000   Scope of Work
03100   Concrete Formwork
03210   Reinforcement Steel
03220   Welded Wire Fabric
03300   Cast-in-Place Concrete
03480   Precast Concrete Specialties

Division 4-Masonry
04000   Scope of Work
04100   Mortar and Masonry Grout
04150   Masonry Accessories
04220   Concrete Unit Masonry

Division 5-Metals
05000   Scope of Work
05050   Metal Fastening
05120   Structural Metal Framing
05530   Gratings

Division 6-Wood and Plastics
06000   Scope of Work
06100   Rough Carpentry
06150   Wood and Metal Systems

FIGURE IV–1
Continued

```
                    06180   Glue-Laminated Beams
                    06190   Trusses
                    06200   Finish Carpentry

            Division 7-Thermal and Moisture Protection
                    07000   Scope of Work
                    07110   Sheet Membrane Below-Grade Moisture Protection
                    07200   Insulation
                    07300   Roofing Tile
                    07460   Manufactured Siding
                    07500   Membrane Roofing
                    07600   Flashing and Sheet Metal
                    07900   Sealants and Caulking

            Division 8-Doors and Windows
                    08000   Scope of Work
                    08100   Metal Doors and Frames
                    08200   Wood and Plastic Doors
                    08250   Door Opening Assemblies
                    08500   Metal Windows

            Division 9-Finishes
                    09000   Scope of Work
                    09100   Metal Support Systems
                    09200   Lath and Plaster
                    09250   Gypsum Board (GWB)
                    09300   Tile
                    09500   Acoustical Treatment
                    09650   Resilient Flooring
                    09680   Carpet
                    09900   Painting

            Division 10-Specialties
                    10000   Scope of Work
                    10400   Identifying Devices
                    10500   Lockers
                    10800   Toilet and Bath Accessories

            Division 11-Equipment
                    11000   Scope of Work
                    11160   Loading Dock Equipment
                    11500   Industrial and Process Equipment

            Division 12-Furnishings
                    N.I.C.   -to be Furnished by Owner

            Division 13-Special Construction
                    13000   Scope of Work
                    13400   Industrial and Process Control Systems
                    13900   Fire Suppression and Supervisory System

            Division 14-Conveying Systems
                    14000   Scope of Work
                    14500   Material Handling Systems
                    14600   Hoists and Cranes
```

FIGURE IV–1
Continued

Division 15-Mechanical
    15000   Scope of Work
    15050   Basic Mechanical Materials and Methods
    15400   Plumbing
    15500   Heating, Ventilation, and Air Conditioning

Division 16-Electrical
    16000   Scope of Work
    16050   Basic Electrical Materials and Methods
    16400   Service and Distribution
    16500   Lighting (General Lighting and Power)
    16600   Special Systems
    16700   Communications

STANDARDS

AIA-American Institute of Architects
ACI-American Concrete Institute
APA-American Plywood Association
ASHRAE-American Society of Heating, Refrigeration, and Air-conditioning Engineers, Inc.
ASTM-American Society for Testing Materials
AWS-American Welding Society
CRSI-Concrete Reinforcing Steel Institute
DHI-Door and Hardware Institute
MIA-Masonry Institute of America
TCA-Tile Council of America, Inc.
UL-Underwriters Laboratories, Inc.
WWPA-Western Wood Products Association

FIGURE IV–1
Continued

SPECIFICATIONS

DIVISION 1 General Requirements

01010   Summary of Work

1.1. The contractor warrants and represents that it has carefully examined all the plans and Specifications, and all of the real property upon which the work is to be conducted, and has satisfied itself as to the conditions existing and the difficulties that may be encountered in the execution of the work which should have reasonably been discovered upon such examination, will not constitute a cause for the reformation or recision of this contract, or a modification of the amount of this contract, or its termination.

1.2. The contractor shall obtain and pay for all permits, licenses, certifications, tap charges, construction easements, inspections, and other approvals required, both temporary and permanent, to commence and complete the work at no additional cost to the owner.

1.3. The contractor shall be responsible for all the work on the site and the adjacent property regarding loss or damage resulting from its operations at no additional cost to the owner.

1.4. Contractor shall receive a full certificate of occupancy before the contractor can receive final payment for the work.

1.5. The contractor may have portions of the work performed by others by use of subcontract agreements. These agreements must be approved by the owner and shall in no way increase the cost of the project.

1.5.a. All subcontract agreements shall automatically include the General Conditions and Requirements between the owner and the contractor.

1.5.b. No contract between the contractor and the subcontractor shall be construed to be a contract between the owner and the subcontractor. No subcontractor has a right against the owner unless the contract has defaulted. Should this happen, the owner shall be liable only for the costs incurred in accordance with the subcontract agreement.

1.6. The contractor shall be fully responsible for any omissions, commissions, or errors committed by the subcontractor, or any person, firm, or corporation, or any of their respective employees, in contract with the contractor.

01020   Allowances

1.1. An allowance shall be permitted by the owner for all lighting fixtures. The fixtures included are for the plant/warehouse overhead fixtures, the office fluorescent ceiling fixtures for the offices and the display room, and the track lighting as may be required by owner. The lighting fixture allowance shall be in the amount of ten thousand three-hundred fifty and 00/100 dollars ($10,350).

01025   Measurement and Payment

1.1. Each subcontractor shall submit a request for payment to the contractor as prescribed in the contract agreement. Each submission shall be made no later than the 10th day or the 25th day of each month. Requests for payment received on the 10th day shall be reimbursed on the 30th day of the same month. Requests for payment received on the 25th day of the month shall be reimbursed on the 15th day of the month following. There shall be only one payment allowed per month.

1.2. No payment shall be approved by the contractor or owner without verification of the measurement submitted with the payment request.

01030   Alternates/Alternatives

1.1. Should any of the materials, procedures, or systems be unavailable for any reason an alternative material, procedure, or system may be submitted. Should there be an alternative submitted, the contractor and/or material supplier shall submit such information and change per Section 01300.

1.2. Alternates shall only be submitted at the request of the owner or the owner's representative.

01035   Modification Procedures

1.1. Upon contract and start of construction, no work shall be done other than that established by contract. Any changes to be made due to construction problems or the owner's request shall be done by one of two (2) methods, work order or field directive.

FIGURE IV–1
Continued

1.1.a. Only authorized personnel shall request any contractor or subcontractor to make such changes. Changes requested shall be by written authorization only in the manner directed above. Authorized personnel include the architect, engineer, appointed superintendent, project engineer, or project manager. All other requests shall be denied.

01040   Coordination

1.1. It is the responsibility of the contractor to supply a Critical Path Chart to the owner, all selected subcontractors, and manufacturers or suppliers so that the work can be accomplished in a timely manner without confusion or delay.

01060   Workmen's Compensation and Insurance

1.1. The contractor, at its own expense, shall be responsible for maintenance of workmen's compensation in accordance with the laws of the state in which the project is being constructed.

1.2. The contractor shall also supply the owner with liability insurance in the amount of one million and 00/100 dollars ($1,000,000) for injury or death and three million and 00/100 dollars ($3,000,000) for property damage. The owner shall be named as co-insurer.

01200   Project Meetings

1.1. It shall be the responsibility of the contractor and all subcontractors, manufacturer's representatives, and/or suppliers to be available for regular project meetings to be held on-site weekly for the purposes of discussing continuity, labor, material, or equipment problems, and safety. The day and time of the meeting is at the discretion of the contractor. The owner may or may not be present at these meetings.

01300   Submittals/Substitutions

1.1. The contractor shall submit to the owner, or owner's representative, for approval, all materials, equipment, and procedures to be a part of the completed project. Submittals shall be in writing and certified to be as per manufacturer's recommendations.

1.1.a. All "or equal" and alternative products or procedures are to be submitted in writing to the owner, or owner's representative, for approval. The reason for the "or equal" or alternative materials or procedures must be explained in the submittal. Such submittals must be available to the owner or owner's representative no less than ten (10) working days prior to the start of work on the project.

1.2. The owner has the right to reject any and all such submittals except in the event the material is no longer available or there is a delay in time in obtaining the material or the procedure must be changed due to the change in material.

01400   Quality Control

1.1. The contractor warrants that all materials and equipment supplied to the owner for the project are new unless otherwise specified. All work shall be free from any defects in material and workmanship.

1.1.a. All warranties or guarantees supplied by the manufacturers to the contractor or subcontractors shall be deemed as supplied to the owner as well. Prior to final payment by the owner, all copies of the warranties, guarantees shall be submitted to the owner and the said warranties/guarantees assigned directly to the owner.

01500   Construction Facilities and Temporary Controls

1.1. The contractor, at its own cost, shall be responsible that all temporary facilities such as telephones, electrical supply, personal care equipment, first aid equipment, potable water, and fire prevention facilities are made available on the project.

1.2. Fire prevention facilities and services and first aid and medical assistance must be prominently displayed so that all persons, firms, or corporations employed on the project may have access to them.

FIGURE IV–1
Continued

01600   Material and Equipment

1.1. At the discretion of the owner, if there is sufficient room, an area may be set aside for storage of equipment and materials. If possible, a fence will be so provided for enclosure of the materials and equipment. It is the responsibility of each person, firm, or corporation to make certain that the area is secure at the end of each workday.

01700   Contract Close-out

1.1. The contractor shall be responsible for maintenance of all records. A copy of such records shall be provided to the owner at the time of completion of project including manufacturers' warranties, guarantees, certifications of workmanship and material prior to final payment and/or retention. Where no manufacturer's warranty or guarantee exists, and, regardless of such warranties or guarantees, all trades shall submit, in writing, a minimum two (2) year guarantee against defects in workmanship and material which are a permanent part of the project.

1.2. The contractor, at its own expense, shall be responsible for a clean worksite. All rubbish caused by the contractor's employees, the subcontractor or its employees, and the suppliers or their employees shall be removed and properly stored in containers for removal to a suitable site for dumping.

DIVISION 2 Sitework

02000   Scope of Work

1.1. Division 1 and the General Conditions are to be considered a part of this division including all materials, labor, and equipment necessary to complete the work of this division.

02010   Subsurface Investigation

1.1. The owner shall provide for subsurface exploration to be conducted by a qualified soils engineering firm. The soils testing and results shall be made available, in writing, to the owner or owner's representative and the contractor and shall become a part of these Specifications.

1.2. The report shall include the type of surface soil, the type, or types, of soil for a minimum of ten (10) feet (3.05 m) below grade, obtained by test borings or core drillings, and shall make recommendations, if any, for correcting substandard soils conditions. During excavation and grading, soils testing shall be performed to ensure the soils meet a minimum of 3,000 psf (1,360.79 kg/30.48 cm^2) design strength.

02020   Demolition

1.1. If, during the soils testing, any hazardous materials, pipes, conduits, or other possible hazards, are located, the owner shall be notified and corrections made at the expense of the owner. All materials shall be properly and safely removed from the site. All pipes shall be tested and capped at a safe distance from the site work.

1.2. No work shall be initiated until after "Call Before You Dig," or equivalent organization, is contacted and permission to proceed is given by all utilities and/or local authorities. Any structural demolition which may be located on the property shall be done by a licensed, qualified demolition and/or salvage company.

02100   Site Preparation

1.1. The contractor shall be responsible that certain vegetation is marked to remain intact or to be removed, saved, and transplanted. This shall be accomplished in cooperation with the owner, contractor, and clearing and grubbing contractor. When all vegetation to be saved is so marked, all remaining vegetation, debris, and refuse is to be cleared and removed.

02220   Earthwork

1.1. Excavate as required to achieve proper grade levels and for the mass excavation of the loading dock ramp and for working room required for laying of retaining walls on both ends of the loading dock area. Excavation for all footings to be on undisturbed earth or minimum 95% compacted soil with the minimum allowable depth, as shown on drawings, or otherwise governed by local codes.

1.2. Should the contractor contact calcite or large rock conditions which would require blasting, the owner will reimburse the contractor for the cost of such work.

FIGURE IV–1
Continued

1.3. Backfill at exterior walls shall be Type II soil, well compacted, to the grades specified on the plot plan. Backfill shall be performed in 8″ (20.32 cm) lifts. Backfill over utilities shall conform with the utility company requirements of sand and/or Type II soil. The remainder of the site shall be graded to assure proper drainage away from the building. Remove all excess soils from the site. Grades not otherwise indicated on the plans shall be of uniform levels or slopes between points where elevations are given.

1.4. Contractor is to notify owner immediately if any excavation reveals fill or ground water.

02270   Slope Paving

1.1. The finish grading shall be completed to conform with the paving swale elevations as indicated on the plans. Rough grading must be such that the base course, aggregate (cementitious) base, and finish surface shall not exceed elevations indicated on plans.

02510   Asphaltic Concrete Paving

1.1. All paving is to be prepared from a combination of cementitious and asphaltic materials as per manufacturer's recommendations, the Asphalt Institute, and local codes and ordinances. All paving shall be installed in areas indicated on plans. Pavement design shall meet ten (10) year minimum design criteria for local areas as established by the Asphalt Institute. The following guide indicates the *minimum* thickness required:

Soil Class	Minimum Pavement
Poor-CBR = 3.5-type, plastic when wet such as clay, fine silt, sandy loam	6″ (15.24 cm) coarse asphalt base binder (1½″ [3.81 cm] asphalt aggregate) and 1½″ (3.81 cm) asphalt topping (maximum ½″ [1.27 cm] aggregate)
Medium-CBR = 7.0-type, hard, silty sands or sand gravels containing clay or fine silt	4″ (10.16 cm) coarse asphalt base binder (1½″ [3.81 cm] asphalt aggregate) and 1½″ (3.81 cm) asphalt topping (maximum ½″ [1.27 cm] aggregate)
Good-CBR = 12-type, clean sand and sand gravel free of asphalt topping clay, silt or loam	3″ (7.62 cm) coarse asphalt base material (1½″ [3.81 cm] asphalt aggregate) and 1½″ (3.81 cm) asphalt topping (maximum)

1.2. Finish paving shall be applied with a 4″ (10.16 cm) asphalt mix at all areas over a 6″ (15.24 cm) cementitious base over 10″ (25.40 cm) approved compacted base, aggregate or sand, at all paved areas. The aggregate or sand base shall be compacted to maintain an 80% compaction rate. Base shall be tested for compaction prior to application of asphalt finish. All paving surfaces shall be properly sealed from weather deterioration as per local codes and accepted workmanship of the trade.

02520   Portland Cement Concrete Paving

1.1. Curb and gutter shall be installed along the perimeter of the driveway and parking areas. Curbs shall be 18″ (45.72 cm) deep by 4″ (5.05 cm) wide (15.24 cm) concrete with 6″ (15.24 cm) exposed above finish asphalt surfacing and/or gutter. 2-#4 rebar shall be installed in curb, one 3″ (7.62 cm) from the top of the curb and the other 3″ (7.62 cm) from the bottom of the curb. The gutter shall be 12″ (30.48 cm) wide by 4″ (5.08 cm) deep with 2-#4 rebar spaced 6″ (15.24 cm) apart. All horizontal reinforcement shall be placed on chairs for proper support and binding of the concrete upon placement. The gutter base shall meet the same specifications as in Section 2510 or shall meet the minimum DOT specifications of the local building and engineering departments.

1.2. Formwork for the approach shall be installed and shall conform to the best standards of the American Concrete Institute. All lines shall be straight and true. Concrete shall be 3500 psi (1,587.59 kg/6.54 cm^2) at 28 days per ASTM C94 using materials from one manufacturer and supplier. Reinforcement shall be installed and inspected prior to concrete placement. The concrete and reinforcement shall meet all ASTM and DOT requirements for

FIGURE IV–1
Continued

approach installations. Should the concrete not meet proper standards it shall be repaired, or removed and replaced, as necessary, at the expense of the contractor.

   1.2.a. See Division 3, Concrete, for complete requirements for concrete installations. If there are any discrepancies noted, the information in Division 3 shall prevail.

02525   Prefabricated Curbs

   1.1. Precast concrete parking blocks, 6'-0" (1.83 m) long and 5" (12.70 cm) high, shall be installed one for each two (2) parking places, spanning one-half (½) per parking space, except at handicapped parking where the concrete block shall be placed one (1) per parking space.

02580   Pavement Marking

   1.1. The paving contractor shall paint parking stalls and directional markings, including entry and exit arrows, center-line striping, and warning signage.

   1.2. The parking spaces shall include two (2) handicap spaces for customer parking in front of office. Two (2) handicap spaces shall be marked at employee parking area along side of structure facing First Avenue. Handicap spaces shall be properly protected from other parking spaces with "Van Accessible" striping and otherwise identified with the necessary ADA signage requirements. All other parking spaces along the front parking area (both sides) and the side parking area shall be standard size (9'-0" [2.74 m] wide by 19'-0" [5.79 m] long). There are no parking spaces inside the chain-link fence and gate (North area of property).

02720   Storm Sewerage

   1.1. A cast iron (CI) drain shall be installed which shall receive drainage from the trench drain and swales and shall be connected to an open storm drain located to the north of the property on First Avenue. The top of the storm drain shall be even with the lowest part of the surrounding area but a minimum of 4" (10.32 cm) lower than the trench drain at the loading dock. See plans for locations and elevations.

02800   Site Improvements

   1.1. An 8'-0" (2.44 m) high chain-link fence and traffic-control, motor-operated, roll-away gate is to be installed across the parking area/driveway on the First Avenue side of the structure as indicated on the plot plan. The fence shall be installed with one section 10'-0" (3.05 m) long abutting the structure and the other section 18'-0" (5.49 m) long with a 12'-0" (3.66 m) long gate.

   A second 8'-0" (2.44 m) high chain-link fence with a 4'-0" (1.22 m) wide personnel gate is to be installed on the opposite side of the structure extending 28'-0" (8.53 m) O/A to the south property line wall across the easement area as per plans. Permission must be obtained from the utility company(ies) for this installation.

02900   Landscaping

   1.1. Provide all labor, material, and equipment necessary to complete the seeding, sodding, landscape planting, earthwork, and edging as shown on plot and/or landscape plans. Landscape bidder shall submit a proposal and drawings for approval by the owner. Proposal shall include size, type, and number of plantings, and exact area to be sodded.

   1.2. Landscape contractor shall be responsible for the installation of the topsoil to finish grade at all the rough grading. All planting areas shall be free of all debris and well drained prior to any planting. An automatic sprinkler system shall be installed in accordance with local codes and ordinances. Total proposal shall include all taxes where applicable.

END OF DIVISION

DIVISION 3 Concrete

03000   Scope of Work

   1.1. Division 1 and the General Conditions are considered a part of this division. All labor, material, and equipment necessary to complete all concrete work including formwork, reinforcing, and cement finish shall be furnished by the concrete contractor.

FIGURE IV–1
Continued

03100   Concrete Formwork

1.1. Formwork shall be installed for footings and sidewalks where required. Footing forms shall be installed along property line retaining wall footings, at the loading dock retaining walls and all other structure footing support. All labor, materials, and equipment necessary for the installation of footings shall include steel stakes, 3'-0" (0.91 m) long and 2× treated lumber or 1" (min) (2.54 cm) treated plywood for forms and any other accessories necessary for proper construction of the footings. Where sidewalks are installed, standard flat forms shall be used.

1.2. All work shall conform with ASTM standards, standards of the trade, and all local codes and ordinances. Where the soil conditions permit, forms may be excluded. Refer to the engineering Soils Report made a part of these Conditions and Specifications for requirements and/or recommendations.

03210   Reinforcement Steel

1.1. Reinforcement bar (rebar) shall be grade 60 (60 kps). Rebar shall be 2-#4 (U.N.O.) laid horizontally and continuous in footings with 48 bar diameters at all laps. Rebar shall be installed on concrete prefabricated chairs 3" (7.62 cm) from bottom of footing. Corners shall have 2-#4 rebar, 4'-0" (1.22 m) long, bent 90° at the center, and shall extend 2'-0" (60.96 cm) each way from the corner. 1-#5 rebar dowel shall be installed vertically in foundation walls or at slab perimeter at 4'-0" O/C (1.22 m) horizontally to match masonry reinforcement (see plans) with the 6" (15.24 cm) hook tied to footing rebar. Dowel rebar length shall extend 2'-0" (60.96 cm) vertically. No rebar shall be heat bent. All rebar shall be installed and inspected prior to placement of concrete.

03220   Welded Wire Fabric

1.1. The manufacturing/warehouse concrete slab shall have W2.9 × W2.9–6 × 6 welded wire fabric installed a minimum 1½" (3.81 cm) below the surface of the slab. The fabric shall be lapped 6" (1.27 cm) on all sides and ends. The perimeter fabric shall extend 6" (1.27 cm) beyond the edges of the slab and shall be turned down parallel at the stem wall and/or footing.

03300   Cast-In-Place Concrete

1.1. Concrete footings and slabs are to be 3,500 psi (1,587.59 kg/6.54 cm²) ready-mix concrete per ASTM C94. Type III cement shall be used. Concrete shall be tested at the expense of the owner at 3 days, 7 days, and 28 days in accordance with ASTM C31 and ASTM C150. If any of the tests fail, the contractor shall, at his/her own expense, make all necessary repairs and/or replacements.

1.2. The manufacturing/warehouse concrete slab, including the loading dock, shall be 6" (1.27 cm) thick and the office slab shall be 4" (0.83 cm) thick. The exterior sidewalks shall be 5" (12.70 cm) thick and the approach apron shall be 6" (15.24 cm) thick. The manufacturing/warehouse slab shall be placed in alternate sections so that expansion joints can be inserted between placements. Flat forms shall be installed with cold key joints. The office slab may be placed as a single unit.

1.3. Concrete components shall be Portland cement, one brand; aggregate-fine sand and maximum ¾" (1.91 cm) DIA coarse gravel free from other deleterious substances; potable water.

   1.3.a. Admixtures permitted shall be:

   (1) air-entrained agent per ASTM C260
   (2) hardener and dustproofer—"Lapodith," or equal
   (3) non-slip additive—"Durafax" or equal
   (4) non-shrink additive—"Sika Set," or equal

1.4. The concrete contractor shall be responsible for all column support pads (footings) and expansion and contraction joints as shown on plans and/or as required by codes and ordinances.

1.5. The concrete contractor shall build into the concrete all materials furnished by others and shall secure same: including plumbing, electrical conduit, concrete inserts, anchors, hangers, hold-downs, sleeving for piping, and so on, when and where required by the other trades.

FIGURE IV–1
Continued

03480   Precast Concrete Specialties

1.1. A 6″ (15.24 cm) wide by 8″ (20.32 cm) deep precast trench drain shall be installed at the bottom of the loading ramp and abutting the loading dock. An open storm drain shall be located at the northeast corner of the drive area (see plans for location) which shall receive drainage from the trench drain and swales and shall be connected to the storm drain located to the north of the property on First Avenue. The drain shall be 3′-0″ (91.44 cm) long by 2′-0″ (60.96 cm) wide by 18″ (45.72 cm) deep. The top of the drain shall be even with the lowest part of the surrounding area and a minimum 4″ (10.16 cm) lower than the trench drain at the loading dock.

END OF DIVISION

DIVISION 4 Masonry

04000   Scope of Work

1.1. Division 1 and the General Conditions shall be considered a part of this division. Provide all labor, material, and equipment necessary to complete the structural and miscellaneous steel work indicated on the drawings. All materials to meet ASTM requirements. Install all embeds, anchors, and accessories as shown on plans or as required for a complete installation.

04100   Mortar and Masonry Grout

1.1. Mortar shall be pre-mixed Type S or Type N as required by code and local ordinances. The pre-mix shall be supplied by one manufacturer and shall be 1800 psi (816.47 kg/6.45 cm^2), consistent with all ASTM requirements as well as local codes and ordinances. All masonry units are to be installed in a ⅜″ (0.96 cm) mortar bed and head.

1.1.a. Mortar may be used for a period of one (1) hour after mixing. Where required, a fluidifier may be used. Care must be taken to ensure that the consistency is not changed by addition of too much water.

1.2. Grout shall be a 2000 psi (907.19 kg/6.45 cm^2) ready-mix concrete with ⅜″ (0.96 cm) pea gravel. All masonry cells shall be grout filled. Where weather conditions permit, a plasticizer may be used to aid in the grout placement.

04150   Masonry Accessories

1.1. All vertical masonry reinforcement shall be 1-#5 rebar spaced at 4′-0″ (1.22 m) O/C, horizontally, to match the dowel rebar placed in the slab or footing. 2-#5 rebar shall be additionally installed on each side of all openings and shall extend three (3) courses above the openings. 1-#5 rebar shall be added on each side of all control joints. 2-#5 rebar shall extend continuously along the east wall in the double bond beam installed over the overhead door openings.

1.1.a. 2-#4 continuous rebar shall be installed horizontally at 4′-0″ (1.22 m) O/C, vertically, U.N.O. 2-#4 rebar shall also be installed at the roof line and 1-#4 rebar at the top of parapet. Rebar extending through control joints shall be taped with cambric a minimum 8″ (20.32 cm) each side of the joint.

1.3. Where required, masonry Rapid Control Joints® by Duro-Wall® are to be installed the complete height of the wall. No wall shall exceed 40′-0″ clear without installation of a control joint.

1.4. All other masonry and non-masonry accessories, although not specified, are understood to be a part of these Specifications to ensure a complete installation.

04220   Concrete Unit Masonry

1.1. All masonry units shall conform to ASTM C-90. All units shall be supplied from one source. The units shall be structural concrete masonry, 8 × 8 × 16 precision, for unexposed retaining walls and exposed manufacturing/warehouse walls, f'm 1565 psi (709.88 kg/6.45 cm^2) and shall meet a total 3125 psi (1,417.49 kg/6.45 cm^2) when cured and grouted. Exposed slumpstone masonry units, 8 × 6 × 16 shall be f'm 1506.

FIGURE IV–1
Continued

1.1.a. All units shall be installed in a common bond. All precision masonry in the manufacturing/warehouse area shall be struck joints on the exterior and hand-tooled joints on the interior side of the units. Retaining walls shall be struck joints unless exposed. All exposed precision units shall be hand-tooled. All slumpstone units shall be hand-tooled both sides. No damaged units shall be installed.

1.1.b. All units shall be stored in a place or in a manner whereby they may be protected. All incomplete work at the end of each workday shall be braced and covered with polyethylene sheets to protect the units from moisture and dust.

END OF DIVISION

DIVISION 5 Metals

05000   Scope of Work

1.1. Division 1 and the General Conditions shall be considered a part of this division. Provide all labor, material, and equipment necessary to complete the structural and miscellaneous steel work indicated on the drawings. All materials to meet ASTM requirements. Install all embeds, anchors, and accessories as shown on plans or as required for a complete installation.

05050   Metal Fastening

1.1. The steel manufacturer shall provide all reinforcement bar as specified in Division 3, Concrete, and Division 4, Masonry. All rebar shall meet the ASTM requirements.

05120   Structural Metal Framing

1.1. The column supports for the glue-laminated beams shall be fabricated by a steel fabricator with all accessory parts included (base plate, 6″ (15.24 cm) DIA column, top plate, and beam hinges) as per plans. The column bottom plate shall be fastened to the concrete pad with ⅝″ (1.59 cm) anchor or expansion bolts. Bolting for the glue-laminated beam shall be ⅝″ (1.59 cm) through bolts, extending sufficiently long enough to expose a minimum ⅜″ (0.95 cm) beyond the flat and lock washers and tightened nuts. The tightened nuts shall be tack welded to prevent loosening.

1.2. Hinge connectors shall be constructed of ¼″ steel plate in the design shown on the plans and details. The hinge connectors may be manufactured or custom-made if a manufactured size is not available. Simpson Strong Tie Company, or equal, may be approved for the hinges.

1.3. Steel materials and accessories shall meet all ASTM, FM, and local codes requirements.

05530   Gratings

1.1. A grating shall be fabricated to fit the top of the trench drain at the loading dock. The grating shall be a total of 55′-8″ (15.97 m) long by 7″ (17.78 cm) wide cast in two (2) sections 5′-4″ (1.62 m) long and two sections 5′-0″ (1.52 m) long. The casting shall have two (2) supports extending 8″ (20.32 cm) to the bottom of the trench on each side of the trench as per plans.

1.1.a. A grate shall be manufactured and fitted over the 3′-0″ (91.44 cm) by 2′-0″ (60.96 cm) storm drain. The grate shall be of sufficient strength to withstand heavy traffic. The grate shall completely cover the precast drain with a ¼″ (0.64 cm) thick by 1½″ (3.81 cm) deep steel plate welded to the underside of the grate placed so as to fit into the precast drain for rigidity and support. All welding shall be continuous ¼″ (0.64 cm) fillet welds on both sides of the extensions for all gratings. Flat plate joints shall be welded with continuous V groove welding both sides of plate. All flat surfaces shall be scarfed and ground smooth.

END OF DIVISION

FIGURE IV–1
Continued

DIVISION 6 Wood and Plastics

06000   Scope of Work

1.1. Division 1 and the General Conditions are to be considered a part of this division. Furnish all labor, materials, tools, and equipment necessary to complete all work under this division and as indicated on drawings. All lumber shall meet the Western Wood Products Association (WWPA) standards for materials. All plate stock shall be DF common or HF utility stock. All studs shall bear identification verifying stud grade. All other vertical structural members shall be DF #2 or better. All horizontal structural members shall be DF #1 or better, U.N.O.

1.2. Provide and maintain temporary enclosures, fences, and barricades as required by local codes and ordinances and OSHA. If required, provide temporary door and window enclosures.

06100   Rough Carpentry

1.1. A rough-sawn 6 $\times$ 12 (15.24 cm $\times$ 30.48 cm), DF #1 or better, beam shall be centered in the demising wall. The top of the beam shall be 12'-0" (3.66 m) A.F.F. and shall be supported by two (2) rough-sawn 6 $\times$ 6 (15.24 cm $\times$ 15.24 cm), DF #2 or better, posts. The beam shall be mounted on the posts in such a way that the connections are not visible.

1.2. A 3 $\times$ 10 (7.62 cm $\times$ 25.40 cm), DF #2 or better, ledger shall be installed on the north and south walls of the manufacturing/warehouse for support for joists. The ledger shall be fastened with ⅝" DIA $\times$ 7" (1.59 cm DIA $\times$ 17.78 cm) anchor bolts embedded in the masonry walls at 48" (1.22 m) O/C, with all necessary accessories. The top of the ledger shall be 12'-0" (3.66 m) A.F.F.

1.3. The exterior walls of the plant office, wash/restroom and break room, shall have ½" exterior grade CDX or OSB™ sheathing. The ceiling over the plant office, wash/restroom, and break room shall be two (2) layers of ½" exterior grade CDX or OSB™.

06150   Wood and Metal Systems

1.1. Open web joists, manufactured by Trus-Joist for the manufacturing/warehouse area. Trusses shall be series TJL, 14" (35.56 cm) deep by 27'-6 ⅛" (8.39 m) long, top chord, connected to the glue-laminated beam with hangers and to the ledger on the masonry walls with beam with hangers. Accessories shall be provided by the manufacturer as required for support and rigidity of the trusses. Trusses shall be spaced at 2'-0" (0.61 m) O/C.

06180   Glue-Laminated Beams

1.1. Structural glue-laminated beams shall be installed as part of the structural roof support system. All beams shall be cambered a minimum 1" (2.54 cm). The center beam shall be 6 ¾" $\times$ 27" $\times$ 24'-0" (17.14 cm $\times$ 0.69 m $\times$ 7.32 m), the two (2) end beams shall each be 6 ¾" $\times$ 18" $\times$ 31'-0" (17.14 cm $\times$ 0.46 m $\times$ 6.47 m). The one end of the two equal beams shall rest on the masonry pilasters for support. The larger beam shall be connected with a hinge connector as designed and required in Division 5, Metals. The interior end of the smaller beams shall rest on the 6" DIA (15.24 cm DIA) pipe column supports provided for the purpose.

06190   Wood Trusses

1.1. Prefabricated wood trusses, 3:12 slope, manufactured by Trus-Joist, for the office area. Trusses shall be constructed with a 2 $\times$ 6 (5.08 cm $\times$ 15.24 cm) top chord and 2 $\times$ 4 (5.08 cm $\times$ 10.16 cm) bottom chord. The trusses shall be constructed so as to provide the shed roof configuration as indicated on the structural framing plan. Trusses are to be mounted on the exterior of the plant west wall on a 2 $\times$ 10 (5.08 cm $\times$ 25.40 cm) top ledger and the bottom of the 2 $\times$ 8 (5.08 cm $\times$ 20.32 cm) bottom ledger at 12'-0" (2.66 m) A.F.F. All trusses, blocking, and accessories shall be supplied by the manufacturer. The truss shall include a rafter tail to extend 2'-0" (0.61 m) beyond the plate line at the eave.

06200   Finish Carpentry

1.1. An oak wood surround shall be installed at all windows on the interior side of the exterior walls. In addition a ½" (1.27 cm) to ¾" (1.91 cm) thick return of the same thickness shall be applied to both sides and head of each window immediately adjacent to the interior side of the window. An apron and stool of matching

FIGURE IV–1
Continued

oak finish shall be applied to the interior side of the exterior windows. All nailing shall be with 6d finish nails, maximum 1½″ (3.81 cm) long. The nails shall be slightly punched for application of a finish putty over each nail head. All joints shall be smooth and even.

1.2. A matching 3″ (7.62 cm) baseboard shall be applied at all areas where carpeting exists and in the showroom area.

1.3. The exterior walls of the plant office shall have a ½″ (1.27 cm) insulating sheathing board installed with panelized ⁷⁄₁₆″ (1.11 cm) T-1-11 siding over.

END OF DIVISION

DIVISION 7 Thermal and Moisture Protection

07000   Scope of Work

1.1. Division 1 and the General Conditions are to be considered a part of this division. Furnish all labor, materials, and equipment necessary to complete all work under this division and as indicated on drawings.

1.2. Work shall include a 20 mil polyethylene sheet horizontally under the slabs and footings; installation of tile and built-up roofing; insulation between office walls and ceilings adjacent to the plant, interior offices, and display room.

07110   Sheet Membrane Below-Grade Moisture Protection

1.1. All retaining walls shall be moisture-protected with a single-ply self-adhering bituminous membrane with ½″ (1.27 cm) rigid fibrous protection board over.

1.2. Acceptable manufacturers are as follows:

Koppers   GAF   Owens Corning   Johns-Manville

1.3. The membrane shall be applied as per manufacturer's specifications and shall be approved by manufacturer with a certificate of approval and a minimum five (5) year warranty.

07200   Insulation

1.1. Install an R-11 combination thermal and batt insulation by Owens Corning in all interior office, hall, perimeter wall framing in the office areas, and the plant office, break room, and wash/restroom. Install an R-30 batt insulation in the ceiling of the offices.

1.2. A 2 × 4 (5.08 cm × 10.16 cm) chemically treated fire-retardant furring strip shall be installed over the interior face of the masonry on the east, west and south walls. The furring shall be applied horizontally, 2′-0″ (0.61 m) O/C, vertically. The strips shall be fastened with concrete nails or anchor bolts or screws.

1.3. A rigid roof insulation system shall be installed over the plywood deck. The system shall be a tapered insulating system by Western Insulation Company, Los Angeles, California. The manufacturer shall estimate the materials required and cut the insulation to properly fit as per the roof plan. All tapered insulation shall be directed to the roof drainage system.

1.3.a. Western Insulation shall properly protect its product from damage and weather. Any materials that must be replaced shall be at the expense of the manufacturer or contractor, whichever is deemed responsible for the damage.

1.3.b. A guarantee shall be provided for the product and its approved installation that covers a period of five (5) years.

07300   Roofing Tiles

1.1. Roofing shall be clay slate tile, variegated colors, as manufactured by EuroTile Systems, or equal. Underlayment shall be a 43 lb (19.55 kg), 36″ (91.44 cm) wide, 5-square felt laid horizontally on the roof sheathing starting from the bottom (eave line). The felts shall have a minimum 4″ (10.16 cm) lap.

FIGURE IV–1
Continued

1.1.a. The tile shall be laid with a maximum 5″ (12.70 cm) exposure. All tiles shall be laid in a straight and true horizontal line. No broken tiles shall be used. All broken tiles shall be replaced prior to final inspection of the roof.

1.1.b. A prefabricated plastic or metal ridge vent shall be installed under the ridge along the top of the masonry wall. (See Section 07600, Flashing and Sheet Metal.)

1.2. Manufacturer shall supply a ten (10) year warranty covering workmanship and material. A certificate of acceptance by the manufacturer shall be submitted to the owner prior to release of retention payment.

07460   Manufactured Siding

1.1. The face of the end trusses above the masonry walls on each side of the office segment of the structure shall be covered with aluminum shiplap siding over ½″ (1.27 cm) insulating sheathing with a minimum 7½ lb (3.41 kg) moisture barrier. Materials shall meet all ASTM criteria and local codes and ordinances. Siding shall be applied with proper flashing and fasteners as recommended by the manufacturer. Siding selection shall be at the option of the owner.

07500   Membrane Roofing

1.1. The plywood roof deck shall be covered with a 2½″ (6.35 cm), 2′ × 4′ (0.61 m × 1.22 m) rigid fiberglass insulation board manufactured by Owens Corning. The insulation shall be in two layers. The first layer shall be 1½″ (6.35 cm) thick and the second layer 1″ (2.54 cm) thick. The first layer shall be adhered to the roof deck with a "spot" mopping and typical insulation nails a minimum 2½″ (6.35 cm) long. The joints shall be staggered and tape sealed. The second layer shall be mopped in place with a minimum 15 lb (6.82 kg) coating of hot asphalt. The joints shall be staggered and opposite the joints of the first layer and tape sealed.

1.2. The built-up roofing system shall be a four-ply BUR system, specification I04G by GAF with decorative white gravel topping, is hereby specified. Asphalt shall be supplied in a pre-heated tank truck. All felt materials shall be supplied by the same manufacturer. All asphalt shall be supplied by the same manufacturer. The asphalt shall be approved for use with the BUR system. The system shall be applied as follows:

Type II asphalt ply coat	@ 25 lb (11.34 kg)
Gafglas Ply 4 sheet	@ 10 lb (4.54 kg)
Type II asphalt ply coat	@ 25 lb (11.34 kg)
Gafglas Ply 4 sheet	@ 10 lb (4.54 kg)
Type II asphalt ply coat	@ 25 lb (11.34 kg)
Gafglas Ply 4 sheet	@ 10 lb (4.54 kg)
Type II asphalt ply coat	@ 25 lb (11.34 kg)
Gafglas Ply 4 sheet	@ 10 lb (4.54 kg)
Asphalt flood coat	@ 60 lb (27.22 kg)
White decorative pea gravel	@450 lb (204.12 kg)
Total weight	650 lb (294.86 kg)

07600   Flashing and Sheet Metal

1.1. All sheet metal flashings and accessories for the roof shall be supplied by the sheet metal contractor. All sheet metal shall be a minimum 26 gauge galvanized steel or aluminum material with the exception of the pipe jacks, which shall be manufactured in 1/16″ (0.16 cm) thick lead and formed in the same manner as the galvanized flashings. 26 gauge galvanized steel shall be used for the coping on the manufacturing/warehouse parapets.

1.2. A prefabricated ridge vent shall be used along the ridges.

07900   Sealants and Caulking

1.1. The contractor shall provide for installation of joint sealants and caulking at all control joints. Caulking shall also be provided around all exterior doors and windows.

END OF DIVISION

FIGURE IV–1
Continued

DIVISION 8 Doors and Windows

08000   Scope of Work

1.1. Division 1 and the General Conditions are to be considered a part of this division. Furnish all labor, materials, and equipment necessary to complete all work under this division and as indicated on drawings. Refer to door and window schedules on the plans.

08100   Metal Doors and Frames

1.1. Exterior doors to be hollow-metal (HM) with hollow-metal frames. The door separating the offices from the manufacturing area shall also be hollow metal w/hollow-metal frame and shall be installed as a fire door to be connected to the emergency alarm system.

08200   Wood and Plastic Doors

1.1. Interior doors to have hollow-metal knock-down (KDHM) frames. See door schedule for door styles and types. All interior doors to have sound insulation fill (STC 60) in the door cores to match the sound attenuation requirements for the walls.

08250   Door Opening Assemblies

1.1. All door hardware is to be supplied by one manufacturer. The hardware shall be Schlage, or equal. The following is the hardware schedule for all doors:
Front Entry-Schlage entry latch w/thumb latch handle and deadbolt, w/matching key, brass. Schlage handle to match latch. 1½ sets butts, brass, each leaf.
Side Exterior Doors-Schlage emergency kit hardware only (no special knowledge). 1½ sets butts, brass.
Offices and restroom-Schlage privacy latch, brass, 1½ sets butts, brass.
1.1.a. All emergency door closers, shall be the "No Special Knowledge" type of release bar.

08500   Metal Windows

1.1. Windows shall be aluminum framed and manufactured to fit into frame or masonry wall openings. All glazing for the exterior windows shall be integrally tinted, gray, dual pane insulated glass, ¼" (0.32 cm) thick, w/½" (1.27 cm) air space between panes. Windows are to be installed as per plans and details. The window schedule is a part of this specification.

END OF DIVISION

DIVISION 9 Finishes

09000   Scope of Work

1.1. Division 1 and the General Conditions are to be considered a part of this division. Furnish all labor, materials, and equipment necessary to complete all work under this division and as indicated on drawings. Work is to include installation of cement plaster on exterior masonry walls, an acoustical suspension system, drywall, floor coverings, wall tile, and painting.

09100   Metal Support Systems

1.1. A metal stud framing system shall be installed for all interior office framing. Interior nonbearing walls shall be 4"-20 ga (10.16 cm-20 ga) galvanized studs and track at 24" (0.61 m) O/C. The plumbing wall between the kitchen and restroom shall be 6"-20 ga (15.24 cm-20 ga) studs and track at 24" (0.61 m) O/C. Hall walls shall be 6"-20 ga (15.24 cm-20 ga) galvanized studs and track at 24" (0.61 m) O/C. All walls shall extend to a height of 9'-0" A.F.F. (UNO). The demising wall between the offices and display room shall be 6"-20 ga (15.24 cm-20 ga) stud and track at 16" (0.41 m) O/C, extending to the underside of the roof structure. All necessary accessories required shall be in

FIGURE IV–1
Continued

accordance with the manufacturer's recommendations, codes, and local ordinances. All materials shall be supplied by American Studco Company, Phoenix, Arizona.

1.2. See Reflected Ceiling Plan for locations of ACT system. All ACT ceilings are to be 8'-0" (2.44 m) A.F.F. Install 1" (2.54 cm) wall angle along perimeter of all supporting walls. Install 1" (2.54 cm) main "T" runners spaced 2'-0" (0.61 m) O/C, with secondary cross runners spaced at 4'-0" (1.22 m) O/C. Center the main runners in each area for aesthetic appearance. In areas where the walls are 4'-0" (1.22 m) apart, only the wall angle and main "T" runners shall be used. All joints shall be fastened with corner clips at the walls and at the cross joints.

1.2.a. The ceiling shall be suspended with 9 gauge tie wire fastened to the wood joists by a screw eye and to the runners with a clip fastener at the corners of the mains and cross secondary members. Tie wires shall be installed so as to offer support every 9 square feet of ceiling area or as necessary for proper support. Additional tie wire shall be added at each corner of the T bar ceiling structure where an electrical fluorescent fixture is to be installed. Add seismic support as may be required by local code and ordinance.

09200   Lath and Plaster

1.1. The exterior face of the exposed precision masonry walls shall have an Exterior Insulation and Finish System (EIFS) cement plaster finish with integral coloring. Coloring shall be selected by owner from standard pigmentation. All materials shall be from one manufacturer. Acceptable manufacturer(s) include:

Senergy   Dryvit   Sto Corp.

1.2. The system shall be installed as per manufacturer's specifications. The contractor shall be responsible for timely work and quality control. The contractor shall supply a written manufacturer's warranty to cover a period of ten (10) years after the manufacturer's inspection and acceptance of the work.

09250   Gypsum Board (GWB)

1.1. The office partition and plant office interior walls shall be covered with one (1) layer of ⅝" (1.59 cm) × (Firecode) by USG, or equal, both sides. The demising wall between the offices and showroom shall be covered with two (2) layers of ⅝" (1.59 cm) × (Firecode) by USG, or equal, on both sides. The perimeter walls adjacent to the exterior masonry shall have one (1) layer of ⅝" (1.59 cm) × (Firecode) by USG, or equal, on the interior side of the framing. The office/showroom area shall also have one layer of ⅝" (1.59 cm) × (Firecode) GWB installed on the underside of the roof trusses.

1.1.a. Drywall shall be laid horizontally with the long side perpendicular to the framing on both walls and ceilings. The sheets shall be placed so that all vertical joints on walls and the ends on the ceilings are staggered. Staggered joints shall be centered on the adjacent sheets.

1.1.b. GWB shall be fastened with a minimum 1⅛" (2.86 cm) drywall screws spaced at 6" O/C (15.24 cm) along the perimeter of each sheet and 9" O/C (22.86 cm) in the field. The screws shall be applied with sufficient force to slightly indent the GWB.

1.1.c. All exposed joints on walls and ceilings shall be sealed with either paper tape or self-adhering tape and multipurpose compound. The first application shall be left to set and, when dry, sanded smooth. A second application is applied to the taped joint, allowed to set, and sanded smooth to match the GWB surface for application of paint or wallcovering. All exposed screw heads shall also be embedded in multipurpose compound, sanded and smoothed to match the GWB surface. See Finish Schedule for textures. All drywall ceilings are 8'-0" A.F.F. (2.44 m), U.N.O.

1.1.d. All areas above the ceilings shall be fire-taped only.

09300   Tile

1.1. See Finish Schedule for location and other information regarding ceramic wall tile to be installed. Tile shall be "Dal-Tile," or equal, 4 × 4 (10.16 cm × 10.16 cm), color to be selected by owner from standard ranges. Bullnose tile shall be applied at all exposed ends of tile.

1.2. Tile shall be applied using a thinset cement wall application and grouted with a color matching the tiles as per manufacturer's recommendations.

FIGURE IV–1
Continued

09510   Acoustical Treatment

1.1. An acoustical ceiling tile (ACT) shall be installed using Armstrong Acoustical Tile, 2′ × 4′ (0.61 m × 1.22 m), 1½″ (1.91 cm) thick, treated wood fiber, fissured, 1-hour rated fire-retardant boards. See Section 09100 for the support system for this installation.

09650   Resilient Flooring

1.1. Vinyl composition tile (VCT) flooring shall be installed with an adhesive directly to the subfloor. Tile shall be placed so that it is properly centered on the floor in each area where it is used.

1.2. The tile flooring shall have a 4″ (5.08 cm) base, or coving of the same height. See Finish Schedule. The coving shall be backed by a 1½″ (3.81 cm) concave quarter-round wood member, color selected by owner to match flooring.

1.3. The contractor shall allow for left-over material, sufficient for repairs, to be left on the project.

09680   Carpet

1.1. See Finish Schedule for location of carpet installation. Carpeting shall be DuPont, commercial grade, heavy traffic, with a rubber pad. Installation shall be by a reputable carpet contractor. Seams shall be kept to a minimum. Seams shall be installed so that the webbing or joint does not show after installation. A guarantee shall be supplied to the contractor and owner by manufacturer as to workmanship and material. A copy of the manufacturer's accreditation shall be in the hands of the owner prior to final payment and retention.

09900   Painting

1.1. See Finish Schedule for location of all interior painting and exterior elevations for exterior paint. Colors to be selected by owner from standard color ranges.

1.2. Acceptable paint manufacturers for standard paints are:

Sinclair Paints	Sherwin-Williams Paints
Dunn-Edwards	Frazee Paints

1.3. The painting shall be applied as follows:

Exterior Walls (to match cement plaster color) and Trim:
Exterior Wood Trim-Oil based stain
Standard colors selected by owner
Underside of Overhang-one coat primer and two coats latex paint
Interior Walls-one coat sealer, one coat primer, and one coat semi-gloss epoxy

END OF DIVISION

DIVISION 10 Specialties

10000   Scope of Work

1.1. Division 1 and the General Conditions are to be considered a part of this division. Furnish all labor, materials, and equipment necessary to complete all work under this division and as indicated on drawings.

1.2. The work shall include installation of all identifying devices and personnel lockers.

10400   Identifying Devices

1.1. Exterior signage and other identifying devices, such as exit signs and restroom identification, shall be a part of this contract and shall be installed as per all codes and ordinances. The exterior sign shall be painted on a

FIGURE IV–1
Continued

wood background with frame and lighting to be mounted over front entry. The design shall be given to contractor by owner for production.

10500   Lockers

1.1. Individual personnel storage lockers shall be installed for each employee and are to be located in the plant restroom for the plant/warehouse employees and in the office restroom for the office employees. The number of employees to be determined by owner (maximum of fifty).

10800   Toilet and Bath Accessories

1.1. The contractor shall be responsible for the purchase and installation of all Restroom and Kitchen accessories including, but not limited to, mirrors, dispensers, waste depositories, and grab bars per ADA requirements.

END OF DIVISION

DIVISION 11 Equipment

11000   Scope of Work

1.1. Division 1 and the General Conditions are to be considered a part of this division. Furnish all materials, labor, and equipment necessary to complete the installation of all of the equipment as indicated on drawings and in these Specifications.

1.2. It is the responsibility of the manufacturers' erector crews to install all necessary equipment for a loading dock with all accessories and the processing system for the manufacturing area.

11160   Loading Dock Equipment

1.1. The contractor shall be responsible for proper installation of the equipment. Where required, coordination shall be applied by the various subcontractors responsible for specialty installations, such as plumbing and/or electrical.

11500   Industrial and Process Equipment

1.1. The owner shall supply the paint booth and mixing equipment used for the manufacture and finishing of residential and commercial plumbing fixtures. The contractor shall be responsible for placement and installation of the equipment as directed by the owner or manufacturer. All codes and ordinances shall be adhered to. See manufacturers' instructions, plans, and shop drawings for proper location and installation procedures.

END OF DIVISION

DIVISION 12 Furnishings-N.I.C. Supplied and installed by owner.

DIVISION 13 Special Construction

13000   Scope of Work

1.1. Division 1 and the General Conditions are to be considered a part of this division. Furnish all materials, labor, and equipment necessary to complete the installation of all of the equipment as indicated on drawings and in these Specifications. Installation of the control systems for the mixing, kiln and finishing system, and the conveying equipment are a part of this division. A systems supervisory for the fire suppression system shall also be included as a part of this division.

FIGURE IV–1
Continued

13400   Industrial and Process Control Systems

1.1. All trades involved with the installation of the process equipment shall also be responsible for the correct application and installation of all operating and safety controls. The drying booth, the mixing vats, kilns, and dryers are all to be installed in accordance with manufacturer requirements and/or recommendations. The contractor shall make certain that all work shall comply with OSHA, ADA, and ANSI regulations and orders.

13900   Fire Suppression and Supervisory Systems

1.1. The mechanical engineer shall supply a complete fire sprinkler system for the office and manufacturing/warehouse areas. A special suppression system shall be installed in conjunction with the kiln and processing units. Shop drawings shall be submitted to the engineer and architect for approval prior to any construction.

END OF DIVISION

DIVISION 14 Conveying Systems

14000   Scope of Work

1.1. Division 1 and the General Conditions are to be considered a part of this division. Furnish all materials, labor, and equipment necessary to complete the installation of any equipment required for material handling as indicated on drawings and in these Specifications. The equipment shall include a floor-operated A-frame crane with proper electrical controls and safety features.

14500   Material Handling Systems

1.1. A conveying system shall be installed in the manufacturing/warehouse portion of the structure for handling of parts and complete units to and from the processing areas and the warehouse storage areas.
1.2. All work shall be in accordance with manufacturer's requirements and/or recommendations as well as with local codes and ordinances. Shop drawings shall be submitted for approval. Warning devices and alarm systems shall be a part of the installation and shall meet OSHA and ANSI requirements.
1.3. Where motorized equipment is used in lieu of a conveying system, the motorized equipment shall be required to include all safety and warning devices as required by ANSI and OSHA.

14600   Hoists and Cranes

1.1. The floor-operated crane shall be installed in the manufacturing/warehouse area by the manufacturer's installation crew. All work shall be coordinated with the contractor to ensure cooperation with all other trades. Shop drawings shall be submitted for approval prior to installation. The equipment shall meet the requirements of both ANSI and OSHA.

END OF DIVISION

DIVISION 15 Mechanical

15000   Scope of Work

1.1. Division 1 and the General Conditions are to be considered a part of this division. Furnish all labor, material, and equipment necessary to complete all work under this division and as indicated on drawings.

15050   Basic Mechanical Materials and Methods

1.1. In addition to the requirements stated in Section 15000, the mechanical contractor shall be governed by the regulations established by professional engineers who have designed the installation and material requirements.

FIGURE IV–1
Continued

1.2. The mechanical contractor shall also be governed by the regulations of ASHRAE, OSHA, and by national, regional, and/or local mechanical and plumbing codes, where applicable. The materials used shall be as specified in the following sections.

15400   Plumbing

1.1. The plumbing contractor shall be responsible for all fee and permit costs in reference to the plumbing and piping applying to this project.

1.2. Plumbing shall include, but is not limited to, installation of all sanitary sewer, storm drainage, gas, and potable water connections from the off-sites to, and including, the appliance or fixture shut-off valves and the appliances or fixtures themselves. Fittings not specifically mentioned shall be construed to be included to make a complete installation.

1.3. Provide and install all soil, waste, vent pipes, and clean-outs for all sewer lines in accordance with local code. Provide proper drainage where necessary and ensure that all stub-outs are properly capped. Pipe and fitting sizes shall be as per plans. Where discrepancies may occur with local codes and installation recommendations, such codes and recommendations shall prevail.

1.4. Provide and install type K copper pipe for all underground potable water service and connections. Use Type K or L copper pipe for all potable water above grade pipe.

1.5. Where gas is used for heating and/or hot water heat, gas piping shall be schedule 40, black steel pipe. All below-grade gas pipe and gas pipe exposed to the atmosphere shall be wrapped with a polyethylene wrapper coating.

1.6. Insulate all cold and hot water piping as required by local codes and ordinances. Hold installation to inside of building insulation to prevent freezing.

1.7. The plumbing fixture schedule is as follows:

Handicap Water closet:	American "Cadet" #2108.408–18″ (45.72 cm) high Church #295 or equal
Lavatories:	Custom designed cultured marble one-piece lavatory tops w/basins integral (color and style to be selected by owner)
Mop Basin:	Stainless Steel by Elkay, or equal
Scrub Basin:	By American Standard or equal

15500   Heating, Ventilation, and Air Conditioning

1.1. Mechanical contractor shall supply shop drawings for the installation of the HVAC system as required.

1.2. All fees and permits for the HVAC installation are at the expense of the mechanical contractor. The HVAC equipment shall be manufactured by Lennox Corporation, or equal. The mechanical contractor shall propose two separate self-contained HVAC units.

1.3. The system for the manufacturing/warehouse area shall include one 5-ton self-contained unit with all necessary accessories. The HVAC contractor shall ascertain that the structure is sufficiently constructed to properly support the unit, controls, and accessories.

1.4. A heat exchanger with all accessories shall be installed in the office ceiling. The unit shall be a split system with the A/C compressor located outside the office on a concrete pad. The equipment shall include, but is not limited to, ductwork, grilles, registers, and other fittings as necessary for a complete installation.

1.5. Separate thermostat controls shall operate both units manually and automatically. See HVAC Plan. Coordinate all work with the plumbing and electrical contractors where required.

END OF DIVISION

FIGURE IV–1
Continued

DIVISION 16 Electrical

16000   Scope of Work

1.1. Division 1 and the General Conditions are to be considered a part of this division. Furnish all labor, material, and equipment necessary to complete all work under this division and as indicated on drawings.

16050   Basic Electrical Materials and Methods

1.1. In addition to the requirements stated in Section 16000, the electrical contractor shall be governed by the regulations established by professional engineers who have designed the installation and material requirements. The electrical contractor shall also conform to the latest edition of the NEC, OSHA, regional and/or local electrical codes, where applicable. The materials used shall be as specified in the following sections.

16400   Service and Distribution

1.1. Provide for an adequate service and grounding system as shown on drawings and as described in the specifications. Conduit shall be used as a continuous ground path from appliance to distribution center. A complete equipment ground conductor shall also be supplied from each appliance to the distribution center.

1.2. All materials shall be new and supplied by one manufacturer with shipping crates intact. The contractor shall be provided with proof of manufacturer's shipping record. All materials selected shall be as indicated in the specifications and/or electrical schedules. All equipment shall have a label and/or stamp from an approved testing laboratory such as Underwriters Laboratories (UL), and all motorized and switchgear equipment shall have nameplates which shall be supplied with the equipment. All disconnects shall be rated NEMA 1 enclosures.

1.3. The electrical contractor shall coordinate all installation with the local utility company and shall provide connections for service when all service is inspected and approved. The electrical contractor shall further coordinate all hook-ups with contractors of other trades where cooperation is necessary for speedy execution of the contract.

Acceptable manufacturers of the switchgear equipment are:

        Square D   General Electric   White/Westinghouse   ITT

1.5. There shall be two (2) distribution panels as a part of the entry switchgear, one (1) for power and one (1) for lighting.

16500   Lighting (General Lighting and Power)

1.1. All standard lighting switches shall be Hubbell 1221–1, or equal. All duplex receptacles shall be Hubbell 5262–1, or equal. All three-wire receptacles shall be by Hubbell, or equal (minimum 25A, 240VAC). All GFCI receptacles shall be GE-TGTR115F, or equal.

1.2. Exterior lighting installations shall be underground using schedule 80 electrical PVC conduit.

1.3. The electrical contractor has the liberty to make the best application with the least cost and still have the installation acceptable to all codes and regulations. Sizes of conduit shall be determined by the electrical contractor with all connections, accessories, and wiring to be in accordance with code. The minimum allowable size and insulation type for conductors shall be #12AWG, THNN, for power and exterior lighting circuits, and #14AWG, THNN, for interior lighting circuits.

1.4. The electrical contractor shall install an empty conduit for thermostat wiring.

16700   Communications

1.1. A special conduit and a special circuit shall be installed for an isolated computer system with additional junctions supplied in each office for networking.

1.2. The electrical contractor shall install an empty conduit for telephone communications and for intercom and fire alarm systems. The systems are to be installed by communications specialists who shall supply drawings and specifications to the owner for approval.

END OF DIVISION

FIGURE IV–1
Continued

Glossary

A

abbreviation   shortening of a word or group of words.

ABS   (acrylonitrile butadiene styrene) plastic pipe used for plumbing construction.

abut   joining end-to-end.

accelerator   a concrete additive used to speed the curing time of freshly poured concrete.

acoustical   referring to the study of sound transmission or reduction.

acoustical tile/acoustical ceiling tile (ACT) a combination of products such as vegetable, mineral, wood, cork, or metal, formed into boards or tiles.

acrylic   a thermoplastic material used with resins, paints, and other plastic materials.

additive   *see* admixture.

adhesive   a bonding material used to bond two materials together.

adjacent   touching; next to.

admixture   any material other than water, aggregate, fiber reinforcement, or cement, added to a concrete mix.

advertisement to bid   *see* Invitation to bid.

aggregate   fine, lightweight, coarse, or heavyweight grades of sand, vermiculite, perlite, or gravel added to cement for concrete or plaster.

air entrainment   minute bubbles of air mixed into concrete or mortar to aid in the plasticity of a mix; also improves resistance to frost.

air handling unit   a mechanical unit used for air conditioning or movement of air as in direct supply or exhaust of air within a structure.

allowable load   maximum supportable load of any construction component(s).

allowable span   maximum length permissible for any framing component without support.

anchor bolt   a J- or L-shaped steel rod threaded on one end for securing structural members to concrete or masonry.

apron   (1) a sloped concrete pad on a property used as an approach for a garage or entry to or from a street; (2) A strip of finish trim installed under the window stool to hide the drywall edge.

arabesque   a design of plant forms or geometric figures formed into a complicated pattern used for decorative purposes.

architect   a qualified, licensed person that creates and designs drawings for a construction project.

architect's scale   a rule with scales indicating feet, inches, and fractions of inches.

area   (1) the calculation of the size of a plane (flat surface) in square units (square feet, square yards, and so on); (2) a designated space.

asphalt   the general term for a black material produced as a by-product of oil (asphalt) or coal (pitch or coal tar).

awning window   a window that is hinged at the top so the bottom swings outward.

azimuth   an angle measured from true north and expressed in degrees, minutes, and seconds.

B

backfill   any deleterious material (sand, gravel, and so on) used to fill an excavation.

backup   a masonry wall used to support an exterior masonry finish.

balloon framing   wall construction extending from the foundation to the roof structure without interruption; used in residential construction only.

baluster   a vertical member supporting a balustrade.

balustrade   a horizontal railing supported by a series of balusters.

barge rafter   an extension of the gable end of a roof structure used to support a decorative framing member or roofing material.

baseboard   a finished trim member applied on the finished wall at the junction with the finished floor.

batt insulation   an insulating material formed into sheets or rolls with a foil or paper backing; to be installed between framing members.

batten   a board strip used to hide the joint between two larger boards, known as *board and batten finish construction.*

beam   a large horizontal structural member made of concrete, steel, stone, wood, or other structural material to support the structure above a large opening.

bearing   the direction of a line given by an acute angle between the line and a north or south meridian; can be measured clockwise or counterclockwise by the letters noting the quadrant (northeast, southeast, northwest, or southwest).

benchmark   an area base reference point elevation above mean sea level.

berm   a raised earth embankment; the shoulder of a paved road; the area between the curb and gutter and a sidewalk.

bibb   also known as a *hose bibb;* a faucet used to connect a hose.

bi-fold   a double-leaf door used primarily for closet doors in residential construction.

bird block   *see* frieze block.

bird mouth   a notch cut into a roof rafter so that it can rest smoothly on the top plate.

bitumen   the general term used to identify asphalt and coal tar.

blanket insulation   *see* batt insulation; available in rolls up to 24'-0" long.

blocking   specifically, a piece of wood fastened between structural members to strengthen them; generally, solid or cross-tie wood or metal cross-tie members to perform the same task.

blueprint   a term derived from the original development process; (1) a single sheet copied from a master copy (velum, and so on) with blue lines on a blue back ground, or with black lines on a white background, showing some part of a construction project; (2) the complete set of drawings of a construction project.

board foot   a piece of lumber 12" long by 12" wide by 1" thick.

board measure   a system of measure used for freighting lumber based on the board foot.

bond   as used with masonry, the interlocking system of brick or block to be installed as running or common bond, stack bond, English bond, Flemish bond, and so on.

brick   a masonry unit usually, of clay base, used for both structural and aesthetic appearance.

bypass door   a sliding or track-mounted door in which the leaves can be moved past one another.

C

calcium chloride   a concrete admixture used for accelerating the cure time.

California Bearing Ratio (CBR)   a system used in determining the suitability of a soil for use as a subgrade or base course material in pavement construction.

cement   a material that, when combined with water, hardens due to chemical reaction; the basis for a concrete mix.

cement plaster   a mixture of gypsum, cement, hydrated lime, sand, and water, used primarily for exterior wall finish.

cementitious   able to harden like cement.

chair   used to support horizontal rebar prior to the concrete placement.

chord   top or bottom member of a truss.

cold key   *see* keyway.

collar tie   horizontal framing member trying the raftering together above the plate line.

common rafter   a structural member that extends without interruption from the ridge to the plate line in a sloped roof structure.

computer-aided design and drafting (CADD)   the computer design program used for drawing a set of blueprints or any component thereof.

computer-aided drafting (CAD)   *see* computer-aided design and drafting (CADD).

computer-aided engineering (CAE)   the same system using software specifically for engineering requirements (structural, mechanical, civil, and electrical).

concrete masonry unit (CMU)   manufactured into primarily modular concrete units in lightweight hollow, heavyweight hollow, and solid block forms similar to brick.

contour line   solid (finish grade—plot plan) or dashed lines (natural grade—site plan) showing the elevation of the earth on a project.

contract documents   the legal documents used with commercial bids and contracts.

corner bead   galvanized metal form (L-shaped) used for protecting outside corners in drywall and plaster installations.

cross brace   wood or metal diagonal bracing used to aid in structural support between joists and beams.

cubic measure   the area of a plane multiplied by the depth or height of a second plane perpendicular to the first; formula: $V = Ah$.

cutting plane line   a heavy broken line with arrows, letters, and numbers at each end indicating the section view that is being identified.

D

dampproofing better identified as moisture protection; a surfacing used to coat and protect concrete and masonry from moisture penetration.

datum point *see* bench mark; identification of the elevation above mean sea level.

dead load the weight of a structure and all its fixed components.

deformed bar steel reinforcement bar with ridges to prevent the bar from loosening during the concrete curing process.

diagonal brace a wood or metal member placed diagonally over wood or metal framing to add rigidity at corners and at 25'-0" feet of unbroken wall space.

diazzo print dry blueprint process developing blue lines on a light background; wet blueprint process in black on white background.

dimension line a line on a drawing with a measurement indicating length.

drywall finishing material for walls made of gypsum and paper; types include Gypsum wall board, Sheetrock®.

E

earthwork excavating and grading.

easement a right, granted by a landowner to another party, to use a designated portion of the landowner's property for a specific purpose (roadway, utility, railroad).

eave the lowest edge on a gable roof.

elastomer synthetic polymer; *see* polymer.

elevation an exterior or interior orthographic view of a structure identifying the design and the materials to be used.

embed any component (anchor bolt, wall-to-joist strap, and so on) that is installed within the foundation, slab, or wall of a structure to assist in the installation of another component.

erection referring to structural steel installations.

estimate a calculation of labor, material, and equipment costs of a project.

F

face the exposed side of a framing or masonry unit; a type of brick (also called *common*).

fascia an exterior trim member used at the eave of a roof to hide the rafter ends.

finish any material used to complete an installation that provides an aesthetic or finished appearance.

fire stop/draft stop/fire blocking a framing member used to reduce the ability of a fire's spread.

firewall/fire separation wall/fire division wall any wall that is installed for the purpose of preventing the spread of fire.

fixed window a window that does not open.

flashing metal or plastic strips or sheets used for moisture protection in conjunction with other construction materials.

flat in roofing, any roof structure up to a 3:12 slope.

flexural strength the ability to resist bending pressure without failure of the material.

fly ash fine, powdery coal residue used with a hydraulic (water-resistant) concrete mix.

footing the bottom-most member of a foundation; supports the full load of the structure above.

form a temporary construction member used to hold permanent materials in place.

found identification of the corner of a property.

foundation the support member(s) of any structure; includes footing, foundation wall, and/or slab.

G

gable roof *see* roof.

galvanize a coating of zinc primarily used on sheet metal.

gauge the thickness of metal or glass sheet material.

glaze to install glass.

glu-lam (GLB) glue-laminated beam made from milled 2× lumber bonded together to form a beam.

grade an existing or finished elevation in earthwork; a sloped portion of a roadway; sizing of gravel and sand; the structural classification of lumber.

gravel earth materials such as crushed rock ranging in size from 1/4" to 3" in diameter.

gravel stop (strip) the edge metal used at the eaves of a built-up roof to hold the gravel on the roof.

green uncured or set concrete or masonry; freshly cut lumber.

ground-fault-circuit-interrupter (GFCI or GFI) an electrical receptacle installed for personnel safety at outdoor locations and near water supply fixtures.

gypsum a mineral (hydrous calcium sulfate) powdered and compressed into wallboard (GWB) and used in plaster.

H

habitable space in residential construction, the interior areas of a residence used for eating, sleeping, living, and cooking; excludes bathrooms, storage rooms, utility rooms, and garages.

hanger metal fabrication made for the purpose of placing and supporting joists and rafters.

hardware any component used to hang, support, or position another component; e.g., door and window hardware, hangers, and so on.

header a framing member used to hide the ends of joists along the perimeter of a structure (also known as a *rim joist*); the horizontal structural framing member installed over wall openings to aid in the support of the structure above (also referred to as a *lintel*).

header course in masonry, a horizontal row of brick laid perpendicular to the wall face; used to tie a double wythe brick wall together.

head joint the end face of a brick or concrete masonry unit to which the mortar is applied.

heating, ventilating, and air conditioning *see* HVAC.

hidden line light, dashed lines used to show edges not visible at the level in which the plan view is taken, or to show the edges or outline of structural members.

hip roof a structural sloped roof design with sloped perimeters from ridge to plate line.

hopper window a window that is hinged at the bottom and with a top that swings inward.

hose bibb a faucet used to connect a hose.

HVAC the term given to all heating and air-conditioning systems; the mechanical portion of the CSI format, division 15.

hydraulic cement a cement used in a concrete mix capable of curing under water.

I

I beam *see* S beam.

index mark a datum point in a survey used as the reference point for the survey.

insulating glass a glazing assembly of dual glass with an air space between and sealed in a framework.

insulation any material capable of resisting thermal, sound, or electrical transmission.

insulation resistance the R factor in insulation calculations; a material capable of resisting electrical flow.

invitation to bid the bid request from an owner, or a representative of the owner, to contractor.

isometric drawing a drawing in which all horizontal lines are drawn at an angle of 30° above the horizontal, and all vertical lines are 90° (perpendicular to the true horizontal), with a 120° angle between.

J

jack rafter a part of the roof structure raftering that does not extend the full length from the ridge beam to the top plate.

jalousie window a movable, louvered, multiple-pane glass window; the individual louvered panes open outward in the same manner as the awning window.

jamb the finish framing member installed in window or door openings.

J bolt *see* anchor bolt.

joint compound a dry (which requires mixing with water) or pre-mixed material used with a paper of fiber tape for sealing indentations and breaks in dry-wall construction.

joist a structural horizontal framing member used for floor and ceiling support systems.

joist hanger *see* hanger.

K

keyway also known as a *cold key;* and interlocking depression formed in concrete used to add structural stability to the next lift or placement adjoining the key.

kiln a heating unit or oven used to bake ceramics, cure and dry masonry units, and dry out lumber; *see* kiln-dried lumber.

kiln-dried lumber lumber that is seasoned under controlled conditions, removing from 6% to 12% of the moisture in green lumber.

king post in conventional framing, the vertical structural roof member extending from the ceiling joist to the ridge; in trusses, the vertical structural member extending from the bottom chord of the truss to the topmost point of the truss.

king stud the full-length stud from bottom plate to the top plate supporting both sides of a wall opening.

kips (kps) a measurement of force equal to 1,000 pounds.

knee wall vertical framing members supporting and shortening the span of the roof rafters.

L

laminate the process of stacking and bonding several layers of material together to form a single unit.

lateral underground electrical service.

lath backup support for plaster; may be of wood, metal, or gypsum board.

lavatory bathroom; vanity basin.

lay-in ceiling a suspended ceiling system; *see* acoustical.

leach line a perforated pipe used as a part of a septic system to allow liquid overflow to dissipate into the soil.

leader in drafting, the line to which an arrowhead is placed and used to identify a component.

ledger structural framing member used to support ceiling and roof joists at the perimeter walls.

legend a description of the symbols and abbreviations used in a set of drawings.

light (lite) a pane of glass.

light-gauge metal framing metal stud framing used in lieu of wood framing; consists of track and studs or joists.

linoleum *see* resilient flooring.

lintel *see* header.

live load any movable equipment or personnel weight to which a structure is subjected.

M

m shape beam *see* structural steel.

mansard roof a combination of a flat roof and steep sloped sides similar to a hip roof.

masonry manufactured materials of clay (brick), concrete (CMU), and stone used as components in the completion of a structure.

mean sea level average height of the surface of the sea.

mechanical plan the layout for heating and air conditioning.

member structural component.

membrane roofing built-up roofing.

mesh common term for welded wire fabric, plaster lath.

metal stud *see* light-gauge metal framing.

meter in measurement, the equivalent to 39.37"; used to measure the flow of water, electricity, gas, and so on.

metrics an international system of measurement based on the meter (length), liter (liquid measure, volume), and gram (weight).

mil 0.001".

minute 1/60th of a degree or angle.

mix design the proportioning of cement, sand or aggregate, water, and additives (if required) to produce the desired concrete.

modular construction design based on 4" square.

module a prefabricated component or structure.

moisture barrier a material used for the purpose of resisting exterior moisture penetration.

monitor roof clerestory; a raised portion of a roof above the ridge where windows and/or ventilators are installed.

monolithic concrete concrete placed as a single unit including turndown footings.

mortar a concrete mix especially used for bonding masonry units.

N

natural grade existing or original grade elevation of a property.

neoprene a highly oil-resistant synthetic rubber.

nominal size original cut size of a piece of lumber prior to milling (surfacing) and drying; size of masonry unit, including mortar bed and head joint.

non-bearing not supporting any structural load.

O

on center (O/C) the distance between the centers of two adjacent components.

open any exposed construction component(s).

open web joist roof joist made of wood or steel construction with a top chord and bottom chord connected by diagonal braces bolted or welded together.

orange peel finish a textured plaster finish for drywall applications creating a slightly roughened surface.

oriented strand board (OSB) a resin and fiber strand mixed with compressed and heated plies of wood chips and strands manufactured into a three-ply panel to be used in lieu of plywood.

orthographic projection opening an object into flat-plane surfaces positioned at 90° to one another.

P

package air conditioner or boiler   an air conditioner or boiler in which all components are packaged into a single unit.

pad   in earthwork or concrete foundation work, the base materials used upon which to place the concrete footing and/or slab.

paint grade   a finish designation for lumber unsuited for stain and lacquer or varnish.

paper-backed lath   plaster lath with a moisture-resistant paper barrier attached.

parapet   an extension of an exterior wall above the line of the roof.

parging   a thin moisture protection coating of plaster or mortar over a masonry wall.

partition   an interior wall separating to rooms or areas of building; usually nonbearing.

plan view   a bird's-eye view of a construction layout cut at 5'-0" above finish floor level.

plaster   a mixture of cement, water, and sand.

platform framing   also known as *western framing*; structural construction in which all studs are only one story high with joists over.

plumbing   the general term used for both water supply and liquid waste disposal; specifically, in drawings and specifications, the waste disposal system.

plywood   thin sheets of veneer wood with the wood grain on adjoining sheets at 90° to one another, compressed and glued together in an odd number of plies (3, 5, and so on).

point of beginning (POB)   a point on the perimeter of a tract of land from which the calls for the perimeter of the tract being described will start; it should be easily locatable and tied to a point of record (datum point).

polyester   synthetic resin used for fabrics as well as an additive for concrete and mortar.

polyethylene   thin plastic sheet material used as a vapor barrier.

polymer   an organic chemical compound used in the manufacture of styrene, urethane, and methyl methacrylate; may be used as an additive for concrete.

polypropylene   synthetic fiber used for carpet backing and roofing materials.

polystyrene   the generic chemical name for Styrofoam.

polyurethane   used as a finishing material similar to varnish; also used as a foam insulation.

polyvinyl chloride (PVC)   a plastic material commonly used for pipe and plumbing fixtures.

Portland cement   one variety of cement produced from burning various materials such as clay, shale, and limestone, producing a fine gray powder; the basis of concrete and mortar.

post-and-beam construction   a type of wood frame construction using timber for the structural support.

post-tensioning   the application of stretching steel cables embedded in a concrete slab to aid in strengthening the concrete.

pressure treatment   impregnating lumber with a preservative chemical under pressure in a tank.

purlin   a horizontal framing member spanning between rafters.

Q

quarry tile   an unglazed clay or shale flooring material produced by the extrusion process.

quick set   a fast-curing cement plaster.

quoin   a masonry unit (stone, CMU, or brick) larger than the field masonry; may be used as a header; more commonly used for aesthetics at masonry outside corners.

R

R factor   the numerical rating given any material that is able to resist heat transfer for a specific period of time.

raceway   any partially or totally enclosed container for placing electrical wires (conduit, tray, and so on).

rafter   in sloped roof construction, the framing member extending from the ridge or hip to the top plate; *see* common rafter, jack rafter.

rake   *see* barge; the angle of slope in a roof structure.

random length   a mix of lumber lengths, such as 8 lf, 14 lf, 24 lf, and so on, without specific length requirements, equaling a total length.

ready-mix concrete   a prepared concrete mix from a batch plant and freighted for use on a project.

rebar   *see* reinforcement steel bar.

red iron   *see* structural steel.

reinforcement steel bar   steel rod with or without deformed ridges used for adding strength to concrete and masonry; in increments of ⅛" DIA.

resilient flooring   a vinyl plastic floor finish material formed into sheets and tiles.

ribbon   in balloon framing, the support for the ledger supporting the floor joists at the second floor level.

ridge   the highest point on a sloped roof.

rise and run   the vertical length (rise) and the horizontal length (run) from plate line to the point where the rise intersects the span (see *span*).

roll roofing   a type of built-up roofing material made of a mixture of rag, paper, and asphalt.

roof pitch   the ratio of total span to total rise expressed as a fraction.

roofing   the materials used for moisture protection on a roof structure including composition shingle, wood shake and shingles, tile (clay, concrete, and slate), and built-up roofing (BUR).

S

saddle   in framing, a support for intersecting beam construction or column mount; in roofing, a metal formed sheet (also known as a *cricket*) placed on the upper side of a chimney or skylight to move water away from them.

scale   a system for measuring proportionate lengths on a drawing.

schematic   a one-line drawing for electrical circuitry or isometric plumbing diagrams.

scissors truss   a truss constructed to the roof slope at the top chord with the bottom chord designed with a lower slope for interior vaulted or cathedral ceilings.

scratch coat   first coat of plaster placed over the lath in a three-coat plaster system.

scupper   an opening in a parapet wall attached to a downspout for water drainage from the roof.

scuttle   attic or roof access with cover or door.

sealant   a material used to seal off openings against moisture and air penetration.

section   a vertical drawing showing architectural or structural interior design developed at the point of a cutting-plane line on a plan view; the section may be transverse—the gable-end—or longitudinal—parallel to the ridge.

seismic design   construction designed to withstand earthquakes.

septic system   a waste system used in lieu of a sewer system that includes a line from the structure to a tank and a leach field.

shear wall   a wall construction designed to withstand shear pressure caused by wind or earthquake.

shoring   temporary support made of metal or wood used to support other components.

sidelight (sidelite)   a narrow, fixed window installed adjacent to a door.

sill plate   also referred to as a *mudsill*; the lowest framing member fastened to the concrete or masonry foundation; may be redwood or pressure-treated lumber (PTMS); used to deter termite infestation.

skew   twisted.

slab-on-grade   the foundation construction for a structure with no crawl space or basement; may be monolithic concrete placement.

slider/sliding door or window   a door or window construction in which one of two halves moves horizontally on a track with the other half a fixed leaf.

slump   the consistency of concrete at the time of placement.

snap-tie/form-tie   a bolt-like rod used as a spacer for concrete formwork (plyform) that can be broken off at each end to remove the forms upon curing of the concrete.

soffit   a framed drop ceiling; enclosure of a roof overhang.

solar panel   also called a *solar collector*; a panel used to collect the sun's rays for heating or electrical power supply.

span   the horizontal distance between exterior bearing walls in a transverse section.

specifications   the written instructions detailing the requirements of construction for a project.

square   in geometric design, a figure that has all four sides equal and all angles at 90°; in measurement, a number multiplied by itself; in roofing, 100 square feet.

structural steel   heavy steel members larger than 12 gauge identified by their shapes, which include the W beam (wide-flanged), the S beam (junior), and M steel (miscellaneous) such as plate and tubular steel and angle iron.

stucco   cement plaster applied in one-, two-, or three-coat applications.

stud   wood or metal vertical wall framing members.

subfloor   the rough plywood flooring placed over floor joists upon which the finish floor material is placed.

symbol   a pictorial representation of a material or component on a plan.

T

tail/rafter tail   that portion of a roof rafter extending beyond the plate line.

tensile strength   the maximum stretching of a piece of metal (rebar and so on) before breaking; calculated in kps.

tensioning   pulling or stretching of steel tendons to aid in reinforcement of concrete.

terrazzo   a mixture of concrete, crushed stone, calcium shells, and/or glass, polished to form a tile-like finish; used for entries, patios, plazas, and so on.

title block   a portion of a drawing sheet that includes some general information about the project.

top chord   the topmost member of a truss.

top plate   the horizontal framing member fastened to the top of the wall studs; usually doubled.

transition piece   in sheet metal ductwork, a reducer.

truss   a prefabricated sloped roof system incorporating a top chord, bottom chord, and bracing.

typical   meaning the same throughout the drawing(s) unless noted otherwise (U.N.O.).

U

underlayment   the material applied over the subfloor upon which finish materials are placed.

urethane   a plastic foam material; *see* polyurethane.

V

valley   the reverse of a hip.

valley rafter   a structural roof member extending from the ridge to the plate or an intersecting roof structure.

vapor barrier   construction material used to resist moisture penetration.

veneer   a thin layer of surfacing material adhered to a base material, e.g., face brick over CMU or wood veneer over a pine trim material.

vent stack   a system of pipes used for air circulation and to prevent water from being suctioned from the traps in the waste disposal system.

vinyl   a resin-based thermoplastic material used for resilient flooring.

W

waler   a 2× piece of lumber installed horizontally to formwork to give added stability and strength to the forms.

water-borne preservative   a coating applied to wood to resist deterioration.

water-cement ratio   the ratio between the weight of water to cement.

waterproofing   preferably called moisture protection since there is no product that will permanently resist water penetration or deterioration; materials used to protect below- and on-grade construction from moisture penetration.

weatherproof   preferably called *weather tight* for the same reason as explained under "waterproofing."

welded wire fabric (WWF)   a reinforcement used for horizontal concrete strengthening.

wind lift (wind load)   the force exerted by the wind against a structure caused by the movement of the air.

wythe   a continuous masonry wall width.

XYZ

x brace   cross brace for joist construction.

yard   lineal measurement consisting of 36".

zinc   non-corrosive metal used for galvanizing other metals.

Index

U

underlayment (*See* thermal and moisture protection)
utilities, 183

V

valley (*See* rough carpentry)

W

wallcovering (*See* finishes)
welded wire fabric (*See* concrete)
wind lift, wind load, 71
windows, 100
work authorization, 156
wythe (*See* masonry)